"Wow! Marriage and Lasting Relationships with Asperger's Syndrome (Autism Spectrum Disorder) is a thorough, finely written, insightful, real-world analysis of neurodiverse interpersonal relationships. Author Eva Mendes knows, really knows, what ASD is all about, how it can bewilder, irritate or even collapse a relationship. Partners trying to communicate through the curves of Asperger syndrome and autism will be able to use Mendes' guidance to great advantage. Couples' lives will be touched and changed for the better, thanks to this book!"

—Liane Holliday Willey, author of *Safety Skills for Asperger Women and Pretending to be Normal*

"Eva Mendes has precisely addressed 'emotional-disconnect' in Asperger/HFA relationships, something that I learned through life...the hard way. I wish I had read this book ten years ago, it would have prevented a lot of pain, discomfort and confusion as I navigated my way through life. The language is comfortable and conversational, the anecdotes and real-life stories seem like they were written about me. This book should be read by everyone who is on the spectrum but more so by those who love someone with ASD. As our numbers grow and more of us find out about our social awkwardness being a consequence of the spectrum, sharing war stories like the ones in this book will help millions of people around the world. Thank you, Eva, for writing about us, talented professionals on the Autism spectrum who are tired of wearing the mask of conformity."

—Qazi Fazli Azeem, South Asian self-advocate for the Autism spectrum

Marriage and Lasting Relationships
with Asperger's Syndrome (Autism Spectrum Disorder)

of related interest

The Other Half of Asperger Syndrome (Autism Spectrum Disorder)
A Guide to Living in an Intimate Relationship with a Partner who is on the Autism Spectrum
2nd Edition
Maxine Aston
Foreword by Tony Attwood
ISBN 978 1 84905 498 0
eISBN 978 0 85700 920 3

The Asperger Couple's Workbook
Practical Advice and Activities for Couples and Counsellors
Maxine Aston
ISBN 978 1 84310 253 3
eISBN 978 1 84642 851 7

Alone Together
Making an Asperger Marriage Work
Katrin Bentley
Foreword by Tony Attwood
ISBN 978 1 84310 537 4
eISBN 978 1 84642 623 0

Troubleshooting Relationships on the Autism Spectrum
A User's Guide to Resolving Relationship Problems
Ashley Stanford
ISBN 978 1 84905 951 0
eISBN 978 0 85700 808 4

Sex, Sexuality and the Autism Spectrum
Wendy Lawson
Foreword by Glenys Jones
ISBN 978 1 84310 284 7
eISBN 978 1 84642 112 9

Been There. Done That. Try This!
An Aspie's Guide to Life on Earth
Edited by Tony Attwood, Craig R. Evans and Anita Lesko
ISBN 978 1 84905 964 0
eISBN 978 0 85700 871 8

MARRIAGE AND LASTING RELATIONSHIPS

with Asperger's Syndrome

(AUTISM SPECTRUM DISORDER)

SUCCESSFUL STRATEGIES FOR COUPLES OR COUNSELORS

Eva A. Mendes

Foreword by Stephen M. Shore

Jessica Kingsley *Publishers*
London and Philadelphia

First published in 2015
by Jessica Kingsley Publishers
73 Collier Street
London N1 9BE, UK
and
400 Market Street, Suite 400
Philadelphia, PA 19106, USA

www.jkp.com

Library of Congress Cataloging in Publication Data
Mendes, Eva A.
Marriage and lasting relationships with Asperger's syndrome
(autism spectrum disorder) : successful strategies for couples or
counselors / Eva A. Mendes ; foreword by Stephen M. Shore.
pages cm
Includes bibliographical references and index.
ISBN 978-1-84905-999-2
1. Asperger's syndrome--Patients--Family relationships. 2. Asperger's
syndrome--Patients--Sexual behavior. 3. People with mental disabilities-
-Marriage. 4. Interpersonal relations. 5. Interpersonal conflict.
6. Man-woman relationships. 7. Couples therapy. I. Title.
RC553.A88M45 2015
616.85'8832--dc23
2015016761

British Library Cataloguing in Publication Data
A CIP catalogue record for this book is available from the British Library

ISBN 978 1 84905 999 2
eISBN 978 0 85700 981 4

Printed and bound in Great Britain

Dedicated to my mentor, Daisaku Ikeda
and his wife Kaneko Ikeda.

And, my parents, Elfrida and Sosthenes Mendes
with deepest appreciation and gratitude.

CONTENTS

Foreword by Stephen M. Shore — 11

Acknowledgments — *14*

Preface — *15*

Terminology, Case Studies, and Strategies — *17*

Introduction: Marriage and Lasting Relationships with Asperger's Syndrome (Autism Spectrum Disorder) — 21

1 Pursuing a Diagnosis—or Not — 27

2 Accepting the Diagnosis — 48

3 Learning About and Understanding ASD — 57

4 Managing Anxiety, Depression, Anger, OCD, and ADHD — 65

5 Self-Exploration, Awareness, and Advocacy — 83

6 Expanding Theory of Mind and Emotional Intelligence — 92

7 Coping with Sensory Overload and Avoiding Meltdowns — 116

8 Meeting Each Other's Sexual Needs — 125

9 Bridging Parallel Play — 135

10 Creating a *Relationship Schedule*™ — 146

11 Improving Communication — 157

12 Co-Parenting Strategies — 169

13 Prioritizing Self-Care for the NS partner — 179

14 Organizing, Planning, and Outsourcing 187

15 Suspending Judgments and Managing Expectations 197

16 Staying Motivated 207

17 Neurodiverse Couples Counseling 215

18 Every Neurodiverse Marriage is Unique 230

Appendix I: The Appreciation and Gratitude Exercise™ 237

Appendix II: The Walking in Your Partner's Shoes Practice™ 239

Appendix III: The Sensation-Emotion Awareness Practice™ 240

Appendix IV: The Emotions List 242

Appendix V: The Sensation-Emotion Awareness Chart™ 243

Appendix VI: The Relationship Schedule™ 246

Appendix VII: The Listen, Validate, and Compliment
Strategy™ 252

Appendix VIII: The Marital Satisfaction Scale 253

References 254

Index 258

FOREWORD

As an adult with autism, married to a woman who is not on the spectrum, I am honored to write the foreword to this groundbreaking book that fills a yawning gap in the literature of supporting long-term relationships where one of the couple has autism.

Beginning by referring to ASD as "Autism Spectrum Difference," this invaluable guide and resource provides a therapeutic road map for couples where one or both partners have Asperger Syndrome and autism, and starts off on a positive note by considering neurodiversity as a different, rather than a disordered way of being. Considering autism and related conditions as a difference rather than pathologizing the condition forms a sturdy foundation for the numerous and brilliant strategies in this book. Devoted to generating greater mutual understanding for couples, this book includes a number of inspiring case studies representing great diversity in culture, race, ethnicities, and socio-economic backgrounds! Based on this knowledge of neurological differences, these stories demonstrate how partners can gain clarity and develop successful strategies that work.

The strategies presented in this book for improving self-awareness are a vital prerequisite for deepening understanding of others. For example, my wife, Yi Liu and I have various differences in terms of neurodiversity, culture, race, and religion. Fortunately, our awareness of these differences make us realize that communication and checking-in with each other is required more frequently than perhaps for a neurotypical couple. Yi Liu and I have fewer misunderstandings when we don't rely on the mystical mind-reading that couples allegedly have. Focusing first on developing greater intrapersonal awareness can serve as a gateway to a better understanding of your spouse, as two individuals often have very different ways of perceiving, processing, and communicating thoughts, ideas, and even love.

Easy to implement strategies in areas such as sensing one's own emotions can be a self-awareness boon to those of us on the autism spectrum. For example, most typical people seem to understand their emotions in real time. In other words, the person is able to identify an emotion before noticing bodily sensations, such as anxiety creating a queasy feeling in the stomach. Whereas a person with autism often needs to learn to recognize how bodily sensations signify specific emotional states. Taking the same example of a queasy stomach, as long as an illness can be ruled out, perhaps the upset stomach can be attributed to anxiety from an upcoming job interview. With knowledge and self-understanding, a calming strategy can help reduce anxiety and even prevent a meltdown.

In addition to knowing my own sensory issues in terms of touch, hearing, and sight, I need to know how to communicate these differences to my wife in a way she can understand and provide support. Whether it's the need for firm rather than light physical contact, keeping a lower volume on the TV, or my insistence on wearing a baseball cap, Yi Liu understands and knows the reasons why. Conversely, self-awareness of my sensory needs generates a greater understanding of the needs my wife may have, that are different from my own.

The stories describing the constellation of challenges, and solutions, are keenly accurate to many neurodiverse relationships. While many intimate relationships require problem solving, Asperger or autistic traits intensify the need for greater creativity and originality in resolving issues. This wise and practical book lays out easy to implement strategies covering all areas of living for the neurodiverse couple. Couples employing these ready to use solutions will find a beacon of hope, helping to pave their way to better understanding and harmonious relationships.

Love conquers all could perhaps be rephrased as *love with knowledge and understanding conquers all.*

Stephen M. Shore, Ed.D.
Clinical Assistant Professor at Adelphi University
Internationally known author, speaker, and
individual on the autism spectrum

Acknowledgments

A heartfelt thank you to Stephanie Loo, friend and colleague, for the long afternoons of chicken soup, talking through chapters, offering suggestions, and assisting in the editing. Thanks to Harriet Simons for reading through the initial chapters, and offering valuable insights, and clinical validation. My deepest appreciation for Nisha Narvekar—friend, colleague, and neighbor—for her constant support, wise encouragement, and affection. I would like to express my gratitude to all my Buddhist friends in the Soka Gakkai International for their ready compassion and guidance and my sister Grace who loves me always.

Thanks to Susan Cherwinski for assuring me, "you're ready to write the book," and Emily McClave, my editor at JKP for recognizing the need for and enabling me to publish this book.

I'm grateful to my colleagues and former supervisors at AANE who influenced many of the thoughts and ideas expressed here: Dania Jekel, Jamie Freed, Grace Myhill, and Erika Drezner. This book would not be possible without the work of the numerous individuals with Asperger's Syndrome (ASD), their partners/spouses, Asperger/autism specialists, and researchers around the world, whose books and articles I've read, and trainings and workshops I've attended over the years, and whose names are too numerous to mention.

Above all, I want to thank each and every neurodiverse couple, individual with Asperger's Syndrome (ASD) and non-spectrum spouse that I've worked with, who inspired me and gave me hope with their tenacious efforts to create happier relationships.

PREFACE

Working with Neurodiverse Couples and Adults with Asperger's Syndrome (ASD)

People often ask me how I came to be working with neurodiverse couples: where one or both partners have Asperger's Syndrome (ASD). Prior to learning about ASD, my graduate studies in psychology were focused on couples counseling and gender relations. In 2009, a professor introduced me to Asperger's Syndrome in one of his lectures. Curious and interested in neurological differences, I sought out an internship at the Asperger/Autism Network (AANE), formerly known as the Asperger's Association of New England—in Watertown, Massachusetts (about five miles outside of Boston).

At AANE I was able to combine my work with Asperger's and couples counseling to develop a specialty in neurodiverse relationships. My work as a couples counselor and group leader for neurodiverse couples, individuals with ASD, and their partners eventually led to my master's thesis on ASD and marriage, "Bridging parallel play in asperger marriage," and many papers and articles. As my internship progressed, I realized that some of my family members had undiagnosed Asperger's. Having been raised in a neurodiverse family may account for my unique understanding, insight, and comfort in working in individuals with ASD and their families.

In my private practice, I see couples, spouses, adults, and teens, including women with Asperger's (ASD) and related profiles. Many of them are professional engineers, physicians, business people, scientists, mathematicians, finance or IT professionals, professors, artists, and musicians; some are students; and there are those struggling to find and maintain employment, or who are receiving disability assistance. I facilitate groups, workshops, and trainings for couples, individuals with ASD, and professionals at AANE, various universities, mental health, and medical centers.

Practical Strategies

In my work as a couples counselor and group leader, I observed that even though the circumstances of each neurodiverse couple were different, they all struggled with similar issues. I saw the same themes come up over and over again. These observations led me to design and create practical strategies for the couples and individual partners I worked with. They came back reporting that the strategies worked and that they were able to minimize some of their challenges. Encouraged by this feedback, I wrote a paper called "Marriage with Asperger Syndrome: 14 Practical Strategies," which has now been translated into four different languages other than English. These well-received strategies are the basis for this book.

For Couples and Counselors

This book will assist couples in neurodiverse relationships. Even if one partner, the non-spectrum partner or partner with ASD reads the book, they will still find strategies that they can apply to numerous situations. I've demystified many aspects of ASD, such as getting a diagnosis. I've attempted to explain the basis for certain ASD behaviors and the strategies that can be useful in neurodiverse situations.

Counselors will also find the book helpful in understanding, diagnosing, and working with neurodiverse couples and individuals in these relationships. They can help these couples and individuals implement the strategies listed in this book, helping them increase the odds of creating successful and lasting relationships.

Terminology, Case Studies, and Strategies

Terminology

Asperger's Syndrome (AS)

In 2013, the American Psychiatric Association released the Diagnostic and Statistical Manual-5 (DSM-5), and excluded the diagnosis of Asperger's Syndrome, along with related conditions, such as Pervasive Developmental Disorder-Not Otherwise Specified, Childhood Disintegrative Disorder and Autistic Disorder. Individuals who used to receive one of these diagnoses now receive a singular diagnosis of Autism Spectrum Disorder, Level 1, 2 or 3, based on their level of functioning.

Asperger's Syndrome is now considered to be Autism Spectrum Disorder Level 1. Although the use of Asperger's Syndrome may be waning in the clinical setting, my hope is that its use as a neurodiversity term will continue.

Autism Spectrum Disorder or Difference (ASD)

For the purpose of the book, I have used the letters "ASD" to indicate Autism Spectrum Disorder Level 1, as mentioned in the DSM-5. However, I am replacing the word "Disorder," with the word "Difference," because I view individuals on the autism spectrum as being neurologically different rather than having a disorder. Please read the acronym ASD to mean Autism Spectrum Difference.

Additionally, this book may be useful to those individuals and their partners diagnosed with Social (pragmatic) Communication Disorder (SCD), Non-Verbal Learning Disorder (NVLD), and Attention Deficit Hyperactivity Disorder (ADHD).

Gender Pronouns

ASD is considered to be more prevalent in men than in women; although, I am acquainted with almost an equal number of females with ASD. I will interchange the pronouns "he" and "she" for equal representation where I can.

The majority of couples who come to see me consist of an NS woman married to a man with ASD; however, in many neurodiverse relationships, the woman is the partner with ASD. The principles in this book are also relevant to couples who are in same sex relationships, and those who do not fall into binary genders.

Marriage and Relationships

Most of the couples I work with tend to be married; however, many are in long-term and short-term relationships as well. I will use the terms marriage and relationships interchangeably.

Neurodiverse Marriage, Relationships, and Couples

Similar to biodiversity, neurodiversity refers to the naturally occurring variations and evolutionary adaptations of the human brain (Armstrong, 2010). Neurodiverse marriages, relationships, and couples are those where one partner has diagnosed or undiagnosed ASD. Similar dynamics also present in couples where both partners have ASD.

Non-Spectrum (NS)

The term "non-spectrum" refers to the partner or spouse that doesn't have ASD. In the past, the non-spectrum (NS) partner has been known as the neurotypical (NT) partner. However, the NS spouse can have neurological differences other than ASD. These can include Attention Deficit Hyperactivity Disorder (ADHD), dyslexia, learning differences, bipolarity, and seizure disorders. Therefore, the non-ASD partner in the neurodiverse relationship is more accurately referred to as the NS partner.

Case Studies

The case studies I've used to illustrate and clarify the various aspects of neurodiverse relationships are fictitious. Although they are not based on any specific individuals or clients, they do reflect the composite dynamics of couples I have counseled.

Strategies

The strategies in this book should be seen as a starting point. Couples must tailor the strategies for themselves as they see fit. It's important not to implement too many strategies and solutions at once as the partner with ASD might become overwhelmed, exhausted, and stressed out. It's better to choose the most pressing issues to problem-solve and build from there.

It can also take a while to know when strategies are working. Seeing changes can take longer than expected. Patience is vital and there is no need to rush. Building a happier relationship is a life-long process.

INTRODUCTION

Marriage and Lasting Relationships with
Asperger's Syndrome (Autism Spectrum Disorder)

The only journey is the one within.

RAINER MARIA RILKE

♥ BEN AND JACKIE'S STORY ♥

Jackie was a recently divorced social worker in her late 20s. She met Ben, a physics postdoctoral fellow at the Massachusetts Institute of Technology, at a friend's party. "I was immediately attracted to his curly hair and erudite wit." Charming and outgoing, with a big smile, she was popular with the opposite sex. At the party, while she had more than one man vying for her attention, it was Ben's quiet stillness that drew her in.

When she gave Ben her phone number, he took it eagerly, but didn't call her right away. Jackie assumed that perhaps he wasn't interested in her. She had almost considered calling one of the other guys who'd pursued her at the party. But then, four days later, Ben had called and invited her on a date.

Jackie had already been seeing me for individual counseling as she had recently discovered that her mother most likely had ASD. She sought me out to discuss her recent divorce and her challenging relationship with her mother. In the beginning of the courtship with Ben, Jackie seemed fine with the slow pace of the relationship. She was still processing her divorce and getting used to the idea of being in a new relationship. As the months went by, however, she began to feel antsy about Ben's slow pace and lack of emotional reciprocity.

Jackie was hoping to hear Ben say, "I love you," and that they were in a committed relationship. When she expressed to Ben that she loved him, he didn't respond. "I don't think Ben loves me. I'm going to break up with him," she said in our session. "From his actions, it would seem like he loves me. He plans these wonderful dates for me and is even planning our next vacation together."

"Have you asked him if he loves you?" I asked.

"Not directly. You think I should?"

"Well, it's one way to know for sure."

"I think so..." was Ben's hesitant response.

"Then, how come you've never told me that you love me?"

"Because, I'm not sure I know what love is."

Jackie felt very confused by Ben's answer. She didn't know what to think. Did he love her? Or did he not? What did he mean by saying that he didn't know what love was?

"I don't understand what other people mean by being in love. Maybe we should look up the definition of love." So saying, he began his favorite game of asking the intelligent virtual assistant on his smartphone, "Siri, what is love?"

"Ben, focus! Put your phone away. I don't care what the definition of love is. Do you love me or not?" Jackie asked him again.

"I don't know. I think I do. I like seeing you and I like having sex with you."

Jackie felt offended by his response and came into therapy saying that she couldn't be with someone who didn't love her.

"It's a shame too, since I really like him. He's a great guy. He makes me laugh. He's kind and decent. He does remind me of my mother. A lot of his little quirks like how formal his speech is. He bought me a present yesterday; it was a set of Isaac Asimov books! Science fiction! Just because he likes it, he thinks I would too."

I asked Jackie if being with Ben made her happy other than the fact that he didn't tell her that he loved her.

"Yes, he does make me happy. He's actually very physically affectionate. So I can often feel like he does love me, but if he doesn't think he loves me, I feel like I'm settling and just wasting my time. I'm so confused."

I advised Jackie that she break up with Ben if she truly wanted to, but I also suggested that she try asking Ben to quantify his feelings for her using a numeric scale. Perhaps that would yield more information from him.

Jackie broached the subject again on her next date with him. "Ben, could you tell me on a scale of one to ten how you feel about me. Ten being that you want to marry me and one being that you're going to break up with me."

"Scale of one to ten? That's not going to work."

"How do you know how much you love me then?"

"I haven't thought about it," he paused, deep in thought. After a few minutes of processing, he declared, "I love you as much as the energy the sun burns up in a day."

Jackie was truly taken aback by Ben's response. The amount of energy the sun burned up in a day sure seemed like a lot! But she wanted more information to clarify things.

"Do you love me more or less than you do Max?" she asked.

"The dog?" Max was Ben's golden retriever and they were inseparable. Jackie could see the wheels turning in Ben's mind. She waited as he processed some more.

"I love you more than Max!" he said confidently, "Max and I don't have sex. I love you more because we have sex and I like it."

"Were there other people with whom you didn't like sex?" asked Jackie mildly flabbergasted at the content of their conversation.

"Yes," he replied, "My ex-girlfriend made me feel uncomfortable sometimes, so I didn't like sex with her as much as I like it with you." While Jackie could have been easily offended by Ben's mention of his sexual relationship with his ex, she realized that that's how Ben processed things in his mind—very matter of fact and literally.

Needless to say, Jackie came to her next session with a new spring in her step. "Guess what," she said giggling, "Ben loves me as much as the sun burns up energy in a single day! How crazy is that!? I'm now convinced he's an Aspie, just like my mother. How else can we explain his bizarre way of processing his feelings for me?"

Neurodiverse Marriages: More Common than You Might Think

Ben and Jackie's story is all too common in today's day and age. In the last two decades, since Asperger's Syndrome (AS) and the Autism Spectrum Difference (ASD) became more recognized in the field of psychology, there has been a monumental increase in the diagnosed cases of individuals with AS and ASD. The Centers for Disease Control and Prevention report that nearly one in sixty-eight children are affected by an ASD (CDC, 2014). Scientific evidence indicates that ASD is largely genetic. Although there is currently no data for the prevalence of ASD in adults one could assume, due to its genetic nature, that the same one in sixty-eight figure might apply to adults as well.

Due to their giftedness in the areas of math, science, technology, medicine, art, and music, many adults with ASD make for highly desirable life partners. Based on prevalence rates alone, one could assume that a significant number of marriages today are neurodiverse relationships.

The Challenges of Marriage

Marriage and relationships in general can be complicated—an obvious reflection of the nature of human beings, and the ups and downs of life. Relationships can be challenged by everything from child-rearing, infidelity, illness, infertility, the death of loved ones, addictions, cultural differences, family, or financial troubles, and other major life-stressors; thus, testing the patience, understanding, coping and communication skills of both partners.

Even under the best of circumstances, sustaining a relationship can push most individuals to the brink of their limits and capacities. As such, 40 to 50 percent of marriages do end in divorce (APA, 2013). That said, the majority of adults still pursue long-term relationships or marriage.

Neurodiverse Marriages or Relationships

Neurodiverse marriages or relationships where one or both partners have ASD or a related neurological profile present additional challenges. These challenges can very quickly deplete the energy reserves of each partner. The strategies and tools that non-spectrum (NS) couples find useful often do not work for those in neurodiverse relationships.

In general, people with ASD can be at an inherent disadvantage in relationships because ASD (although marked by many other physiological and psychological idiosyncrasies) is primarily a social-communication-emotional difference. In a neurodiverse marriage, where one or both partners struggle to communicate, expressing emotions can be even more challenging to facilitate. Some adults with ASD end up in multiple marriages in their lifetime, due to the difficulties they face in communication, mood regulation, stress management, anxiety, depression, and sensory integration on a daily basis.

Couples in neurodiverse relationships may need to create an entirely new structure for their lives and their interactions with each other. They may have to work much harder to stay connected to each other, and manage aspects of ASD such as sensory issues, executive functioning challenges, ADHD, mental health and medical issues if they coexist.

Successful Neurodiverse Marriages

Since the vast numbers of individuals with ASD, in particular those in neurodiverse marriages remain undiagnosed, little is known about the success rates for marriages where one or both partners have ASD. As a couples counselor, specializing in neurodiverse couples, a majority of couples I see choose to stay together in the relationship. Some couples come to me with a significant number of years already invested in the relationship. They may have children, assets, community, and a life built together.

In my own experience with the couples I see, they tend to exhaust every option before they opt for a divorce. Many times, their efforts to improve their marriage in the past have been in vain because they haven't viewed the relationship through the ASD lens. The strategies they tried weren't specific to the neurodiverse relationship. Despite their best efforts and hard work, psychotherapists and couples counselors who are uninformed about ASD and not trained in working with neurodiverse couples, can cause more harm than good. Due to the pervasive and sometimes disabling nature of ASD, many neurodiverse couples do get divorced. The choice to stay married versus the decision to get divorced is very personal and unique to each couple.

This book is for couples that are seeking the right assessment and understanding of their neurodiverse relationship. While they may have figured out some strategies on their own, or with their couples counselor, they could use more assistance in building a better marriage. Not every strategy will be applicable for every relationship. The strategies in this book are a starting point and will inspire couples to create even more solutions for their relationships.

Chapter 1

PURSUING A DIAGNOSIS—OR NOT

If a man does not keep pace with his companions, perhaps
it is because he hears a different drummer. Let him step to
the music which he hears, however measured or far away.

HENRY DAVID THOREAU

How Most People Come to Suspect ASD

In the majority of neurodiverse marriages, it can be several
years before either partner has any idea that ASD is at play in the
relationship. More often than not, it is the NS partner who first
comes to realize that her partner might have ASD. She might
find out about ASD from an article, book, or television program.
Sometimes when a child receives an ASD diagnosis, the father
may self-diagnose by seeing his own traits reflected in the child.
At other times it may be a well-informed friend, family member,
co-worker, psychotherapist, or acquaintance who might bring up
the possibility of ASD.

Even if the NS partner is at first unfamiliar with ASD, she
may have noticed that something was different about her partner
early in the relationship. However, she may have ascribed these
differences to her partner's difficult childhood, cultural differences,

or the newness of the relationship. She may have hoped that over time, the relationship would deepen and that she and her partner would be able to work through their differences.

When the relationship doesn't improve, or their differences do not get resolved, the NS partner might begin looking for additional explanations for her husband's behavior. For example, she may wonder why her partner brings home dinner just for himself, but none for her, or why he never tells her he loves her. Why he doesn't buy her birthday or anniversary presents, or initiate holding her hand? Why does he march twenty steps ahead of her every time they're walking somewhere? Why does her partner, so loyal and devoted in some ways, say, "You should stop wearing dresses, they don't flatter you!" When she expresses hurt feelings, he shows no empathy—and even may argue why he's right!

For his part, the partner with ASD is confused by his wife's unhappiness. He doesn't understand why she repeatedly says, "I feel like you don't love me." Doesn't he work hard at his job so that he can financially provide for his family? After work, even though he's exhausted, he still does his share of the household chores. Yet, his wife thinks that he doesn't care about her! Why does she constantly criticize him? Why is she so dissatisfied?

Many individuals with ASD often lack awareness about how different they are from NS individuals, and what a relationship entails. A man with ASD may not realize how different he is from NS men. Even the nonverbal autistic Japanese teenager, Naoki Higashida, in his book, *The Reason I Jump* (Higashida and Mitchell, 2013), states that he wasn't aware that he was different from other people. Without the feedback from his partner, a man with ASD might never consider that he has certain relational-communication challenges. If on occasion, he does seek help, it's likely to be for depression, anxiety or ADHD.

When the NS partner begins looking into ASD, she may experience a combination of shock and relief: "As I read the traits about Asperger's Syndrome and relationships, I felt as if someone had knocked the wind out of me... I was so shocked! I had to read the article twice to make sure that I had read correctly. I felt as if the world shifted on its axis, and my life came into clear focus." Or she may say, "At first, I couldn't believe it. I had a hard time believing that my partner could be autistic. But then, I begin to feel enormous relief. I finally had the answers I had been looking for."

The Un- and Misdiagnosed

Renowned ASD expert Dr. Tony Attwood estimates that 50 percent of children with ASD may currently be undiagnosed or misdiagnosed due to their ability to mask their difficulties (2007). One can perhaps assume that over 50 percent of adults with ASD, too remain undetected due to their ability to compensate and camouflage their social-communication-emotional challenges. ASD is not a mental disorder, but a neurological difference. Even though the prevailing perspective of ASD is that it is a disability requiring substantial interventions, not everyone with ASD requires special accommodations at school or work, or assistance in their day-to-day life. Individuals with ASD are often intelligent in the average to superior range; they can easily be a cut above their peers in terms of their ability to think outside the box and innovate. In fact, many adults with ASD have highly successful careers due to their intelligence and hyperfocus. Many rise to prominence in the fields of technology, engineering, science, math, medicine, art, and music. And, they may use their high intelligence and ingenuity to mimic behavior that helps them achieve social acceptance.

The majority of individuals with ASD who are successful at work may go their whole lives without feeling the need to seek a diagnosis, or viewing their life in the context of ASD. Even though adults may experience distress, instead of seeking professional help, they may self-medicate with alcohol or marijuana or excessive sex. For individuals with ASD who are able to hold jobs and have social relationships, marriage may be the final frontier—the last arena where anybody challenges them to grow beyond the limitations of their ASD nature. Even though they may have some struggles with social-communication or sensory issues, these issues are most evident in the context of a romantic relationship. Their colleagues, parents, siblings, and even children might consider them quirky, unusual, or different, but it's their romantic partners who will have expectations that are the hardest for them to meet.

Many mental health professionals aren't able to recognize ASD in adults and are ill equipped to help neurodiverse couples. Many psychiatrists, for example, provide medication during a 20-minute appointment, but not counseling. If the partner with ASD visits a psychiatrist or his physician complaining of depression, he might receive a prescription, but not be self-aware enough to report accurately on the struggles in his marriage, and his wife is unlikely to accompany him to these appointments. Even if the patient does reveal social-communication-emotional and marital challenges, the clinician may be unfamiliar with ASD and may not see the necessity to refer him to an ASD specialist. In instances when the patient does mention the possibility of having ASD, based on his limited understanding, the clinician may dismiss his patient's concern. He may even insist that his patient "can't have ASD!"

Prevalence and Cause

In 2014, as we have seen, the Centers for Disease Control and Prevention (CDC) estimated that 1 in 68 children (or 14.7 per 1000 eight-year-olds) in the United States has been diagnosed with an Autism Spectrum Disorder (ASD). This new estimate is roughly 30 percent higher than the one reported in 2012 (CDC, 2014). The prevalence of ASD is on the rise. Autism Spectrum Difference (ASD) is mainly genetic, although environmental causes cannot be completely ruled out (Insel, 2009). Another explanation for the prevalence of ASD is neurodiversity.

Neurodiversity "is the idea that neurological differences like autism and ADHD are the result of normal, natural variation in the human genome. This represents a new and fundamentally different way of looking at conditions that were traditionally pathologized" (Robison, 2013). Individuals with ASD are well suited to and often do well in technology-based professions. They can often be financially secure and stable life partners; thus, increasing the likelihood of neurodiverse marriages and more offspring with ASD. Regardless of the reasons for the increasing rates of ASD, it's important to invest in solutions rather than focusing solely on causes or cures. Rather than perpetuating a culture that is fearful about autism, we need to focus on creating an inclusive society of neurodiverse individuals.

Core Features of ASD

The autism spectrum is a neurological difference, rather than a mental disorder. It is not a disease that needs to be cured. ASD is characterized by a collection of traits, or a behavioral profile with certain core features. The criteria for an Autism Spectrum Disorder (see the Terminology section) diagnosis include:

- Social-interaction and social-communication issues, namely impairments in social-emotional reciprocity, struggles in keeping a conversation flow, very limited or no sharing of interests, and emotions.

- Difficulty in nonverbal communication, such as, understanding gestures and facial expressions.

- Challenges in pursuing and sustaining relationships, and displaying flexible social behavior, and an absence of interest in peers.

- Repetitive and narrow behavioral patterns, including an intense focus on special interests. A need for routines and structure, combined with trouble with transitions, and inflexible, black and white thinking patterns.

- Hyper- or hypo-reactivity to sensory input.

- Traits may or may not become fully manifest until life-stressors and social-emotional demands become unmanageable. Coping strategies may also mask traits.

- Traits cause clinically relevant impairment in work, social and personal relationships.

- The behavioral profile is not explained by any other intellectual developmental disorder.

(American Psychiatric Association [APA], 2013).

If the individual demonstrates traits in the listed domains, he will receive an ASD diagnosis. If he fits a profile similar to Asperger's Syndrome in DSM-IV (APA, 2000), he will receive an Autism Spectrum Disorder Level 1 diagnosis according to DSM-5. The second and third levels include those who are visibly impaired, disabled, and require considerable assistance for all or much of their lives (APA, 2013).

ASD Traits Vary in Severity

The severity of ASD traits varies from person to person. In order to arrive at a diagnosis, clinicians assess the severity of traits. For a diagnosis, traits have to be clinically significant, that is persistent and severe in nature. Individuals with ASD often have extreme traits. For example, one individual with ASD might be an expert at traveling and planning trips, while another might completely lack any such knowledge and ability. One NS partner might find that her husband is obsessed with cleanliness. He won't go to bed until the entire kitchen is spotlessly clean and disinfected with several anti-bacterial cleaners. Whereas, another NS partner might report that his girlfriend doesn't ever clean up after herself and that "her apartment resembles a garbage dump." Another individual might be a great cook because food is his special interest, while another might not even know how to boil an egg.

These inconsistent features can have clinicians as well as the neurodiverse couple doubting whether ASD is really a factor in their relationship. The partner with ASD may say, "See? I don't have ASD. That guy with ASD never stops talking, but I'm a man of a few words." Differences in traits and the severity to which they manifest vary so greatly, that I've never met two people with ASD who are exactly alike.

ASD is a Constellation of Traits

It's tempting to think of an individual with ASD as having a score on a numeric autism scale—neatly lined up according to his level of functionality. However, using such a linear scale wouldn't represent an accurate picture of the individual. Rather it's easier to view each individual with ASD as having his/her own unique constellation of traits. The clusters of ASD traits vary from person to person. It's extremely rare for one individual to have all the traits listed in the DSM-5 or on the online ASD quizzes. For example, one partner might have 15 traits while another 30. The combination and severity of traits is what makes each individual with ASD different.

ASD is Invisible

Although people with autism look like other people physically, they are in fact very different (Higashida and Mitchell, 2013). It's difficult to tell if someone has ASD from his/her outward appearance. Autism Spectrum Difference is largely invisible. If visible at all, the features of ASD can appear to be subtle on the surface, especially in adults that are undiagnosed or diagnosed later in life. Most clinicians are yet to receive the specialized training required to identify ASD in adults. They may not understand or recognize the complex and varied manifestations of ASD. They also have biases on what autism looks like and what it doesn't. Many harbor misconceptions on the causes for some of the ASD traits they see in adults.

If a spouse comes in with his partner saying that she has trouble with empathy, the clinician may either think that the spouse is being oversensitive, or that the partner with ASD has unresolved mother issues. They may attribute her perceived coldness and anger problems to dysfunctional parenting, childhood trauma, or psychological problems rather than to a neurological hard-wiring. Many times, even when she goes to her doctor and therapist saying that she's read up on ASD and is convinced that she is on the autism spectrum, they might brush her off, and attribute her ASD traits to a string of other diagnoses or causes. Therefore, obtaining a diagnosis is often not a straight, or easy path.

Pursuing a Diagnosis is Challenging

Diagnosing ASD, particularly in adults, remains challenging. It is a science and art—requiring the trained eye of a specialist who has seen a wide variety of adults on the spectrum. To decide whether an adult has ASD or not, it is necessary to view his cluster of traits in the broader context of his relationships, life history, and lived experience.

While there are a myriad of valuable books about ASD-NS relationships, understanding ASD in the context of a neurodiverse relationship is the work of a specialist—someone who has training and experience not only with adults with ASD, but with couples in neurodiverse relationships. Clinicians also need to listen to the NS partner. While knowledge gained from books and research papers can provide clinicians with a lot of information, the adults and their partners themselves are incredible sources of information.

Why Clinicians Rule Out ASD

Severity of traits are not the same across the board, they vary according to each individual, making diagnosis really difficult. Many adults with ASD that I've met report that they've seen more than one counselor, social worker, psychologist, psychiatrist, or physician who has explicitly told him that he doesn't have ASD. These clinicians rule out ASD by saying, "You don't have tics. Adults with ASD usually have tics." Or, "You've been married for over 20 years, how can you be autistic? People with autism aren't interested in relationships."

The majority of individuals with ASD qualify for a number of other common mental health diagnoses such as anxiety, panic disorder, depression or ADHD (Miller, 2012). Clinicians often focus on the diagnosis that is strongest at the particular moment in the time that the individual goes to see them. For example, if an individual with ASD goes to see a therapist or psychiatrist for having anxiety about a new job, they may diagnose them with anxiety. If the individual with ASD isn't specifically seeking an ASD diagnosis, they may not screen them for underlying issues such as ADHD or ASD.

Self-Diagnosis

John Elder Robison (2013) said about being on the autism spectrum:

> As an adult with autism, I find the idea of natural variation to be more appealing than the alternative—the suggestion than I am innately bad, or broken and in need of repair. I didn't learn about my own autism until I reached middle age. (para.5)

More and more adults are self-identifying as being on the autism spectrum. Many of them prefer a self-diagnosis. A self-diagnosis can lead to the individual with ASD evaluating his strengths and weaknesses in the context of ASD. He can help him finally make sense of why he has always felt so different from his peers. He can feel empowered to learn strategies to help himself. A self-diagnosis can be as beneficial if not more beneficial than a clinical diagnosis.

There is a great sense of relief in knowing that her "alternate mindset" is what makes her different. A self-diagnosed individual may also take more responsibility for her traits, and actively seek out the necessary interventions and support. More often than not, her struggle may be being unable to find clinicians who understand adult ASD and teach her strategies that work.

Ronaldo, an adult with ASD, once said to me, "For years, I would brush off my wife trying to tell me that I had ASD. Then, one day,

I saw a documentary on neurological differences, and how autism was just a different kind of intelligence. From then on, I began reading about ASD for myself. I felt internally changed. Everything about my life began to make sense. Not only my own life, but even the lives of my parents, who are probably autistic. I didn't want to hear about ASD when I thought it was some psychobabble to make who I am wrong. As a neurological difference, I can accept it. And of course, I'm convinced I have it!"

The *Aspie Quiz*

There are a few online tests available for people investigating ASD on their own. The *Aspie Quiz* is one such example. It is a set of roughly 100 questions that ask a person to rate if they strongly or mildly identify with certain ASD traits. For many individuals with ASD and their partners, such quizzes can be a good starting point and might even be a useful tool in self-diagnosing. However, it's important not to substitute the online quizzes for an expert's clinical judgment. I have more than one NS partner emailing me to tell me that her partner took the online quiz and "passed it"—or came out to be—"not Aspie" perhaps because her partner wanted to outsmart the test and deflect the diagnosis. He may have felt attacked or blamed because he may feel like his partner was trying to pathologize him. The NS partner is then disappointed that she lost an opportunity for a conversation with her husband about ASD and neurological differences.

I recommend that, unless the partner with ASD is open to the possibility that he is neurologically different, then an online quiz might be best avoided. It might be more valuable to read books and articles on ASD and relationships, or consult an ASD-specialist instead.

Neuropsychological Testing: Is It Necessary?

Neuropsychological testing is most commonly conducted for children and teens requiring special educational accommodations. First, the neuropsychologist meets with the parents to elicit a detailed developmental life history of the child, including information about birth, physical and social developmental milestones, family history, and educational reports. Next, she would administer the neuropsychological tests in order to measure the child's cognitive functioning in a number of domains such as intelligence (IQ), reading, writing, and verbal skills, reasoning ability, processing speed, memory, and learning differences. If she deems them necessary, the neuropsychologist will administer scales that measure depression, anxiety, and/or ADHD. She will then review the test scores against the life history interview, and the various DSM diagnostic criteria in order to arrive at a diagnosis. For children, a neuropsychological evaluation can be really helpful for the parents and educators to understand their academic and learning challenges.

Diagnosing ASD, even in children, is a complicated process. It's not unusual for many children to have five or more diagnoses before finally receiving an ASD diagnosis. The interpretation of the test scores is also based on the training, breadth of experience, and clinical judgment of the neuropsychologist. The tests don't automatically indicate ASD, the way a blood test can indicate tuberculosis. Therefore, despite the battery of tests and life history interview, it is still possible for the neuropsychologist to rule out an ASD diagnosis, or for the diagnosis to be inconclusive.

As we have seen, there are many reasons why it's even harder for adults to get an ASD diagnosis, especially if they are professionally successful, have advanced degrees, are married, and have children. While some adults may prefer a neuropsychological evaluation as part of their diagnosis, others may be satisfied with getting the expert opinion of a counselor or a psychiatrist specializing in adults with ASD, and neurodiverse marriages. When an adult goes for an evaluation, it's very valuable, indeed almost essential for the clinician to interview the NS partner.

Still other adults are happy to claim an ASD identity after reading books and articles by ASD specialists or by other adults with ASD. In any case, the insight that a neuropsychological evaluation and diagnosis provides can be a valuable tool for the individual and for the neurodiverse couple.

For adults with ASD obtaining a neuropsychological test is somewhat of an individual choice. Diagnosis is largely contingent on how well the neuropsychologist is trained in recognizing and working with adults with ASD. In the context of neurodiverse couples, it's necessary to understand that neuropsychologists seldom provide psychotherapy or couples counseling, and are thus limited in their understanding of neurodiverse relationship dynamics. Hence, the couple can leave feeling even more confused, if the clinician lacks the proper expertize.

Best Practices for an ASD Diagnosis

It's important that an ASD diagnosis be based on a detailed overview of several domains of a person's life. In my own experience, in addition to the DSM-5 diagnostic criteria for ASD, it's important that an individual diagnosis include:

1. A comprehensive overview of an individual's life. Everything from:

   a) a person's childhood development

   b) his educational, and

   c) employment history

   d) psychological profile

   e) head trauma/medical conditions, and

   f) any prior mental health diagnoses need to be considered.

2. Additionally, when diagnosis is precipitated by a troubled marriage, an interview of the spouse or partner is key. When

possible, parents, siblings or adult children, and close friends might also contribute to a more comprehensive profile.

3. It's important that the clinician is experienced and has seen a wide variety of adults with ASD. The clinician must be able to notice traits during the diagnostic interview.

4. Finally, the diagnosis process is most valuable when it is a collaborative process between the individual with ASD and the clinician.

A Comprehensive Overview of an Individual's Life

In my practice, when I conduct a diagnosis, I use a multi-page *Life History Questionnaire* adapted from Lynda Gellar, Ph.D., to gather information about a client in a number of different categories. The questionnaire includes details about the individual's birth, developmental milestones, a family history of parents and other blood relatives, and a detailed understanding of their education, employment, social life, relationships, and life experience. This questionnaire is a guide to sift through information about a person's life, and carefully review every aspect of his existence.

I evaluate the individual through an in-person interview over a period of almost four hours, preferably over a few days. This allows me to look for variations in the individual's ASD traits, and behavior over the course of our interactions.

An Interview of the NS Partner is Key

NS partners in the neurodiverse marriage have a unique experience. There is much written about their experiences and the majority of the literature is by the spouses themselves. The mental health field is lagging behind in understanding how being in a neurodiverse relationship can affect the NS partner. There have been a couple of different terms coined to understand the experience of the NS partner, such as Cassandra Affective Deprivation Disorder, and currently Affective Deprivation Disorder (AfDD) (Simons and Thompson, 2009).

The NS partner's experience is important for the diagnosis within the context of a neurodiverse marriage. It's really important that clinicians understand AfDD even though it might not currently be a part of the DSM-5. Just because it's not in the DSM-5, doesn't mean that it doesn't exist. Also, the majority of NS partners I've met do not seem to exaggerate their partner's traits, or their own experience. No NS spouse that I've ever met is out to simply *get* her spouse, or pin a label on him. That said, even without an ASD diagnosis, the neurodiverse couple could begin to see positive changes, once they learn to problem-solve in the context of ASD.

Another barrier that some adults face in getting a diagnosis is the fact that many adults can have trouble observing, identifying, and verbalizing their relational issues due to their limited perspective on their emotional differences and social-communication challenges. They are often unable to accurately report to the clinician their whole gamut of ASD traits. Therefore, it is essential that the NS partner be part of the diagnostic process.

A Clinician Who Knows ASD and Neurodiverse Relationships

It's important that the clinician is a specialist in ASD and that she understands the neurodiverse relationship dynamic. In general, a diagnosis of ASD in adults requires a highly trained eye. A specialist who's worked with and seen numerous adults with ASD is usually best equipped. Clinicians who are generalists or specialists in other areas tend not to have the training, or experience to make such a complex diagnosis. That's probably why many adults and even children end up with several diagnoses, before clinicians arrive at ASD. These prior diagnoses most often include depression, anxiety, ADHD/ADD, OCD, bipolar, schizophrenia, or even personality disorders. Many of these diagnoses may be misdiagnoses; however, many individuals with ASD qualify for dual or even triple diagnoses. Individuals with ASD tend to have complex profiles; it is common for adults with ASD to have multiple diagnoses over their lifetime.

An ASD-specialist can be a psychotherapist, psychiatrist, neuropsychologist, neurologist, psychologist, or couples counselor.

The key is that the clinician be familiar with the neurodiverse couple experience. Even with an ASD-specialist, receiving a diagnosis can be fraught with challenges and obstacles if he does not understand the various iterations of the neurodiverse relationship.

In the context of a neurodiverse marriage, it's important that the clinician understand that the couple is seeking an ASD diagnosis to explain the unique set of challenges that they are facing. If the couple wasn't together, the individual with ASD might not even be in the doctor or counselor's office. Clinicians need to understand that the NS partner may have read the ASD-NS relationship literature prior to making the critical phone call for a diagnosis for her partner. She may have gathered information and confirmed her experience from reading the experiences of other NS partners and realized that her experience is consistent with that of a neurodiverse marriage.

Diagnosis is a Collaborative Process

Finally, the diagnosis process is most valuable when it's a collaborative process between the clinician, the individual with ASD, his partner and other family members when possible. A diagnosis of ASD should be an empowering event. Preferably, the individual with ASD is a full participant in his own assessment and wants to understand how his mind works and why. Once he understands himself in the context of ASD, he can ask for the help he needs, learn compensatory strategies, and develop better relationship skills.

Even if a clinician does diagnose him with ASD, unless he wants to engage in counseling, a diagnosis may not always force him to do so. Diagnosis thus shouldn't be seen as the be-all end-all to the couple's problems; however, it is a big step in the direction of creating change. Diagnosis is an empowering experience only when both partners choose to acknowledge, understand, and work on their relationship in the context of ASD.

♥ SARAH AND BRIAN'S STORY ♥

Sarah contacted me over the Internet about her marriage. She had been married for several years to her husband Brian, who was a renowned surgeon in Philadelphia. She expressed that she'd read an article, and realized that Brian fit the description of ASD. She scheduled an appointment to come see me along with Brian, and over a period of four days, we scheduled six counseling sessions.

In that time, I reviewed Brian's *Life History Questionnaire* and spoke to both Sarah and him extensively about his ASD traits and their relationship challenges. I also observed how the two of them interacted with each other, and the manner in which he answered many of my questions. To me, Brian fit the textbook profile of an individual with ASD. Sarah also had a classic experience of an NS partner of a man with ASD. She said that she felt emotionally deprived, exhausted, had trouble sleeping, and was depressed. She felt alone and experienced a complete lack of empathy from Brian.

"I feel so disconnected from him. I feel like I'm alone. He's always complaining about something or the other. He's so hard to be around."

Brian was somewhat quiet; he seemed anxious and a little angry. I explained how many individuals with ASD can't help but notice things that could be better or need to change. "It must be hard not to verbalize what you notice knowing that it would upset your wife." Brain began to feel like he had an ally in me. He calmed down and began to open up.

"I guess I am grumpy sometimes. I feel like I never have time to relax anymore. Work is so stressful and the only thing that makes me happy is pot and sex."

"Yes," said Sarah, "he likes having sex all the time. I feel used and objectified."

After the first session Brian began using some strategies I prescribed to better manage his anxiety. Sarah and him seemed happier at the second session with me. Brian took a lot of notes on his computer tablet in our sessions. By the time they ended their sixth and last in-person session with me, they both seemed excited about continuing to apply and practice the solutions we had discussed. I suggested follow-up sessions as a way to maintain the gains made, and to continue to troubleshoot new issues that came up. I recommended that Brian go see a psychiatrist, specializing in ASD, so that he could get a medicine evaluation for his anxiety. Using medication might after all prove to be a more reliable, consistent and long-term solution to his anxiety, than marijuana and sex.

Feeling better about his marriage than ever, Brian went to a psychiatrist in his home town. The psychiatrist listened to him describe his visit with me, and within 20 minutes dismissed him by saying, "You don't have ASD! A lot of wives these days are bringing their husbands in saying they have Asperger's. Sounds like you had a traumatic childhood with a narcissistic mother; of course you're having trouble expressing your emotions to your wife. It's pretty common. You have anxiety for sure. I can prescribe something for that. I've seen plenty of people with ASD. You're definitely not one of them!"

In an instant, the psychiatrist set back several weeks of progress that Brian and Sarah had made in their marriage. Brian began to question the couples counseling trip, and his wife's perception of him. Sarah became very angry with both the psychiatrist and Brian. She vented her frustrations, to which Brian responded by stonewalling, as was his usual pattern.

When Sarah contacted me again to follow up on the situation, she said she was sadder than before they came to me. She said that she felt hopeless once again. I told her that despite what the psychiatrist had said, she should follow her heart. If she felt like she still wanted to continue working on her marriage, then she should do so. If the ASD-specific strategies were working, then regardless of Brian's ownership or acceptance of his ASD, they should continue doing the work. Viewing her marriage through the ASD lens had been very valuable for Sarah, and wasn't lost just because one doctor didn't understand their neurodiverse relationship.

After that, Sarah decided that she was going to apply the strategies that worked, even if Brian and the doctor didn't think he had ASD.

Thus, well-meaning doctors and clinicians can often be insensitive to the NS partner's perspective and experience. Many clinicians also have their own preconceived notions of what ASD may look like in a person, and they can within a span of minutes dismiss an ASD diagnosis. An NS partner once narrated how a renowned psychiatrist dismissed the fact that his wife might have ASD by saying, "She offered you a tissue when you were crying. A person with ASD would never be able to do that. They have no empathy."

Some clinicians might also see ASD as a mental disorder and a negative label, rather than just an alternate way of thinking and processing the world. This mindset might influence their clinical judgment. The biggest reason though that clinicians rule out ASD, even when they are familiar with ASD in adults is that they just aren't familiar with the experiences of the NS partners and the neurodiverse marriage.

Women on the Spectrum

The majority of children and adults diagnosed with ASD are males, with a current male to female ratio of 4:1 (CDC, 2014). There is growing consensus in the field that the seemingly low prevalence of ASD in women is due to the fact that girls and women tend to remain largely unidentified or misdiagnosed. Women with ASD are better able than their male counterparts to compensate for social-communication issues, and mask their challenges. In addition, not as many women on the spectrum fit the stereotypical geek/computer-nerd representation of ASD that is common (but not universal) among men with ASD. While many NS women may be attracted by the quiet, gentle personality of a man with ASD, NS men might find the childlike innocence of a woman with ASD intriguing.

Autobiographies written by women on the spectrum, for those who suspect that their female partner might have ASD, can be a valuable resource. Women with ASD often get misdiagnosed with

Borderline Personality Disorder, Bipolar Disorder, Schizoaffective Disorder, ADHD, OCD, anxiety, or depression.

Additionally, accomplished and professionally successful women are more likely to go undetected even by clinicians who may be familiar with ASD. This is due to the fact that many individuals with ASD are very capable in certain areas. They can often have average to high IQs and may even seem more resilient to adversity than their NS counterparts. To illustrate this point, let us look at Nancy's case.

♥ NANCY AND BILL'S STORY ♥

A successful real estate owner in a Boston suburb, Nancy grew up in a tough inner-city neighborhood in Indiana. From a young age, her special interest was real estate. She loved going to open houses even as a teen and knew all about mortgage rates, and property values. She had an encyclopedic memory for the sales and purchases of various homes by neighborhood and street addresses.

Nancy married her childhood sweetheart and they had one daughter. After a few years, her husband became disabled with multiple sclerosis (MS). Nancy found a job in real estate. Even though the pressure of meeting with people was difficult for her due to her communication challenges, she was very smart, and direct. She could easily calculate figures in her head for her clients, which made them feel like they could trust her. Even without a college degree, she became one of the most successful real estate agents in her company. Eventually, she became successful enough to own several properties around Boston.

Twenty-five years into their marriage, at the behest of her husband, Bill, Nancy went to a local hospital to get a neuropsychological evaluation. He had read about ASD in a magazine and thought that his wife might fit the criteria. He wanted her to get checked out. Their relationship had becoming increasingly difficult with Nancy not being able to contain her anger at the slightest misunderstanding. Also, she seemed to misunderstand him much more than before.

In the evaluation, Nancy scored in the average range on most of the neuropsychological tests. The evaluating diagnostician asked her many questions about her life history and by the time the interview was over, Nancy reported that the psychologist was rather impressed with her accomplishments. The diagnostician told Nancy that she had some unspecified attention issues and a mild short-term memory issue. Nancy was confused, and went home without an ASD diagnosis.

Nancy and Bill's hurdle in to getting an ASD diagnosis is common. Many clinicians rule out ASD because they see the accomplishments of the person, but not the relationship or social-communication-emotional challenges.

Although discouraged, Bill didn't give up. He looked online for resources for ASD and finally came to see me for a couples counseling session. Nancy was very well put together. She had no makeup on, but her clothes were very formal. She wore a beige pantsuit and her straight blonde hair was in a neat ponytail. She looked about 20 years younger than her chronological age. Bill walked leaning on a cane, had a firm handshake, and a ready smile.

Bill began by saying, "We came to see you because I think my wife has Asperger's Syndrome. She went to get a diagnosis, but they told her she didn't have it. From everything I've read about Asperger's, I really believe my wife has it."

"Yes, I don't know why my husband insists on me having Asperger's. What difference does it make?"

"We've been married for twenty-five years now and not once in that whole time has she said, 'and I love you' or 'and I miss you' to me."

"I don't see why I have to tell you I miss you. We live in the same house. If I go away, I always call you, so how can you miss me?"

Even without the diagnosis, Bill and Nancy saw me for couples counseling for almost two years. Nancy did need some assistance with her attention issues. She became aware of how her attention lags when Bill was talking affected her communication and outbursts with him. Nancy began exercising more to help her concentrate better and she saw a psychiatrist who prescribed her with a small dose of an antidepressant to help smooth out her anger outbursts. Bill and Nancy added more structure to their lives, so that they could spend more time together, engaged in activities they enjoyed.

They attended a couple of ASD-focused workshops and conferences, where Nancy met other women with ASD. Towards the end of their work with me, Nancy had on her own, begun to seek out information and learning about ASD. She found it to be an enormous relief to understand that she wasn't being deliberately mean, and that Bill wasn't just trying to blame his unhappiness on her.

Thus, a formal diagnosis of ASD isn't always necessary. Even in the absence of an ASD diagnosis, if the couple is able to acknowledge ASD traits, and neurological differences they might be able to work together to apply specific strategies. Even if the partner with ASD refuses to get an evaluation, the NS partner may be able to use his understanding of ASD to modify his behavior towards his partner.

CHAPTER 2

ACCEPTING THE DIAGNOSIS

If a man does not keep pace with his companions, perhaps
it is because he hears a different drummer. Let him step to
the music which he hears, however measured or far away.

HENRY DAVID THOREAU

♥ MARIA AND SAM'S STORY ♥

Maria and Sam came to see me four months after Sam's diagnosis by
a psychiatrist. The session began with Maria saying, "Receiving the
diagnosis is good. I realize why Sam is the way he is, but nothing in our
marriage has changed. I really thought that he'd start making more of
an effort now that he knows that's he's responsible for the difficulties
in our marriage. Instead, I feel even more depressed knowing that he
is neurologically different and that it's not something he can change."

Maria said that while she understood that Sam couldn't really help
the fact that he had ASD, she was angry with him for having ASD. In
the weeks after receiving the diagnosis she had to really be careful not
to use the ASD diagnosis to shame or blame him. As the non-spectrum
(NS) partner, Maria was worried that Sam might use his ASD diagnosis
as an excuse not to be the partner she needed. She also wanted to

know where she could expect Sam to change, and what were the things that she would just have to live with.

For his part, Sam stated that he was "confused about the whole ASD thing." He had always seen himself as different, but he just attributed this to his being very intelligent and focused on his own special interests and work. Being driven and ambitious in his career had also made him very successful and he was a well-respected leader in his field. Sam really didn't feel like he needed or wanted a diagnosis to explain what he saw as his personality.

Accepting the diagnosis can be a hard road, not just for the partner with ASD, but for the NS partner too. Understanding ASD can be a life-long ASD process and an ongoing journey for both partners for many reasons.

A Paradigm Shift

The diagnosis can create a paradigm shift in perspective for both partners. It can help the NS partner put into perspective all of the couple's marital struggles. The NS spouse often says that the "pennies keep dropping" with regard to her partner's ASD traits. He is now able to view his marital challenges—both past and present—in the context of ASD (Myhill and Jekel, 2008). For the partner with ASD, the diagnosis can often bring about mixed feelings. She may at first deny or make light of her diagnosis, even if deep down she suspects that she is different and struggles with relationships. While some are defensive about their ASD, others are relieved and more readily accepting.

The NS Partner's Grieving Process

Right after finding out about ASD and the diagnosis, the NS partner might go through a grieving process of anger, denial, bargaining, depression, and finally acceptance to cope with the loss of the partner he thought he had versus the partner he actually has. He may not only grieve the loss of having a neurologically different partner, but also the loss of having a typical marriage. It is necessary to recognize that the grieving process is not linear and in a neurodiverse marriage, it can even be cyclical. Just when the NS partner thinks he's done grieving for his atypical partnership, his partner with ASD may make yet another stinging comment causing him to feel upset once again.

It's not uncommon for a sense of hopelessness to sometimes set in. The NS partner may ask, "I finally understand that it's not her mother issues that are causing her to behave like this. Her brain is actually wired differently. Does this mean that she won't be able to make any progress at all?" The NS partner may feel like he's trapped in a marriage that he didn't sign up for. Therefore, it's important that the NS partner fully understand ASD and what this means for his marriage and life. For many an NS partner, ASD can feel like a death sentence, and he may feel like he needs to end the relationship while he still can.

For many an NS partner, the grieving process can bring hope. He may think, "I now understand the way she is. I no longer feel like I'm going crazy. It's not what I thought my marriage would be, but I'm interested in working on solutions."

He may weigh the positive qualities of his partner with ASD such as being a good financial contributor, problem-solver, and a good mother. He may also begin mobilizing around his own unmet needs in the marriage. He may realize that he has to supplement his social and emotional needs by spending time with friends, family, and counselors. He might also find that being involved in support groups, spiritual endeavors, and community causes help to further broaden and expand his horizons.

In cases where the female partner has ASD and the NS partner is male, the male partner or husband might have a harder time getting his needs met outside the marriage. Female NS partners generally tend to have a better support network in their friends and close family relationships. It can be harder for men, as the NS partner, to find other men to lean on for emotional support. Male NS partners can often have it harder in a neurodiverse marriage.

How the NS partner responds to their partner's ASD diagnosis is very individual. It can depend on factors such as if the couple has children, and if the positive aspects of their life together outweigh the challenges.

The ASD Partner's Relief

For the partner with ASD, receiving the diagnosis can often bring about a huge sense of relief knowing that there's finally an explanation for his relational challenges. Many undiagnosed adults, consciously or unconsciously, have been seeking an explanation for their ASD traits. They are the ones that often embrace the ASD diagnosis 100 percent.

The partner with ASD can thus feel enormous relief at the discovery that his brain is wired differently. He can feel better about himself knowing that he wasn't being deliberately difficult towards his NS partner. He may learn that his NS partner isn't to blame for their relationship challenges either, and that she wasn't "overreacting or being too demanding." Realizing that his challenges of anger management, emotional reciprocity, and communication are neurologically based can be liberating. Acceptance can set him on the course to learn and implement strategies to better his neurodiverse relationship.

Diagnosis Denial

That said, accepting an ASD diagnosis can sometimes be a tough journey. The partner with ASD may reject the diagnosis at first because it is a new idea. It may take him some time to get used to the idea of ASD. When appropriate, I advise the NS spouses I work with "to plant the ASD seed, and water it often" iterating the fact that ASD is an alternate mindset, rather than a disorder. I recommend that they provide this information in small, digestible nuggets. If he views the ASD as a disorder rather than a neurological difference, he may resist the diagnosis. He may insist that there is nothing wrong with him and that it's his NS partner who is "crazy!" He might be blind to his faults and traits. Especially if he is successful in his career, and feels like his so-called ASD traits of hyperfocus, high logic, and rigid pursuit of solutions are highly rewarding at work.

While one could assume that it is often the accomplished men with ASD that are resistant to the ASD identity, I've also met women with ASD, brought in by their NS partners, who are adamantly unaccepting of their diagnosis. When the wife with ASD is in denial about her diagnosis, she may turn around and attack her partner for being unreasonable and wanting to pin a label on her. Often, due to her analytical bent of mind, she may turn the question of whether she has ASD into a battle of wills—played out in endless and exhausting discussions about the minutiae of each ASD trait. Her logical mind can also be particularly wired to trump up all manner of counterpoints with the aim of disproving her NS partner's point of view.

Because the diagnostic process is so complex and long in coming, perhaps after many misdiagnoses, the partner with ASD might think, "What's different this time? First it was a personality disorder, then my wife accused me of being bipolar. For a while she was reading books on ADHD, and now suddenly it's autism!" Acceptance can also be hard because ASD in adults is invisible even to many clinicians who may also reinforce his view that he doesn't have ASD. Negation of ASD, particularly by uninformed clinicians, who are also authority figures with credibility, can be particularly detrimental, and can hinder progress made on the path to acceptance. Well-meaning family and friends may also say things like, "You don't have Asperger's Syndrome. You have friends. You're so social. You don't lack empathy. Don't autistic people lack empathy? I know someone with ASD and you're nothing like him," further reinforcing the partner's denial of his ASD.

The cycle of acceptance versus denial for the partner with ASD also ebbs and flows. He might pretend "to be normal" by imitating others, or adopting personas of individuals he sees around him.

He may be so good at mimicking that he may not only fool others, but even himself. I had a woman with ASD comment after years of ongoing ASD-specific counseling and interventions, "I went to visit my family for Christmas, and realized that I totally have ASD! They are so non-Aspie compared to me."

On some days, the partner with ASD may be rested, and comfortable enough that his ASD traits can be minimized, and he may feel "less Aspie." However, when he is stressed, his ASD traits might become stronger. There is a direct correlation between the amounts of stress an individual with ASD feels and his autistic traits. Sometimes, "feeling Aspie or not" can happen in the span of one evening. For example, a man with ASD explained how he felt like the most charming person in the room as he was giving his best man's speech. He was funny, witty, and had great timing. But after the toast ended, he had to sit and make small talk to those at his table, and felt "his awkwardness return again." Thus, it can be hard to accept the ASD diagnosis based on the inconsistent social experiences an individual on the spectrum can have.

The NS partner may also report that her partner exhibits the Dr. Jekyll and Mr. Hyde effect. For example, the couple might be on vacation, enjoying a nice time sitting on the beach. The NS partner may notice that her husband is being very attentive and considerate. He may listen to her intently, make her laugh, and even be physically affectionate. She may wonder, "Does he really have ASD? He's being so romantic right now, and I feel so connected to him. He even planned this vacation. This feels nice." Depending on the circumstance, the partner with ASD may be very accommodating, affectionate, and appropriately responsive for a few hours, or even days at a time. The NS partner might then make an innocent comment, "Isn't it so nice to be here, just you and me with no phone and television?" Without any warning, her husband might react with an outburst, "What? It would be so much better if I had my phone with me!" Things can thus change in an instant. One moment the couple may be having a nice conversation and the very next, all hell may break loose. If his wife asks him why he's so angry, he may further decompensate and even start screaming, sometimes without knowing that he's doing it. He may then need the rest of the day to recover, possibly even leaving his wife to have a solo vacation for the next few days. These are the incidents that reinforce to her that her husband does in fact have ASD. It's normal for both partners in the neurodiverse marriage to cycle through bouts of acceptance and denial.

Denial Can Perpetuate Pain

The problem with denial is that the couple can stay stuck longer in their rut of negative behaviors, more often than not leading to a break up of the relationship. When the partner with ASD is in denial, the NS partner can often feel further betrayed and hurt. The NS partner often has the experience of being invalidated, lonely and like no one "gets" his relationship experience. His wife denying that she has ASD can feel like she doesn't see, nor understand even a fraction of his reality and pain. The hope he may have initially felt after finding out about ASD may be quickly extinguished. He may then try giving his wife an ultimatum saying, "You either accept that you have ASD, or I'm out of this marriage!" While it's best when both partners accept the diagnosis, even one partner working in the context of ASD can make a positive difference for the neurodiverse relationship.

In cases of denial, engaging the help of an ASD-specific couples counselor can help enormously. The majority of couples I see in my practice come to me having just found out about ASD, and it's rare that the partner with ASD fully accepts this perspective. When in denial, the partner with ASD may feel, "So, I'm responsible for your suffering? I can't accept that. And even if I do accept it, then ASD sounds like a horrible thing to have. Like my having it makes you suffer. I don't have it. I'm not ready to accept that I have ASD!" If and when this is the case, it might be best for the NS partner to back off broaching the subject. Working with a counselor on his own, or in couples counseling without bringing up the subject of

ASD right away, might be a way to strategize around his wife's denial.

Even though the partner with ASD might initially deny having ASD, in time, she can begin accepting that her brain is wired differently. Once again, acceptance is more likely to occur, if ASD is understood as neurological difference versus a medical condition needing a diagnosis. Hopefully, the neurodiverse movement will in time eliminate the medical perception of an autism disorder in favor of an autism difference.

What to Expect After Accepting the Diagnosis

In Maria's case, she wanted to know, "I've read about neuroplasticity. How much change can I expect from Sam with couples counseling?" The answer to this question is that in most neurodiverse couples, it is the NS partner who has to make the majority of the adjustments. That said, the partner with ASD could change, although the change is slow, and painstaking.

The husband with ASD often says to me, "I feel like I'm running a marathon every day, it's exhausting and she doesn't even notice! She only notices all the things I don't do. I get no credit for all the things that I've been working on." The hardest thing for the NS partner is to accept that ASD is neurologically based and that her husband can't just "lose" his ASD traits and turn into an NS person. Even though he can learn new social skills and learn to better communicate, he may continue to struggle with these challenges for a long time.

Change in the ASD partner can be slow and should be seen over months and years rather than days and months. More than one NS partner has described the pace of change in her partner as "glacial." I often use the analogy of watching a tree grow. A glacier moving, and a growing tree are imperceptible to the naked eye, but a time-release camera would capture every little millimeter the glacier moved or the tree grew. Over a period of time, one would be able to see significant changes. Nevertheless, for many couples, time does run out. One or both partners may feel that they've tried everything to change the situation, and that they are just too unhappy to stay in the marriage.

Accepting NS-ASD Differences

Having a discussion about the differences in NS-ASD neurology can be useful for both partners. Often, the partner with ASD has no clue how the NS mind thinks. He might also not understand the correlation between emotional reciprocity and the well being of his NS partner. He may have to learn to embrace NS cultural values, such as, conversation as a means of connection rather than information sharing. Similarly, the NS partner may also have to become more accepting of her partner's ASD concrete way of demonstrating his love, such as him refinishing her kitchen floor. An open discussion can help bridge the gap between the NS-ASD neurological and cultural difference.

Open Dialogue and Strategies

Open dialogue can help couples not only understand how their neurological differences cause relational struggles, but also strategize around them. Couples often say to me, "We finally have the ASD diagnosis, now it's time to focus on how we can learn to live with our differences and find solutions."

The purpose of diagnosis is to find strategies specific to the NS-ASD relationship. Otherwise, the couple can feel like they've been going around in circles, trying things that don't work and speaking to counselors who "don't understand." Rather than skirting around the issue, and simmering in silent resentment, the NS partner can finally open up to her partner about her need for a deeper connection. The partner with ASD too can express his own need for more structure in the household. He might express that he doesn't always know what to do, or say, to connect emotionally with his wife. He might have to accept that he has to intellectually learn social-communication skills, and start learning them.

CHAPTER 3

LEARNING ABOUT AND UNDERSTANDING ASD

The roots of education are bitter, but the fruit is sweet.

ARISTOTLE

Accepting and learning about ASD go together. Learning about ASD is important for both partners. When neither partner is aware of ASD, the neurodiverse relationship can become a source of long-term misery for both partners. Struggling in isolation and confusion can lead to hopelessness.

For the NS partner, learning about ASD can help her understand her husband better. She can now understand how the disconnect in her marriage is due to her partner's neurologically based ASD traits, rather than choices he makes. As the NS partner realizes that neither her husband nor she is responsible for the problems in the marriage, she can embark on the road to healing. She can reclaim her sense of self and self-esteem. Sometimes, the NS spouse can assume that she is powerless to change things, when the truth is that even one partner learning and understanding about ASD can have a favorable effect on the relationship. Understanding ASD can help her find solutions that work. Opening the door to learning and understanding ASD can be the beginning of a slow and steady rebuilding of her marriage and life.

For the partner with ASD, educating and learning about ASD can be a major step towards having a better understanding of himself. By learning about ASD, he can find ways to manage his more difficult traits such as anger, anxiety, and aversive thinking. He can also find strategies around challenges in his marriage such as initiating affection, or conversation with his wife. Instead of getting frustrated with his wife, he can begin to understand her point of view. As much as the NS partner can bring about positive changes in the relationship by learning about ASD and implementing behaviors that get her what she wants, the partner with ASD can have an even greater impact in the marriage. For the NS partner, often just seeing her partner try to meet her needs, and make an effort, can go a long way in feeling like he really cares about her.

By learning and understanding how ASD manifests in neurodiverse marriages, both partners realize that they are working with two completely different operating systems. The ASD-brain and the NS brain just don't work the same, and it's important to know how to work with these differences.

♥ SUE AND HELEN'S STORY ♥

Sue and Helen had been married for close to 15 years. They had one child, a 10-year-old daughter. Helen came into see me for the couples counseling session openly declaring, "So, I don't know if Sue has Asperger's. For a long time, I just thought she was a narcissist— self-centered and arrogant! She looks all sweet and gentle here sitting in front of you, but at home she's constantly critical, openly mocking and explosive. We have to figure out why this is and what we can do, or I'm ready to file for divorce." She continued, "We haven't been intimate in four years due to her hurtful behaviors." Helen was very angry. After a pause, she began to cry. "I feel so hopeless. I don't know what to do or where to turn. We are here to know if she has ASD. I really need to know once and for all, so that we can either put this marriage together or go our separate ways."

Sue and Helen heard about ASD only a few weeks ago after their daughter was diagnosed. While reading about ASD traits, it dawned on Sue that she shared many of her daughter's traits. When she shared her thoughts with Helen, she felt like Sue was just trying to justify all of her difficult behavior by saying that she had ASD. After she read up some experiences of NS spouses on the Internet and in books, she felt like her whole world had changed. At first, she was angry that they were just now finding out what was going on with Sue. Helen was upset that none of the couples counselors they had been to over the years had been able to figure out what was going on in their marriage, or how to help them.

Sue and Helen began viewing a lot of their interactions gone awry through the ASD lens. They both felt an enormous sense of relief as they began conversations around Sue's behavior in the context of ASD. Sue finally realized that she tended to sound angry almost 80 percent of the time even when she wasn't meaning to. She also realized that she had a tendency to say the opposite of what Helen, or their daughter said to her. For example if Helen said, "Looks like your weight-loss program is really working. You're looking really trim, almost like when we were dating." Sue would respond with what her partner described as a "cutting tone," "You're wrong, when we were dating, I weighed a 135 pounds! I'm nowhere near that. I'm still significantly overweight!" "She can't even take a compliment, she's responds to a compliment with criticism! How does one deal with that?"

Helen had always seen Sue as a narcissist with anger issues. It seemed to her that she would fly off the handle at the slightest provocation. While someone with ASD can come across as a narcissist due to their tendency to only see her own point of view, this has to be understood in the context of ASD. The word autism is derived from the Greek word "autos," which means self; thus, autism translates to self-ism. Therefore, many individuals with ASD tend to come across as self-absorbed and narcissistic. With increasing thoughtfulness on her part, and with a little help from Helen, Sue was able to shift her focus to Helen. She was able to see Helen's point of view when her attention was guided there.

Helen had always assumed that her partner was just being mean. Most of her interactions were thus based on this premise. She would react with anger, or tears at which point Sue would just shut down. In counseling, I explained how Sue's ASD wiring predisposed her to focus on flaws, making her more critical than the average NS person. Her brain thrived on precision and she was good at picking out inaccuracies in facts, figures, vocabulary, and grammar. I explained to Sue that while her talent in this area made her a successful software developer, in her marriage, it caused her to inadvertently hurt her partner. Helen's understanding of Sue's ASD and thinking style helped her understand that Sue wasn't deliberately being mean.

Sue realized how her behavior was taking a toll on her partner. She started making a conscious effort to slow down her thoughts, and become more responsive rather than reactive with Helen. Once Sue understood how her brain worked and how her eruditeness could sound like arrogance and rudeness, she learnt to guide her attention to the negative statements she made and apologize. Saying sorry was something she had never learnt or practiced before. In couples counseling, Sue tried out a few ways of apologizing, and slowly incorporated these into her interactions with Helen.

For her part, Helen too learnt that she had to be careful about not reading into what Sue said. She reported that she always interpreted many things she said to be negative and deliberately hurtful to her. She realized that maybe it was Sue's ASD that caused her to think and react the way she did. She also learnt how to manage conversations that typically had the potential to escalate into debates. If she tried to talk through what she had actually meant, for example, and how Sue had misunderstood her, she would often try and debate her by trotting out numerous logical data points. In the past, she had assumed that Sue was having an ego trip at her expense. After discussing Sue's tendency to process facts and get stuck on ambiguous information, we came up with a plan to either abort the conversation, shelve it for a couples counseling session, or to guide both of their attention to the outcome of the conversation. I explained how if the goal of the conversation was to gauge whether Sue's weight-loss program was working, for example, to discuss in exact pounds how much weight she had lost, and how much she had left to go and how she was feeling about the process.

Helen worked on her deep-seated belief that Sue was deliberately trying to put her down, invalidate and cut her down to size. She began to change her view that Sue was a narcissist. By becoming more self-aware, her ability to not take every single thing Sue said personally also matured. She became stronger by realizing that Sue actually did really love her, and that she just showed it in her actions. Helen's confidence in her marriage grew, as she saw Sue softening her approach towards her.

Sue continued working hard on changing how she reacted to Helen. In the past, she would also point out whenever Helen left the garage door open, the lights on, or the showerhead dripping. Helen saw this as Sue's controlling nature. When she tried to adhere to Sue's strict admonishments, she had to constantly monitor her behavior and felt like she was "walking on eggshells." At times when she ignored Sue's comments, she would find that Sue would get increasingly frustrated and ask her if she was deliberately trying to provoke or anger her.

When questioned about this in couples counseling, Sue explained that there were all these things that irked her and that Helen knew all of them and yet she continued to do them despite knowing that they bothered her. I explained to Sue that she could make it a choice to get angry, or not, about the things that bothered her. We also came up with a rating scale to rate the things that really bothered her on a scale of 1 to 10, with 10 being the things that had the ability to cause her to have a meltdown. Then we sorted out the stuff that bothered her that was lower on the scale, and discussed why they bothered her and which of these things she could work on letting go.

With training and lots of practice, the human mind is malleable, and able to adapt to new ways of thinking and processing. Thus, Sue and Helen made new strides in their relationship based on an understanding of ASD and each other. This newfound understanding helped them both to learn and adopt new behaviors.

Why Learning About ASD is Important

Learning about ASD is important for both partners. For the partner with ASD, the understanding and acceptance of ASD marks an important time to start a new journey toward self-awareness. He can finally start learning about his partner's NS outlook and traits.

Despite ASD traits, such as rigidity and the tendency to be self-focused, my experience as a couples counselor has been that the partner with ASD will work hard to change and evolve when motivated by the right set of circumstances and loving support from the NS partner.

ASD in Books, Articles, Television, and Film

There are many books and articles on ASD and marriage written from the point of view of the NS partner. Reading personal narratives can help the NS partner to validate her experience and feelings. She may want to share these with her partner with ASD. They can both learn how ASD manifests in relationships. It's important to note that some narratives can paint a painfully negative picture; while it may still be helpful to read these accounts, it is good to keep in mind that every relationship is unique.

There are also many television programs and films with ASD characters. Most are positive and encouraging, while others might be caricatures. The news and media also often over-emphasize crime stories where a perpetrator might have ASD. The media may choose to focus on the individual's ASD diagnosis versus his deep-seated mental health problems, traumatic upbringing, and access to weapons thereby perpetuating false stereotypes about ASD. Individuals with ASD are often more likely to endure bullying and mistreatment from those at school, work, and even home, rather than be the perpetrators (Jekel, 2012).

Understanding ASD

Understanding ASD for both partners is a lifelong process. As life evolves and changes on a daily basis, so do the dynamics of the marriage and relationship. It is not just that the ASD needs to be understood, but also the NS partner's traits in the context of the couple's neuro-differences. NS partners often say that they behave differently because of their partner's unique qualities. Understanding how the NS partner has evolved to cope with their partner's ASD is important.

While ASD itself isn't a mental disorder, individuals with ASD often struggle with mental health issues, especially depression, anxiety, OCD, and anger management. They may have attention issues or ADHD. They often have a lower emotional intelligence quotient, and may struggle to express empathy and share their feelings. Many are challenged with organizing time, space, and managing mundane tasks—executive functioning issues. Some have learning differences, sensory and sleep issues. They might have medical challenges such as gastro-intestinal issues, and a propensity for allergies, and environmental sensitivities. Understanding how these traits interact with each other and cause difficulties in the neurodiverse marriage enables us to strategize the right combination of solutions.

Understanding ASD as a Neurological Difference

The ASD brain is different in how it regulates emotion, organizes and plans tasks, memorizes, processes and learns information (Hua *et al.*, 2013; Mottron *et al.*, 2014).

Therefore even though the partner with ASD might try very hard to make changes or implement strategies, his brain may be working against him. For example, the partner with ASD may admit to his anger issues. He may admit that he has "a short fuse." Even though he understands this intellectually, and knows that reacting with anger is detrimental to his relationship, he may not be able to control his anger. It often takes an enormous amount of effort in the form of a prolonged course of cognitive behavior therapy, mood regulation strategies, mindfulness meditation, and psychotropic drugs to be able to manage his mind.

One way to think about the NS-ASD neurological difference is that the ASD brain is the opposite of the NS brain, especially when it comes to relationships and communication. Where the NS partner thrives on social-emotional connection, the partner with ASD much rather prefers intellectual endeavors. The ability for visual processing and logical analysis in the autistic brain can be highly developed. This can mean that areas necessary for emotional-relational intelligence are underdeveloped or slower to develop (Mottron *et al.*, 2014). This slow development might be why ASD is also considered by some to be a developmental delay.

The NS partner might have to accept that while his partner with ASD may be able to make significant changes, she will still remain different because of her neurology.

Learning and Understanding is a Lifelong Process

Due to its complexity, learning about ASD is a lifelong process. ASD traits and behaviors evolve through the couple's life and it's important to keep learning. Similarly, NS traits and behaviors are often mysterious and surprising to the partner with ASD. There is always more to discover about one another.

CHAPTER 4

MANAGING ANXIETY, DEPRESSION, ANGER, OCD, AND ADHD

Facing it, always facing it, that's the
way to get through. Face it.

JOSEPH CONRAD

Many brain studies conclude that differences in the ASD brain can put individuals with ASD at a higher risk for depression and anxiety (Grandin and Panek, 2013). ADHD, Obsessive Compulsive Disorder (OCD), and anger issues can also feature on the list of ASD traits. Most adults whom I see in my practice have diagnoses of depression, anxiety and ADHD, in addition to either diagnosed or undiagnosed ASD. It's common for clinicians unfamiliar with ASD to diagnose an individual's anxiety, depression or ADHD, but miss the underlying ASD.

Even if the partner with ASD does not have depression, anxiety, ADHD or OCD at clinically diagnosable levels, it's important to understand how these mental health issues impact the neurodiverse marriage. Untreated mental health issues can derail her from fully functioning in her life and marriage. It is therefore necessary to thoroughly evaluate and treat any mental health conditions that she might be struggling with.

I will discuss the most common mental health issues that the partner with ASD experiences, followed by specific strategies and treatments such as Cognitive Behavioral Therapy (CBT), Dialectical Behavioral Therapy (DBT), medication, mindfulness, yoga, and exercise. We'll conclude by discussing the mental health of the NS spouse.

Anxiety

Most individuals with ASD experience anxiety. A study of children with ASD found that 84.1 percent of them struggled with some form of an anxiety disorder—a specific phobia, separation anxiety, social phobia, avoidant disorder, obsessive-compulsive disorder, and/or panic disorder (Muris *et al.,* 1998). In my own work, adults with ASD exhibit a similarly high rate of anxiety—the most common forms being generalized anxiety disorder and social anxiety.

The amygdala, a region of the brain thought to help us detect and respond to threats, is known to be larger in individuals with ASD; researchers hypothesize that the larger amygdala is linked to increased anxiety (Amaral and Corbett, 2003). Regardless of the cause, the reality is that the partner with ASD most likely struggles with anxiety in one form or another.

For the following reasons, an ASD individual's anxiety might go undiagnosed for a long period of time:

- He may be self-medicating with alcohol, marijuana, food, or sex.

- He might have always had a low-level of anxiety throughout his life, and he sees it as a normal part of being human.

- He is unaware of his anxiety and may struggle to express the distress he feels.

- He may blame his partner, job, or environment for the fear and discomfort he experiences.

- He may unload his anxiety onto his partner. He may feel better after such an outburst or meltdown.

Undiagnosed and untreated anxiety is a major problem for the partner with ASD, and can lead to deeper manifestations of ASD traits like impulsivity, meltdowns, rage, and withdrawal. Left untreated, these behaviors can of course have an adverse effect on the neurodiverse marriage.

Depression

Differences in brain structure and the neurotransmitters that regulate mental wellness seem to put individuals with ASD at a higher risk for depression (Marc and Olson, 2009). The vast majority of individuals with ASD struggle with depression, either long-term or in recurring episodes. Some experience a low-grade depression or a general feeling of malaise. Others suffer depression severe enough to require a psychiatric hospitalization, for example, depression leading to thoughts of suicide or even a suicide attempt. Many individuals I treat have a history of depression and some are already being treated with antidepressant medication.

The giftedness that many individuals with ASD have in areas of science, technology, design, mathematics, art, and music can also predispose them to depression. Many of these occupations require precision with little or no room for error. The ASD mind is uniquely wired to hyperfocus and perseverates on imperfections and flaws. While the ability to hone in and solve a mathematical problem can make a man with ASD thrive in academia, this same "zero-defect" thinking when unleashed on himself can induce feelings of self-doubt and inadequacy, culminating in bouts of depression.

A man with ASD has a mind that is well suited to noticing an error, whether it be a painting that is hanging askew, or a grammatically incorrect sentence. Oftentimes, he won't hesitate to point it out, and proceed to fix it. This criticizing and "nit picky" behavior can be intensified if he is also struggling with depression.

Depression in the individual with ASD can often go undiagnosed for a long time, because symptoms can manifest differently than they do for NS individuals. Withdrawal, low affect, detachment, lack of motivation, explosive outbursts, and unpredictable anger can all be symptoms of depression. Directed towards the NS partner, these behaviors can cause a lot of damage.

Obsessive Compulsive Disorder (OCD)

Anxiety coupled with a tendency to perseverate, to hyperfocus on flaws, and to engage in repetitive behaviors, can predispose individuals with ASD to develop obsessions and compulsions. Although, rates of OCD in individuals with ASD seem to be lower than that of other anxiety disorders (Muris *et al.*, 1998), when the partner with ASD develops OCD or manifests traits or tendencies of OCD, it can put a severe strain on the neurodiverse marriage.

♥ FREDERIKA AND JOHANN'S STORY ♥

Frederika and her husband, Johann, a middle-aged German couple, long-settled in the U.S. came to see me because Frederika's house-cleaning routines had become all consuming, and Johann complained that they hadn't been spending any time together.

"Frederika is spending up to 30 to 40 hours per week just cleaning! She's always been obsessed with cleanliness and minimalism, but ever since our son left for college last year her behaviors have gotten worse. At the end of every winter she throws out all her winter accessories—gloves, hats, coats and scarves—because…"

Frederika interjected, "I can't stand to have them around when I'm not using them."

"She stays up late cleaning and can't seem to stop. Sometimes it's the almost brand new car, or the nearly empty attic, on top of her regular cleaning of the bathrooms, kitchen, and hardwood floors—plus organizing and weeding out clothes, books, grocery items, and knick-knacks. Even our drawers are empty!"

"I now have to do things in a sequence. That's a new thing. Especially cleaning my hands, I have to use several cleaners in a particular order to decontaminate." She showed me her hands, which looked dry, raw and red.

I referred Frederika to a psychiatrist for medication, and an OCD program at a local hospital (both of which were very helpful). Johann and she continued couples counseling to increase awareness of how her compulsive behaviors and "irritations" were affecting him. The irritations that Frederika mentioned were in fact mini meltdowns, reactions to what she saw as Johann's inability to spotlessly clean up coffee grinds off the kitchen counter, dust particles from the window sills, and sand grains off the floor of the car. Johann was tired of having to clean and stack the dishes in exactly the same order every night after dinner. If he didn't do it the way she liked it, he risked being yelled at. Frederika wasn't aware of her own tone of voice as she criticized Johann. He felt unappreciated for his work, and his wife's constant anger was wearing him down.

Learning more about ASD and how these traits fed into her OCD helped Frederika come up with coping strategies. Understanding how hurtful she was being to Johann helped her make significant changes. She worked on increasing her emotional self-awareness by using the *Sensation-Emotion Awareness Chart*™ (see Chapter 6 on Emotional Intelligence). Johann and she began using *The Relationship Schedule*™ (see Chapter 10 on *The Relationship Schedule*™) to consciously plan more leisure and fun activities. Johann reported that his wife went from being "uptight, angry and obsessed" to being more humorous and relaxed.

Attention Deficit/Hyperactivity Disorder (ADHD)

A majority of adults with ASD seem to also have ADHD. There seems to be a significant overlap in the symptomatology of ASD and ADHD, and up to 60 to 70 percent of children with ASD have traits that overlap with ADHD (Rosenn, n.d.).

Similar to ASD, ADHD is a spectrum condition, made up of a cluster of traits, which can vary from one individual to another. Like adults with ASD, adults with ADHD also struggle with depression and anxiety and often have relationship issues as well. Due to the overlap between ADHD and ASD, at the severe end of the ADHD spectrum and the milder end of the autism spectrum, clinicians may often chose one diagnosis over the other (Rosenn, n.d.). While almost 70 percent of individuals with ASD also have ADHD, individuals with ADHD may or may not have ASD.

The neurology of individuals with both ADHD and ASD point towards differences in executive functioning, judgment and decision-making, reasoning, problem-solving, and processing complex information compared to NS individuals as we have seen (Nigg, 2012). Brains in both ADHD and ASD tend to feature a smaller corpus callosum, which connects the right and left hemispheres of the brain, contributing to a lack of emotion recognition and processing challenges (Nigg, 2012). The differentiating factors between ASD versus ADHD is that individuals with ADHD don't struggle as much with social/emotional reciprocity, Theory of Mind, understanding nonverbal cues, facial recognition, and misunderstanding the social context (Rosenn, n.d.).

Many individuals with ASD who come see me already have an ADHD diagnosis and are on medication for it. When ADHD is present along with ASD, understanding and treating these traits is important because of the problems they can cause the neurodiverse couple.

♥ VIVEK AND SUSAN'S STORY ♥

Vivek and Susan were college seniors at one of the universities in Boston. Vivek was an international student from India, and Susan was Chinese-American. Susan came in saying that Vivek had been increasingly frustrated and angry with her, and that his anxiety was at an all-time high; he kept complaining that he was tired, and had stopped wanting to have sex with her.

Vivek said that he was constantly behind on school assignments, and everything in his life was a blur. Formerly, Susan and he had shared many of the same classes and she had been helping him to stay organized. Vivek in turn helped Susan with her physics and math homework; everything went smoothly. Recently though, as their last year of university drew to a close, Susan found it challenging to manage both Vivek and her own life. She pulled back on the amount of assistance she was giving him, and without her support, his struggles became more obvious.

Susan had ADHD herself and had been successfully taking medication for a number of years. She recognized traits of ADHD in Vivek and recommended that he see the campus psychiatrist, who prescribed medication for ADHD. Due to his poor eye contact, complaints of anxiety, sensitivity to noise, and trouble with his girlfriend, the doctor suspected that Vivek might have ASD and referred Susan and him to me.

At first, I recommended that Vivek get more organized. We looked at his class syllabi, broke down his assignments, gave each step a due date, and put the deadlines on a calendar. The medication was helping him. He was more focused and able to complete these tasks. He was less anxious and irritable with Susan. However, he was still feeling tired a lot, and falling asleep around 9 p.m., leaving little time or energy for sex. Every time Susan tried to broach the subject, Vivek would tell her that she was making him feel anxious.

We discussed the possibility of putting sex on a schedule, possibly finding time to be intimate during class breaks rather than waiting until after 9 p.m. at night. We spoke about how much sexual activity would be satisfactory to both. We tried to understand the breakdowns in their communication. Vivek said that when he felt misunderstood by Susan, he became more anxious.

After only a few weeks of couples counseling, Susan and Vivek were feeling much better about their relationship. Vivek begun to understand that his way of thinking was completely different from Susan's. He realized that he had to slow down, reflect, and learn not to take everything she said as a criticism of him. Putting sex on a schedule had helped him reduce his anxiety about not being able to please Susan. Learning to handle his ADHD challenges with medication and organizational skills made her feel less burdened. An increase in intimacy made her feel closer and more connected to Vivek.

Anger

The partner with ASD often has significant anger issues, which it is necessary to address. Due to neurological factors, she may experience emotional extremes and struggle to regulate these extremes. If she has anxiety, being in an anxious state could make her more likely to be triggered, and less likely to maintain control over her anger.

When the partner with ASD has anger issues, her explosive words and behavior can "terrorize" and traumatize the NS partner. Due to her literal thinking and logical processing, even a simple comment about a movie could trigger her and escalate the conversation. Without intending to, she might "go from zero to 80," become enraged, and blindside her NS partner with cruel remarks.

In the aftermath of an explosion, she might react in the following ways. She might be clueless about her behavior, not realizing how destructive her angry outburst was to her partner and relationship. She may assume that her husband, the NS partner, is overacting, or that he's too sensitive. She might blame him for provoking her. She may not hear the anger in her voice, and may downplay her words and actions. If she does realize that she has truly hurt her partner, she might express remorse over her behavior and apologize.

In order to have better conversations without getting triggered, she might need to learn that even if her partner doesn't think the way she does, his perspective is still valid. She may have to become aware of her black and white thinking, and be able to hear his thoughts without feeling threatened. The partner with ASD might need to broaden her social skill repertoire and ability to tolerate different points of view.

While there are cognitive and behavioral strategies to manage anger, medication can be essential for mood regulation and anger management. Medication can make the partner with ASD slower to anger, giving her "a longer fuse." She might then be able to deploy anger management strategies and exercise new social skills. In favor of medications, a woman with ASD once said to me, "My brain is different, and the medications I take are like vitamins! I see them as supplements, chemicals my brain needs in order for me not to be such a hothead. I can't keep losing boyfriends over my anger problem."

Strategies to Manage Mental Health Issues
Cognitive Behavioral Therapy (CBT)

Cognitive Behavioral Therapy (CBT) has proven to be effective for many individuals with ASD struggling with depression or anxiety (Gaus, 2007). Individuals with ASD take in, hold, process, understand, and output information differently from NS individuals. This especially applies to social-relational-emotional information.

Even though the partner with ASD can be highly intelligent, he is prone misinterpreting his interactions with his NS partner. He might not be able to perceive her feelings and intentions. He can make inaccurate assumptions and stay stuck on some preconceived notion that can then dictate how he interacts with her. He might seldom express these peculiar concepts and schemas and therefore never have the opportunity to challenge and correct them. He may harbor these negative and even harmful ideas for years. CBT can provide the opportunity to for the husband with ASD to talk about these ideas whether they be about his partner, their relationship, or anything else and subject them to a reality check.

For example, when Pete's wife suggested that he think about a few topics of conversation before a dinner party, he automatically assumed that his social awkwardness embarrassed her, and that she secretly hated him. In counseling, we were able to explore the possibility that perhaps she had been attempting to help him because she loved him. Instead of perceiving what his wife said as criticism, based on his premise that she secretly hated him, he was able to entertain the idea that there was another explanation for her behavior.

CBT is based on the premise that our thoughts, emotions, and behaviors are inexorably linked and that each has an effect on the other. Thoughts result in emotions, which in turn result in behaviors. When left unchecked, negative assumptions can fuel negative behavior such as anger, resentment, and defensiveness. For individuals with ASD, the knowledge, understanding, and reality testing that CBT provides can reverse the process.

Persistent thinking patterns that are responsible for depression, anxiety and OCD can also be reset with CBT. Using CBT, the counselor can help the partner with ASD draw out these thoughts, examine them, and replace them with more balanced and positive schemas. Understanding how his thoughts reflect a version of reality based on his unique mindset can help him realize that there might be an alternate way to perceive reality. CBT strategies can help him stop his thoughts from spiraling down a dark path.

CBT can help the partner with ASD to not only recognize the negative emotion, but also to identify the thought that triggered it. He can then choose to change his emotional state by reading something inspiring to lift his spirits, taking a walk, showering, making a gratitude list, or watching his favorite movie, listening to music, speaking to a friend or counselor. Over time, he can became a master of circumventing his negative thought spirals, and creating a positive mindset.

Positive behaviors promote an increase of happy emotions and thoughts. Exercise, laughter, or deliberately smiling can trigger "happy chemicals" in the brain and give his mood a boost. For example, I often suggest that the partner with ASD do something kind that he knows will please his partner even if he's not feeling especially positive about her at the moment. He might be surprised at how quickly this can bring him out of his negative state of mind.

Putting CBT strategies into practice can be challenging at first, but with deliberate practice and continued hard work, the thoughts, feelings, and behaviors of the partner with ASD can become more balanced and positive.

Dialectical Behavioral Therapy (DBT)

Dialectical Behavioral Therapy (DBT) is typically used for individuals who are self-harming, suicidal, or have eating disorders or addictions. If a partner with ASD struggles with handling stress, anger, and regulating his emotions, DBT can be very useful. It combines the cognitive-behavioral aspects of CBT and the mindfulness meditation practices of self-awareness, acceptance, and distress tolerance. Individuals are taught to integrate seemingly contradictory thoughts and passionate feelings in order to tolerate and manage extreme emotional distress (Sanderson, 2008). Using DBT techniques, the partner with ASD can learn to slow down her reaction time and become more resilient to stress. By being less reactive, and reducing behaviors that sabotage her relationship, she can build a more stable life.

♥ PAUL AND STACEY'S STORY ♥

Twenty-seven-year-old Paul was referred to me for individual counseling by his girlfriend, Stacey. She said that Paul was spending more than eight hours a day playing video games. We discussed the reasons for his addiction.

Paul had been recently laid off and was feeling depressed about it. His negative feelings were so intense and painful that he compulsively went online to avoid them. Losing himself in the fantasy world of video games was a welcome escape. In the online gaming world, he had become very adept, which gave him a feeling of accomplishment and importance. Gaming alleviated his boredom, and soothed his distress.

Paul agreed to keep a thought and mood log; when we examined his log together, it became obvious how many of his thoughts were negative. Over time, he came to realize how this type of thinking was having a detrimental impact on his feelings and behavior. I suggested that Paul practice sitting in silent meditation twice a day for at least 15 minutes each time. This exercise helped him to become aware of the feelings and thoughts that lead him to escape into the gaming world. With his newfound mindfulness skills, Paul was able to identify and tolerate his distress and then make a decision not to react to it by succumbing to his video game. Instead, he filled up his daily schedule by attending networking events in his industry and looking for a new job in earnest.

Paul also began working with an organizational skills coach to balance his bank account, sort his mail, and pay his bills on time. Eventually, he found a job in his field that he enjoyed. Two years later, Paul is employed at a job that he enjoys. He and his girlfriend Stacey are now planning to move in together and get engaged.

Planning Ahead

For individuals with ASD, anxiety is often related to sudden changes and a fear of the unknown. For example, a man with ASD might experience a spike in anxiety because he does not know what is expected of him at an office party or what present his wife would like for her birthday. This distress can not only affect him, but also his wife; therefore, it's important that he learns to manage his anxiety by planning ahead and preparing for things that are likely to stress him out. For example, a couple might plan ahead by taking the time to discuss in detail the upcoming Christmas trip to his parent's house. Doing so would minimize his stress and he might be better able to support his wife during the visit. On the other hand, if there is no discussion and the wife feels like her husband is not sticking up for her or not helping her enough with the children, she might get angry with him. Without a plan, not knowing how to react or what to do to change the situation he might become anxious and withdraw.

Strategies such as conversation scripts, a step-by-step breakdown of the event, looking at pictures of the venue, visiting the venue ahead of time, and gathering other pertinent information can make the partner with ASD feel more prepared and less anxious. Scheduling solitude and downtime before and after a social event is another good strategy to reduce anxiety. Knowing that he has time planned to relax and rejuvenate after, might allow the partner with ASD to cope better and even enjoy the event.

Routines and structure can help the partner with ASD feel more in control and less nervous in an otherwise chaotic world. Working with calendars and *The Relationship Schedule*™ (see Chapter 10 on *The Relationship Schedule*™) can also lessen anxiety.

♥ JOHN'S STORY ♥

John, a man with ASD, said that he became highly anxious every time he went to see his in-laws, even though they had been doing so for six consecutive years. His in-laws lived in Ireland on a remote farm. Once a year, his wife, kids, and him took a six-and-a-half hour flight, followed by a five hour drive to see them. He said it took him a while to work out the sequence of events for the trip every single time. He often felt overwhelmed by the airport security and stimulation of unfamiliar people, lights, smells, and sounds. He explained, "Every time I'm at the airport, I have to pretend like I know what I'm doing. If the children are with us, which they always are, I'm even more on edge."

In order to ease things for John, his wife and him came up with a detailed, written sequence of events and a list of "to dos" for him on each leg of the trip. I advised John to write everything on a three by five (about 7 cm by 12 cm) inch index card. "Armed with the index card in my pocket, I had a much better trip this time," John reported, "I felt less anxious knowing I had a plan for what was next."

Medications

Medications can alleviate anxiety, treat depression, and even reduce the obsessiveness and rage that the partner with ASD might struggle with. Due to a lack of awareness or communication difficulties, the partner with ASD may not always report his anxiety, depression, or anger issues to his doctor. He might instead self-medicate or distract himself with alcohol or marijuana, video games, pornography, and special interest obsessions. He may be embarrassed to admit his dependence on these substances and interests to his doctor.

When an individual does go to the doctor for a mental health complaint such as anxiety or depression, it is important that the prescribing psychiatrist be knowledgeable about ASD. Many individuals with ASD have a tendency to be sensitive to drugs, and respond better to lower doses (Cell Press, 2014). A comprehensive and thorough conversation with the psychiatrist is essential. I also suggest that the NS spouse accompany her partner with ASD to the doctor's office in order to provide a more complete picture of her husband's mental health profile. When possible, the psychiatrist might want to communicate with the counselor, in order to share pertinent information.

There are a wide variety of medications available to treat mental health issues. When treating depression, anxiety, OCD, or ADHD, it is vital to combine pharmacological treatment with counseling. Medications can be really useful for many adults with ASD, but it's important to supplement them with therapies and coping strategies.

The partner with ASD will often ask me how long they should be on medications. Although I'm not a medical doctor, I've observed that some of the individuals with ASD in my practice benefit from short-term treatments and others require a longer course.

Mindfulness Meditation

Many individuals with ASD struggle with the mind-body connection; therefore, mindfulness techniques can help the partner with ASD to develop more awareness of his body. A regular meditation practice that involves focused breathing and body-scanning exercises for 15 to 30 minutes each day can increase body self-awareness. The regular practice of tuning into his body can help him monitor and alleviate his reactions to stress.

The partner with ASD can have a tendency for "sticky attention," which means that once he gets started on a train of thought it can be very hard for him stop. Thoughts tend to barrel down a well-laid out track, unable to change course. Mindfulness meditation involves observing one's thoughts, which can help the individual become more self-aware of his tendency to get stuck on certain negative thoughts. He might then learn to stop himself from accelerating into a downward spiral. He might use the same technique to help him become more mindful when speaking to his wife. By creating pauses between thinking and speaking, and editing and refraining from voicing his negative thoughts he can minimize some of the potentially insensitive things he says.

♥ JORGE'S STORY ♥

Jorge, a 32-year-old graduate student with ASD, would often get anxious around visits with his girlfriend's parents. His girlfriend brought him in to see me after he had abruptly left a dinner with her parents who were visiting from out of state. Jorge felt like they didn't like him because he was Latino and his girlfriend was Caucasian.

In couples counseling, Jorge was able to speak about his true feelings and his girlfriend was able to reassure him of her love and respect for him. They decided to have Jorge take breaks when spending time with her parents, so that he would have time to monitor his anxiety levels and replenish his energy. Jorge also learnt to "breathe into his anxiety" and stop his thoughts from spiraling into a negative loop of self-doubt.

He started meditating 15 to 20 minutes a day in order to increase his mind-body connection. He became aware of all the uncomfortable bodily sensations he carried with him on a daily basis. Over time, Jorge was able to notice that whenever he felt anxious, insecure, or self-doubtful, his shoulders felt tensed. His tense shoulders were a signal for him to start using his coping strategies.

Jorge also used a 1 to 10 numbers scale to assess the level of anxiety he felt (1 being the lowest and 10 being the highest). Eventually, Jorge also took up yoga classes along with his girlfriend, which further helped him with his mind-body awareness.

Yoga

Practicing yoga can reduce stress, help with emotion regulation, improve mood and well being, boost cognitive functioning, enhance respiratory function, improve physical flexibility and muscular strength (Khalsa, 2013). A research study on yoga and children with ASD demonstrated similar positive effects. Children with ASD who followed a specific yoga routine each morning had improved "concentration and focus, and improves their strength, motor coordination and social skills" (Barclay, 2012, para. 5).

The partner with ASD can enjoy practicing yoga because it can help him with his anxiety and depression, reduce ADHD issues, improve self-awareness of the body, and even help with sensory integration. There are numerous yoga classes, books, and videos available. Yoga involves rhythmic breathing while stretching, strengthening, and toning the body. The relaxation of the mind and body that comes from yoga also improves resilience to anxiety and stress.

Exercise

Exercise in any form can help individuals with ASD reduce their negative behaviors, alleviate their anxiety, and increase their ability to deal with stress (Elliot *et al.*, 1994). I recommend a regular exercise routine for all my clients whether they have ASD or not. A sedentary lifestyle is linked to a myriad of health problems, but can also exacerbate ASD traits. An active lifestyle is beneficial for both partners. Vigorous exercises such as running and aerobics have been proven to improve mood. The good mood caused by exercise is due to an elevation in several neurochemicals involved in feelings of happiness and well being such as endorphins, serotonin, dopamine and glutamate. Endorphins as the name suggests are naturally produced morphine-like neurochemicals that can actually reduce pain and produce a happy feeling. Similar to mindfulness studies, exercise has unequivocally been proven to reduce cortisol levels and the impact of stress, improve test scores, increase resilience, memory, sexual performance and prevent many diseases (Ratey and Hagerman, 2008). If initiating and sustaining a consistent exercise routine can be a challenge, working with a personal trainer at the gym can provide the necessary motivation and accountability in order to establish and maintain a consistent, long-term exercise routine. Couples can make exercising together a part of their "playtime" and go running, walking, skiing, bicycling, dancing, or kayaking together.

The Mental Health of the NS Partner

The NS partner can often have his own mental health issues separate from his wife with ASD. He may have entered the relationship with pre-existing mental health or neurodiverse conditions of his own, or/and the stresses stemming from being in the neurodiverse marriage may have affected his mental health after the fact. No matter the source, the mental health issues must be addressed and treated. Many of the treatments we've discussed above are useful not only for the partner with ASD, but also for the NS partner.

Pre-existing Mental Health or Neurodiverse Conditions

I have found that many of the NS partners in my practice have depression, anxiety, bipolar, PTSD, or ADHD. Here, we'll limit the discussion to ADHD.

As with ASD, the partner with ADHD has her own unique profile of traits and needs. For example, she may be impulsive, susceptible to stress, and have sensory and executive functioning issues. Her ADHD traits can often exacerbate the stress of the partner with ASD. If she speaks fast or acts impulsively, he may feel overwhelmed. She may run metaphorical circles around him, overtalk and conduct their life at a pace that he finds hard to keep up with. It's important that the partner with ADHD understand what her traits are, and have strategies to cope with them for her own well being and that of her partner.

Stresses Stemming from the Neurodiverse Marriage

The NS partner can often experience mental health issues such as Affective Deprivation Disorder (Simons and Thompson, 2009), Post-Traumatic Stress Disorder (PTSD), anxiety, and depression as a result of being in a relationship with an undiagnosed, and untreated partner with ASD.

The lack of emotional reciprocity and anger issues of the partner with ASD can sometimes result in the NS partner developing Affective Deprivation Disorder. (See Chapter 6, "Expanding Theory of Mind and Emotional Intelligence".)

The anger issues of the partner with ASD can make the NS partner become traumatized; he may even develop symptoms of PTSD. It's important to understand that even after the anger outbursts and hurtful behaviors have stopped, healing from past trauma can take time. What's difficult in these situations is that the partner with ASD seems to move on fairly quickly from the negative interaction, while the NS partner may require time to heal over an extended period of time.

Chapter 5

SELF-EXPLORATION, AWARENESS, AND ADVOCACY

The first thing you have to know is yourself. A man
who knows himself can step outside himself and
watch his own reactions like an observer.

ADAM SMITH

Self-exploration (Merriam-Webster, n.d.) involves the examination and analysis of one's own unrealized spiritual or intellectual capacities. In the neurodiverse marriage, it needs to include the tendencies, motivations and behaviors of both partners. It also means investigating how individual life experiences influence relationship behaviors. When couples undergo a process of self-exploration, they can become aware of their own set of issues, blind spots, and family of origin patterns that influence their relational behavior. They can transform their relationship by being mindful of their own behaviors, and changing them for the better.

Even though the ASD traits of one partner can significantly impact the neurodiverse marriage, the reality is that it takes two partners to create relationship patterns, both negative and positive. The NS partner can sometimes fall into the trap of solely blaming the partner with ASD for their marital problems, instead of examining his own role in the relationship. The same goes for the partner with ASD. She can often come in with a list of complaints against her NS partner. She can have significant blind spots which makes her unable to see her own role in how her NS husband reacts to her. With each partner blaming the other for their problems, the couple can find themselves in crisis on a daily or weekly basis. These volatile interactions can really burn out both partners, and leave them confused and frustrated. Therefore, self-exploration of individual traits, bringing awareness to one's actions and how these play out in the marriage is crucial.

Once the NS partner understands how his own behaviors exacerbate the relationship, he can begin to feel a sense of empowerment that allows him to make positive changes. The NS partner's family of origin issues, personality traits, past trauma, prior relationship experiences, and psychological mindset often influence how he interacts with his partner. Once he understands the personal factors that influence their relationship, he can learn to better manage it.

When the partner with ASD learns about her traits, she can develop better coping strategies, and learn positive behaviors to help the marriage. In any marriage, it is best if both partners examine their own traits, and how those affect their relationship.

Once each partner understands himself or herself, the couple can work towards advocating for themselves. The partner with ASD, often unaware of her own needs and boundaries, might need to investigate what these are and self-advocate accordingly. The NS partner too, can often feel guilty for doing things outside of the marriage to fulfill his social-emotional needs. Discussing needs and self-advocacy is necessary for the NS partner as well.

Self-Exploration and Awareness for the NS Partner

For the NS partner, understanding why she chose her partner with ASD is an important step towards self-awareness. The NS partner may be a super nurturer, manager, and organizer. She might have entered the relationship motivated by a desire to assist and guide the partner with ASD. She might have thought that she could change or fix her partner, and help him grow. While the match of a man with ASD and an NS woman might at first feel like a good fit, overtime the NS wife might become resentful of the fact that her husband is always disorganized, and that he has trouble problem-solving seemingly minor day-to-day issues.

Many NS partners report having at least one parent with ASD. The NS partner may have been drawn to the partner with ASD because she felt familiar and safe. She may also have been going through a vulnerable time in her life, and the quiet, intelligent, and loyal presence of the ASD partner provided her with a sense of stability and security.

In the Partner's and Spouse Support Group, participants make a list of traits of their partners' ASD. Then, as a way to self-explore, they make another list of their own NS traits. The second list serves as a mirror for better insight into themselves. Exploring her own traits can help the NS partner become more self-aware—a necessary precursor to cultivating behaviors that work in interacting with her partner with ASD. Both lists serve the NS partners as a reminder of the ASD-NS confluence of traits in the relationship. It's important that the NS partner understands that she too has a significant effect on the quality of her marriage. Placing the burden of relationship troubles solely on one partner isn't wise or useful, as evidenced by the story below.

♥ RACHEL AND MICHAEL'S STORY ♥

Rachel and Michael were a Russian immigrant couple, living in the United States for over a decade. Michael strongly suspected that Rachel had ASD after their first child was diagnosed. Michael himself was stubborn and Type-A, but wasn't very self-aware. While his wife's ASD traits seemed challenging, his own rigidity and critical behavior were difficult as well.

In particular, Michael was most irked by his wife's knitting habit. Rachel used knitting as a way to calm her anxiety, and also as a way to keep her hands from fidgeting. Michael didn't understand Rachel's anxiety, or her need to calm herself by knitting. He pointed out that she even knit while they were watching a movie and cuddling on the couch. He was very resentful and took it personally that his wife didn't want to hold his hand while watching movies.

Even after Rachel agreed to only do her knitting in the beginning of the movie until she got into the storyline, Michael continued to complain. He insisted that she deliberately kept her hands occupied, because she wanted to minimize the amount of time she was touching him. Rachel admitted to having sensory issues with touch, but tried to convince Michael this wasn't the issue here. Despite having a neuropsychological evaluation to confirm her diagnosis, which Michael read, he remained stuck on the idea that his wife was deliberately trying to hurt him.

Michael's rigidity and inability to understand his wife's point of view made me suspect that he himself had difficulties processing information and being cognitively flexible. While Michael might not have qualified for an ASD diagnosis himself, his slow processing and inflexibility intensified this couple's difficulties. Through prolonged counseling, Michael was finally able to see his wife's point of view, but doing so took many months of intensive counseling.

Self-Advocacy for the NS Partner

An aspect of self-exploration and awareness for the NS partner is to rebuild his own life. He might need to reintroduce activities and interests into his life that he may have given up after marriage. He may have had to cut down on his social activities, due to his wife's reclusive nature, or because he's had to shoulder a higher than average share of the household responsibilities, due to her executive functioning issues. The NS partner may also need to seek emotional support outside the marriage, because of his wife's limited social-emotional reciprocity. Spending time with friends, family and a counselor who is emotionally nurturing can be something that the NS partner requires as part of his basic self-care. Typically, the partner with ASD might be fine with her partner's absence from the house because it gives her the solitude she needs; however, sometimes the NS partner might have to explain and advocate for his needs.

NS partners can also have their own neurological differences, and might even have special needs themselves. An NS partner with ADHD, for example, may require a lot of time to exercise and engage in activities that he finds stimulating and engaging. Making sure that he advocate for his own needs is important.

Self-advocating in a manner that the partner with ASD understands is vital. Often she will need to be told information in simplified, concrete terms, and even then she might not "get what her partner is referring to." Sometimes the neurodiverse couple will need to work with an ASD-specific couples counselor who can interpret and explain the NS partner's needs to his wife.

Self-Exploration and Awareness
for the Partner with ASD

Does the partner with ASD know that he is neurologically different? Does he realize that the difficulties in relating to his partner are based on these neurological differences? This depends on whether he's had prior relationships in his life where his partners made him conscious of his traits and the difficulties they posed. Often, even when an individual with ASD has had multiple divorces, he might still not be aware of his contribution to the breakdown of these relationships. He might say, "My ex-wives were difficult... They were sweet and accommodating while dating, but they became mean after marriage."

Until the partner with ASD understands and takes full responsibility for his own neurological makeup and idiosyncrasies, it may be difficult for him to change. Making a list of his ASD traits and learning his about strengths and weaknesses can be useful.

In many neurodiverse marriages, the partner with ASD might have had a rough template or a list of requirements for what he wanted in his partner. Aware of his own social and executive functioning limitations, he might have wanted a spouse who is organized, and who would act as his social liaison. The traits in the NS partner that were attractive in the beginning of the relationship, can often become troublesome later. Years into the marriage, the partner with ASD might complain that his NS partner is always taking him to parties. Or that he is frustrated with her for not being able to balance the family budget.

Regardless of the frustrations that arise later in the marriage, if he wants their marriage to last or be a happy one, the partner with ASD will need to take responsibility for his own contributions to the marital problems.

♥ MARIKO AND KIM'S STORY ♥

Mariko and Kim were married for 10 years with one child. Mariko was Brazilian, of Japanese ancetry, and Kim was from Korea. They had both met as engineering students at the Massachusetts Institute of Technology in Cambridge, Massachusetts. Mariko had recently begun to suspect that Kim was on the autism spectrum after she read an article about Asperger's Syndrome. At first, she thought she was being crazy and that she was making things up. Both of them spoke English as a second language, which was also the primary language between them. Therefore, in the first few years of marriage, Mariko just assumed that all of Kim's idiosyncrasies were cultural, and the language barrier also left her a little confused about some of his ASD traits.

Mariko began reading every book on Asperger's Syndrome and relationships that she could find. She then came to see me to confirm her suspicions. After our meeting, Mariko felt validated in her perspective and went home and informed Kim about her investigation into ASD. Kim carefully listened to her and surprised her by saying that he had heard a radio program on ASD a few months ago and had wondered the same thing himself! Of course, he hadn't mentioned it to his wife because he felt that she wouldn't be open to it and might think that he was making excuses for his odd behaviors.

At the next appointment, Kim accompanied his wife and at length discussed his ASD traits. He came in prepared with a list of his traits and with a print out of the online *Aspie Quiz* that he'd heard about on the radio program. Kim was genuinely interested in learning more about ASD, and how he could improve his marriage.

Mariko said that one of the biggest challenges with Kim was that he could not hear his own tone of voice. He often sounded like he was shouting when he didn't mean to. Even though she knew that he wasn't doing this deliberately, she still wanted him to be mindful of his volume and tone as it was beginning to affect their three-year-old daughter. Mariko said that their daughter would get really upset and cry when she heard her father raise his tone of voice. The situation was painful not only for Mariko, but for Kim as well. The last thing he wanted was for his daughter to be traumatized by his inadvertent outbursts.

Kim decided to take up yoga and meditation. When that wasn't enough to manage his anger outbursts, he decided to consult with a psychiatrist about medication. The medication, a low-dose of an anti-depressant, immediately helped him to stretch out his reaction time. It also reduced his anxiety and smoothed out his mood. He was able to pause between thoughts and actively chose a positive thought over a negative one. He felt his resilience to stress increase; he became more patient with his wife and daughter, and began sounding a lot gentler. He also continued with regular couples counseling sessions, which resulted in a lot of insight and behavioral changes for both his wife and him. Kim always took notes in therapy, and was always willing to see how he was contributing to the challenges in his marriage and family.

Kim continues to learn about himself and from his mistakes, as does his wife. Encouraged by the positive changes she experienced in her marriage, Mariko decided to have another baby—something she had long wanted, but held off due to her marital difficulties.

Self-Advocacy for the Partner with ASD

The partner with ASD often doesn't know or understand her own boundaries or needs. Even when she does, it can be incredibly challenging for her to verbalize her thoughts and feelings. Add to this her slower than average processing time, and it can mean that she is rarely able to verbalize her needs in real time. Unmet needs can often result in stress that is built up over a long period of time. Due to this unresolved stress, the partner with ASD might have frequent meltdowns causing distress for the couple.

Many times, the NS partner might intuit his partner's needs, and accommodate them in whatever way he can. However, having to always accommodate the needs of his partner can leave him feeling burnt out. Therefore, it's best that the partner with ASD learns what her own needs are and develops the necessary coping skills. While she may be able to handle most of these needs herself, she might need her husband to collaborate with her on some of these plans.

Due to the demands of social-communication in the workplace, the partner with ASD might need to plan for a daily dose of quiet time—where she can just decompress and unwind. If the couple is hosting a dinner party, being around people for long stretches can feel overwhelming. She might therefore plan short intervals where she steps out of the "social zone" for a quick respite. If she has sensory sensitivities, using earplugs at a dance party, sunglasses daily, a noise machine and a weighted blanket might improve her quality of life.

Another important aspect of self-advocacy for the partner with ASD can be engaging in things that they like doing. Oftentimes, in the beginning of a relationship, the partner with ASD, perhaps particularly if she's a woman, will roll back on her own special interests and needs. Ridden with self-doubt that her significant other wouldn't like her if she revealed her true self to him, a woman with ASD might go out of her way to please her partner. It's important that she learn to balance her own needs with what's required in a romantic relationship, perhaps with the help of a good friend, family member, or a counselor who is aware of her challenges. A counselor can also help her to identify healthy boundaries and practice how to convey her needs in a way that is understandable to her NS partner.

CHAPTER 6

EXPANDING THEORY OF MIND AND EMOTIONAL INTELLIGENCE

Most smiles are started by another smile.

FRANK A. CLARK

In people who are at good at or skilled at interpersonal relationships, two capacities are very highly developed. One is Theory of Mind (TOM) and the other is emotional intelligence (EI). TOM could be considered a cognitive aspect of EI. Unlike their NS counterparts, individuals with ASD struggle with TOM and EI.

What is Theory of Mind?

Individuals with ASD tend to have weak TOM, meaning a relatively limited ability to "read" another person's thoughts, feelings, or intentions. Another individual's words or actions can induce different emotions in people. A perceived insult can cause a person to cry, or being given a gift can cause a person to feel happy. A person can feel hurt, or become happy based on what was said or done to/for them. Studies show that four- to six-year-old NS children understand the cause and effect between a stimulus and an emotional response; whereas, children with ASD at the same age may not seem to understand the correlation between the two (Baron-Cohen, 2001). Most adults with ASD find it harder to consider or hypothesize about another person's mental or emotional state. It bears mentioning that not every individual with ASD struggles with TOM to the same degree. TOM is a spectrum and some individuals with ASD struggle with it more than others.

An NS man may interpret the other person's state of mind based on verbal and nonverbal cues and what he knows about human emotions. He is then able to put all this information together in order to make a correct guess of other people's minds. In short, he has a theory of another person's mind. If for example, he happens to say something hurtful to the other person, he might be able to recognize his mistake and apologize. He may say something like, "I never meant to hurt your feelings," or he might make light of his faux pas and say something self-deprecating like, "I'm so sorry, I have a tendency to put my foot in my mouth!"

Even if the individual with ASD is able to belatedly realize that he's caused hurt feelings in the other person, she or he may not be able to repair the situation quickly enough. This is often because someone with ASD may not know what to say or by the time they've figured out what to say, the moment has passed. Others with ASD may not notice that anything's wrong, and may just carry on making the insensitive remarks.

Many individuals with ASD can and do improve their TOM; however, it does require constant and deliberate effort. Anxiety and depression can make it harder for those with TOM issues to make improvements. In such cases, anti-anxiety medications, psychotherapy, and other mental health strategies may be necessary while working on expanding TOM.

A marital partner with weak TOM may unintentionally say and do things in a relationship that can come across as insensitive and hurtful to her NS partner. The NS partner may mistakenly assume that his wife is deliberately being hurtful. Over time, the hurt feelings, pain, and suffering of the NS spouse can cause a breakdown in the neurodiverse marriage. The partner with ASD and TOM issues may be constantly surprised and confused by communications and relationships that suddenly go awry, blow up, and end. These kinds of repeated experiences can lead her to develop anxiety and mild paranoia. It's useful for both partners to learn about TOM, so that the NS partner realizes that his wife isn't knowingly being cruel to him and the NS partner finds ways to minimize her insensitive remarks.

The partner with ASD struggles with a weak TOM due to neurological differences. The partner with ASD can also understand how her husband isn't being overly sensitive, or emotional, and that he is being hurt on many occasions even when she doesn't realize it. In order to change each partner's mindset and pattern of communication, acknowledging that TOM is part of the equation is key. Both partners can then start exercising curiosity and learn about each other's thinking processes. Every individual has their own unique life experiences, which informs who they are. Having an open and flexible mind about one's partner's thinking, rather than making assumptions and jumping to conclusions, can lead to a meaningful dialogue. Verbalizing details about one's thoughts, in a non-judgmental atmosphere, gives both partners an opportunity to understand and feel closer to each other.

♥ AUDREY AND JACOB'S STORY: PART 1 ♥

Audrey, an Australian woman with ASD in her late-twenties, had been married to her American NS partner, Jacob, for five years. Audrey and Jacob came in for couples counseling because their marriage was on the rocks. While they had been to couples counseling before, it hadn't improved things for them. "In fact, they made it worse," said Jacob. They felt like ASD-specific couples counseling was the last resort to see if they could turn things around for the better in their relationship.

Jacob reported that Audrey's tendency to say exactly what was on her mind had caused a lot of strife between his friends and family. He said that he was beginning to feel like there was no way that she would change, and that divorce was the only option. The most recent example of her "rudeness and biting comments" as Jacob put it, was when his mother came to visit them from Israel. In the three weeks that his mother had stayed with them, Audrey and her had gotten into numerous fights. Things became so bad between them that his mother abruptly left a week earlier than planned after a particularly difficult time with her daughter-in-law.

Audrey narrated her version of the story. She said that her mother-in-law had been against their marriage from the very beginning because she wasn't Jewish. Audrey said that she said the meanest things to her to rile her up on a daily basis that caused her to be upset and angry all the time. When I asked for an example of how her mother-in-law caused her to be upset, Audrey described a typical conversation:

"I said, 'Jacob's new job pays him really well. I think we should be able to buy a house soon.' To which she replied, 'Is that why you chased my son then, because he's a good earner?' That was such an unexpected insult and I replied, 'I make almost twice as much as your son, and he'd been out of a job for a whole year, which meant that I was supporting us. And if you really want to know, it was he who chased me for months before I would relent to dating him!'"

Audrey was visibly upset even as she recalled the incident. Jacob interjected at this moment and said that his mother often said things she didn't mean and had a "sharp tongue" herself.

"I admit that my mother says awful things. She's that way with everyone, but it's really Audrey's equally acerbic tongue that escalates the problem."

"Well, what can I do?!" Audrey asked, "She really does get me terribly worked up! And that's not all. She comments on my hair, on my makeup, my clothes, she can be horrible!"

Jacob cut in, "Audrey, you have to understand, she's old, she's 75 years old. She says stupid things, she wants the best for us. She's my mother! See, this is what I mean. She takes things too far and this is exactly why I've lost friends and which is why she has no friends."

"Well, what do you want me to do when people say stupid things?" Audrey demanded.

"This is exactly why I don't think this marriage is going to work out. She says the meanest things without thinking how it makes others feel. Then there's the anger. She goes from zero to sixty in seconds and escalates even the simplest conversations into a big fight."

"And Jacob never supports me with regard to his mother! He never defends me on anything. Even with our friends and neighbors, he's always siding with them saying that I say cruel things."

"Well, it's true. With our neighbors, for example, she picked a fight with our next door neighbor because he believes in astrology. Audrey insisted that astrology isn't scientifically valid and that he should read some books debunking this. Can you believe this?! Our neighbor is a sweet guy who walks dogs for a living! You do seriously want to debate him to death over horoscopes?!"

"I[…]" Audrey began to interrupt him.

"I haven't finished Audrey! I just don't see how this is going to work. She's ruined numerous friendships of mine and no one even wants to visit our house anymore. At first I thought, if I just gave in to this request or demand, she'd be happy, and reciprocate…make sacrifices for me. But it never happens. I give and give and give and she's never happy. I can't live like this! I think it's best if we got a divorce."

"Maybe we should get a divorce! But he tells you all the things that he finds wrong about me. He's not telling you about his gambling habit and flakiness." Jacob shifted uncomfortably in his seat. "He's had an online gambling addiction for several years now. He's also not good at keeping time and is always stressing me out by changing things at the last minute. Even now that he knows I have ASD, and need structure and routine, he continues to constantly surprise with his last minute plans."

"It's not an addiction. I sometimes play online poker to de-stress from the week. And maybe, I wouldn't be gambling if you were nicer to me."

This couple's relationship problems were at least in part due to Audrey's weak TOM. However, Jacob too had his own issues. Unable to cope with the stress in his life and marriage, he had developed unhealthy coping mechanisms. His flexible style around time and life in general exacerbated Audrey's stress in turn making her more anxious and prone to outbursts.

Audrey's weak TOM, inability to be flexible in her thinking, having a low tolerance to frustration and taking things too literally led to her pattern of high relational conflict with everyone from her husband and mother-in-law to her co-workers, neighbors and friends.

Improving Audrey's TOM and broadening her emotional intelligence wasn't something that was going to be easily achieved. Both Audrey and Jacob were going to have to commit to making changes and doing things differently. Relationships that are primarily challenged by a partner's poor TOM, can in my experience be the most problematic.

Accepting and Understanding the Challenges of TOM

The partner with ASD must understand that his words and behavior can have a profound effect on his partner. Once, he acknowledges this fundamental truth about relationships, he can then stop accusing his partner of being overly sensitive or overreacting.

For example, an NS woman who was dating a man with ASD reported that, in the throes of lovemaking, her boyfriend once blurted out that her face was asymmetrical because one of her eyes was smaller than the other. Shortly after this episode, the woman broke up with her boyfriend. A few years later, she realized that this boyfriend probably had ASD and was simply expressing his observation, not realizing that his comment was rude and insensitive.

For the partner with ASD, it's important to accept and understand that his words and actions, however logical and factually correct, can sound harsh and demeaning and that they can take a significant emotional toll on his partner. At first, TOM can often be confusing for the partner with ASD to understand. It may require many moments of discussion and teaching for him to realize what TOM is and why his words and actions might be disturbing to his partner. Only by taking responsibility for behavior that causes pain to his partner, and learning new and improved ways of thinking, can he hope to make any improvements in his marriage. He can begin to monitor what he says to his NS partner. He might also need to be told, for example, that certain types of comments are absolutely unacceptable, for example, giving his partner critical feedback about her body. If and when he does inadvertently blurt out something hurtful, and if his partner reports being hurt, he must train himself to apologize, even if he doesn't immediately see the "logic" behind it.

The NS partner might also want to understand that her partner's TOM challenges stem from his neurological differences, and that he's probably not trying to be deliberately hurtful. When she feels that he has said something stinging, she might want to bring it to his attention and try to talk about how and why that is hurtful to her.

Creating a Mindset of Appreciation and Gratitude

People's thoughts, feelings and behavior are inexorably linked. Therefore, it's really important that both partners become aware of their mindset. Are the majority of thoughts towards the partner negative or positive? Do you find things to appreciate and be grateful for in your partner, or are you always picking and focusing on his flaws? If your thoughts are mostly negative, it might be time to evaluate whether the relationship needs to end, or if it's worthwhile going to couples counseling and finding strategies to improve things.

Constant complaining can erode relationships; gratitude can result in an increase in empathy and connection. Of course, creating a mindset of appreciation and gratitude is easier said than done. It takes daily practice; and it can greatly improve the relationship.

THE APPRECIATION AND GRATITUDE EXERCISE™

1. Each partner may separately create a list of things that they appreciate and are grateful for in their partner. This list can include anything and everything; nothing is too big or small! Don't worry if you only start with a few items.

2. Write down the list on a piece of paper or index card, or use your smartphone or computer, to easily access it—at least twice a day. The more places you post it, the more likely you are to use it.

3. As you practice appreciation and gratitude, every day, twice a day, it can easily become second nature to how you think. You may find that you are more easily able to notice the positive qualities and behaviors of your partner. Keep adding new items to the list as you notice your partner doing nice things for you.

4. Repeat the exercise for days, weeks, months, and years—until a "gratitude attitude" sets in, transforming your mindset into one of appreciation, gratitude, and positivity.

Being deeply grateful and appreciative of one's partner can transform a partner at a fundamental level. He or she might become more positive and empathetic, resulting in a reduction in marital conflict. Becoming a more appreciative, grateful, and positive person may result in more harmonious relationships in other areas of your life as well.

♥ NITARA: WALKING IN EACH ♥ OTHER'S SHOES

Nitara, an African-American woman, is a meditation teacher, and has ASD. She credits her two-decade-long meditation practice with helping her manage her anxiety and depression. She came in saying that she wanted a way to expand her Theory of Mind.

"How about we find a way for you to experience what it's like walking in another person's shoes."

"Should I take an acting class?"

"You might try that to if you want, but how about if we create a meditation for imagining the day-to-day experiences of certain people that you encounter. Especially those that you find difficult to deal with."

"That sounds like a good idea. Will you help me process my theories on what I think the other person might be thinking? It's going to be hard."

Nitara said that she wanted to begin the meditation right away and do it every day for a whole month.

"I'm going to begin by imagining the person's day, from waking up to falling asleep."

Theory of Mind is based on being able to imagine another person's thinking-feeling state and realizing how this can be affected by our own words and behavior. At first, Nitara found it difficult to imagine being in another person's shoes. Guessing details about another person's day was a challenge. However, Nitara talked to some of her NS friends and me to broaden her picture of the individuals she met at work and those in her personal life.

Though it was a challenge, she pushed herself to do this exercise every day for a whole month. "I think I'm beginning to get slightly better at realizing that every person has a unique inner life based on their life experiences. Day to day, their behavior is influenced by the things that happen to them. Good things make them feel good, bad things bad. I never realized before that I could be part of the good things that happened to them."

"What do you mean?"

"I've realized that people in general like compliments. I've been experimenting paying all my meditation students at least one compliment each time I see them."

"I see."

"I've been picking a theme because doling out spontaneous compliments isn't easy for me. So, on Monday, I complimented a few clients on their clothes. Nice scarf, nice shirt, pretty blouse, etc. On Wednesday, I focused on how they looked. 'You're looking great.' Of course, on Wednesday I see mostly women, so that worked. Anyway, I think it went well. Many of my students returned the compliments and seemed to be smiling more."

Through her exercise in empathetic thinking, Nitara was able to become more aware of the people in her environment. By bringing her focus to the thinking-feeling states of the people around her, Nitara was able to find ways to connect with them, even if it was in the context of a formal working setting. She was able to monitor her thoughts, feelings, and words towards the people she was interacting with. This exercise made her feel more relaxed and less anxious. Nitara continues to use this practice for everybody in her life. "It deepens my understanding and empathy for my students and my boyfriend."

It can be equally important for the NS partner to do this exercise. The NS partner might assume that he knows what his partner with ASD is thinking and feeling, but just like in any relationship, it's best not to make any assumptions.

THE WALKING IN YOUR PARTNER'S SHOES PRACTICE™

1. Imagine and write in detail what you think your partner's day might be like—starting from the time they wake up to bedtime. Really try to imagine your partner's thinking and feeling states at certain times of the day, whether they are at the office, commuting, or at home. Write down everything in as much detail as you can.

2. Pick a time to sit down with your partner using *The Relationship Schedule*™ to process your ideas about his experience, thoughts, and feelings. Read your notes to your partner to see if you were right in imagining and guessing your partner's details about their day, and their thinking/feeling states. If you imagined or guessed wrong, ask your partner to fill in the parts that you missed or guessed wrong.

In comparing notes with each other, your partner and you will learn about each other's day and the thinking-feeling states corresponding to the events that happened. Doing this exercise with some frequency can help both partners expand their Theory of Mind and lead to a more empathetic view of the other.

No matter how hard someone works on strengthening their TOM, there is no substitute for honest, open dialogue between partners. Both partners need to clearly communicate their thoughts, feelings, and needs. They can talk to each other face to face, via email, written notes, phone calls, or text messages. It is best if neither partner assumes that the other person can read their thoughts, feelings, or intentions. And that they know the right actions to take based on these thoughts and feelings. In some cases, the partner with ASD may not be able to improve her TOM beyond a certain degree, or the progress might be slow. Patience and understanding from both partners is essential.

Emotional Intelligence

For success in relationships and even at many jobs, having a high intelligence quotient (IQ) isn't enough. An individual's emotional intelligence (EI) can be an important factor for success in both love and work (Goleman, 2005). Emotional intelligence is roughly characterized as the ability to identify, label, and express one's emotions. Understanding the emotions of others is another aspect of EI, as is being able to influence them by one's words and actions. The same way that IQ is on a spectrum of low to high, EI is similarly on a spectrum as well. Individuals with Down Syndrome, for example, aren't known to possess high IQs, but they do possess good EI (Hinshaw, 2010). A high IQ doesn't predict a high EI.

Individuals with ASD typically have lower EI compared to their NS counterparts. They struggle with their emotions in numerous ways: they may have a weakness in regulating emotions, they may experience emotional extremes, they may have difficulty understanding, tolerating, and responding to the emotions of others, and they may have trouble identifying, labeling, and expressing their own emotions (also known as alexithymia).

Alexithymia

Alexithymia is part of the EI profile in individuals with ASD. It means that individuals with ASD may have trouble putting their feelings into words. Even if they intellectually know that they should be expressing their emotions, identifying their feeling state and verbalizing it can seem like a monumental task. To an individual with ASD, this can feel puzzling and complicated. The clinical term for this is alexithymia. Defined as an inability or weakness in recognizing emotional nuances and content (Bermond et al., 2007)—the word *alexi* means no words and *thymia* means emotions: no words for emotions.

Affective Deprivation Disorder

Affective Deprivation Disorder (AfDD), is a term that was coined by Maxine Aston, a British counselor working with neurodiverse couples (Aston, n.d.). Formerly known as the Cassandra Phenomenon, AfDD is a term modelled on SAD (Seasonal Affective Disorder, i.e. depression caused in the winter months due to sunlight deprivation). Symptoms of SAD and AfDD are very similar, namely: sleep problems, lethargy, overeating, sadness, loss of libido, anxiety, and mood changes (Aston, n.d.). AfDD is caused by having constant unmet emotional needs; creating a feeling of affective deprivation (Simons and Thompson, 2009).

AfDD is most severe when the partner with ASD has a particularly low EI. With an undiagnosed partner with ASD, the NS partner can become confused, lonely, and depressed by the lack of emotional reciprocity and reassurance in the relationship. Not understanding why her partner is emotionally inexpressive, she may then try in vain to get his love and attention. When her efforts yield no results, she may mistakenly think that her partner's emotional aloofness is her fault.

It is important to note that AfDD isn't just the sole result of being in a relationship with a partner with ASD. Not knowing that your partner might have ASD and not having alternate sources of having your emotional needs met can also determine AfDD.

♥ SALMA'S STORY ♥

Salma was a woman of Egyptian origin, who had grown up in the U.S. In her thirties, after a brief courtship, she had married Ahmed, a Moroccan immigrant who was an economist. Salma called me about a year-and-a-half into her marriage. She had found out about ASD on the Internet and thought that Ahmed might fit the criteria. She said she had begun to feel depressed after just six months of being married, and that over the last year, she had been feeling worse. She had no history of depression and was satisfied in her job as a school teacher. She reported that her sense of self had eroded since being married to Ahmed.

"If I was a basket, I feel like over the course of our relationship, my weave has come undone. I feel that I'm fraying at the edges to the point where the basket has lost its shape and there are leaks in it. I feel as if the bottom could fall off at any moment. I have trouble sleeping and some days I don't feel like getting out of bed. I've gained thirty-five pounds. I fall sick frequently and I've lost my desire for sex. I feel sad and cry a lot. I no longer enjoy much of anything. I can't remember the last time I was truly happy. Do you understand what I'm trying to tell you?" I told her I understood, and that what she described was known as AfDD.

Salma mentioned that when she told Ahmed that they weren't connecting on an emotional level, he didn't even know what she was referring to, let alone respond to her. Even when she asked Ahmed for physical affection explicitly, he almost never reached for her. He was however happy to cuddle with her when she initiated it. Salma said that she found asking her husband for emotional and physical affection to be exhausting. "Even when we are together, I feel alone. It feels as if I don't have a husband. Why do I feel this way?"

I explained to Salma that her AfDD was due to her husband's low EI. Since Salma had already unsuccessfully tried ways in which to get Ahmed to connect with her emotionally, I recommended that she break down her requests into even smaller steps. I suggested that she ask him to post reminders for him to remember to tell her that he loved her, missed her, and thought about her on a daily basis. I recommended that *The Relationship Schedule*™ (see Chapter 10) might be useful to show him what she meant. I told her to detail the choreography of the physical affection that she desired, in concrete steps.

After several weeks of attempting to get Ahmed to demonstrate physical affection, Salma still felt that things still weren't progressing. Her depression persisted. She then made the decision to go on antidepressants, as she tried to get make sense of her husband and marriage.

Salma felt very conflicted about whether or not she wanted to be with her husband. "If I need antidepressants to be in my marriage, I'm not sure this is the right relationship for me. It's just really hard. Even with the antidepressants, I have to exercise daily to keep my mood up. I feel as if I'm in an empty marriage. I'm a shell of my former self."

As evidenced by Salma's story, the low EI of the ASD partner can often impact the mental health of the NS partner. It's important to note that not every ASD-NS relationship results in AfDD for the NS partner. It's only when the partner with ASD is significantly weak in his EI that his partner may suffer so much.

In Salma's case, her husband, Ahmed eventually did agree to couples counseling. In counseling, Salma broke down in steps exactly all the gestures of physical affection that she wanted Ahmed to make towards her on a daily basis. Ahmed and Salma also came up with a list of terms of endearment and words of affirmation that he could say to her every day. They implemented these solutions working with their customized *Relationship Schedule*™ (Chapter 10).

Salma also realized that she needed to spend more time on self-care. She began getting regular massages, facials, and foot rubs so as to not feel touch-deprived. She increased the amount of time she spent with her friends, so that she could receive the emotional input that she so badly needed. She began training as a dance instructor and volunteering her time at an animal shelter. As her own life expanded, and her strength and resilience grew, she found that she was able to feel less dependent on Ahmed for her needs.

As evidenced by Salma and Ahmed's case, a low EI and a lack of emotional reciprocity can cause depression in the NS partner. It's imperative that couples address the issue of low EI and take immediate steps to treat the AfDD and counter its effects with a variety of strategies.

Increasing Emotional Intelligence

It's important for the partner with ASD to work on increasing his EI even though at first he may find it confusing and challenging. There are numerous ways in which he can increase awareness of his feeling-states and learn to better express his emotions. EI can be strengthened by practicing sensation-emotion awareness, building empathy, and relational consciousness.

Sensation-Emotion Awareness

Once the partner with ASD begins to better understand the sensations in his body and the emotions corresponding to them, he can begin expressing what he's experiencing to his partner, perhaps after a little editing. Doing so can help him increase his emotional reciprocity once he learns to tune in and express his positive feelings to his partner. He can also use his increasing sensation-emotion awareness to better manage stressful situations. A copy of this (and the other exercises in the book) is provided in the Appendices.

THE SENSATION-EMOTION AWARENESS PRACTICE™

Tuning into bodily sensations can help you identify and name your feeling states. You can increase awareness of the physical sensations that occur in particular situations and the emotions connected to these sensations. Learning to express your sensations and feelings to your partner can help you become more emotionally expressive towards him or her.

In a negative situation, you can use your sensation-emotion awareness to practice soothing self-talk, and reduce your stress response. You can then express your feelings of stress or anxiety to your partner if needed.

1. *Situation or event:* Notice and write down (see Table 6.3 and the blank *Sensation-Emotion Awareness Chart* in Appendix V) the particular situation or event. For example, perhaps you just finished watching your favorite television program with your partner.

2. *Physical sensations:* Every person's mind and body is unique, so it's important to notice your own specific physical sensations in response to the situation or event. The situation can be positive or negative. Notice and recognize the physical sensations in your body, no matter how slight or intense they may be. For example, sitting with your wife on the couch after watching your favorite television program gives you a warm and comfortable sensation in your body.

3. *Felt emotions:* Physical sensations in your body can signal different emotions. For example, a warm and comfortable sensation in your body can mean that you're happy and content to be spending time with your partner. Using *The Emotions List* (see Table 6.1 and Appendix IV), you can begin to develop a broader vocabulary for the emotions corresponding to your physical sensations.

4. *Self-talk:* After you label the emotions you're feeling, you can then use self-talk to articulate your sensations and feelings to yourself. Knowing how you're feeling can help you become more aware of your own emotions. For example, you may summarize how you're feeling to yourself, "I feel warm and comfortable in my shoulders and upper arms. She (or he) looks sexy in her (or his) new pajamas. I want to have sex with her (or him). Wait, maybe I should start by telling her (or him) that I love her (or him) and that I'm happy that we're spending time together."

5. *Edited communication:* After noticing your physical sensations arising from the situation or event, labeling the corresponding emotions, and self-talk, you can now express how you feel to your partner. However, it's important for you to edit what you say in your mind prior to orally expressing it. For example, you now have exactly the words you want to say to your partner, "Sweetie, I love you. I'm happy that we're spending time together."

The Emotions List

Table 6.1 is a selected list of emotional words adapted from *Emotional Knowledge* (Shaver *et al.,* 2001). Psychology books, psychotherapy, movies, television, plays, novels, poetry, and songs can further provide emotional learning. There are many new software technologies and smartphone applications that can assist in building an emotional vocabulary.

TABLE 6.1: THE EMOTIONS LIST

CATEGORY	EMOTIONS
Love and longing	adore, affection, love, fond, like, attracted, care, tender, compassion, desire, passion, infatuation
Positive emotions	cheerful, gay, joy, delight, enjoy, glad, happy, elated, satisfied, ecstatic, euphoric, excited, thrilled, content, hope, optimism, bliss
Surprise	amazed, surprised, astonished
Anger	rage, outrage, fury, wrath, hostile, aloof, bitter, hate, loathing, scorn, spite, dislike, resentment disgust, contempt, envy, jealousy torment, irritation, aversion
Sadness	suffering, hurt, anguish, depressed, despair, hopelessness, gloom, unhappiness, grief, sorrow, woe, misery, disappointment, dismay, displeasure, shame, guilt, shame, regret, remorse, isolation, neglect, loneliness, rejection, homesickness, defeat, dejection, insecurity, embarrassment, humiliation, pity, sympathy
Fear	alarm, shock, fear, fright, horror, terror, panic, hysterical, mortified, nervous, anxiety, tenseness, uneasiness, apprehension, worry, distress, dread

The Sensation-Emotion Awareness Chart™

The partner with ASD can also use the *Sensation-Emotion Awareness Chart*™ in stressful situations. Once he identifies how the situation or event can trigger him, what are the sensations he experiences, the emotions he feels, using self-talk to sooth himself, and express himself to his partner can revolutionize how he is able to manage his stress.

TABLE 6.2: *THE SENSATION-EMOTION AWARENESS CHART™* EXAMPLE

SITUATION OR EVENT	PHYSICAL SENSATIONS	FELT EMOTIONS	SELF-TALK	EDITED COMMUNICATION
You just finished watching your favorite television program with your wife.	A warm and comfortable sensation in your body, especially shoulders and upper arms.	Happy and content	"I feel warm and comfortable in my shoulders and upper arms. She looks sexy in her new pajamas. I want to have sex with her. Wait, maybe I should start by telling her that I love her and that I'm happy that we're spending time together."	Express your *edited* thoughts to your partner: "Sweetie, I love you. I'm happy that we're spending time together."
Being stalled in the car in rush hour traffic.	A queasy feeling in the stomach.	Anxiety	Positive self-talk "There's no need to rush. Just take some deep breaths. One, two, three, four, five. Everyone is sitting in the same traffic. Ok, focus. Let me think what I want to say to my wife."	Express your *edited* thoughts to your partner: "Sweetie, I feel a bit queasy in my stomach. I'm feeling anxious in this traffic. I'm so sorry. This is real y hard for me. I'm sorry you have to experience me like this."
After sex.	A warm feeling in the chest.	Contentment	"I like having sex with my wife. We fit nicely."	"Being with you feels so good. I love you."
You're coding software. Your wife interrupts you. She's reminding you to take the garbage and recycling out.	Snooting sensations in the head.	Irritation	"I'm irritated, but I need to calm down. It's ok, I can code later. I'll plan to work for two hours longer in the office tomorrow. My wife isn't deliberately disturbing me. Tomorrow is garbage day after all. I'm so glad that she's there to remind me. I'm so grateful for a partner that stays on top of things around here."	"I need ten minutes to transition into taking the garbage out. I'm just wrapping up. I'll do it at exactly 7:25 p.m."

TABLE 6.3: *THE SENSATION-EMOTION AWARENESS CHART*™

SITUATION OR EVENT	PHYSICAL SENSATIONS	FELT EMOTIONS	SELF-TALK	EDITED COMMUNICATION

♥ LEVI'S STORY ♥

Levi had severe social anxiety. He worked from home as a computer programmer, and only went to the office very infrequently. His anxiety was worse when he and his wife Tia went out together. His palms would start sweating in the last ten minutes of having to leave the house. It could be that they were preparing to go to the grocery store, a party, or even just a walk around the neighborhood. As his heart rate and sweating of his palms escalated, he would begin to feel overwhelmed. He would then become irritable and speak in monosyllables with Tia. She would in turn get frustrated with him because he wouldn't express his emotions.

Once Levi decided to work on becoming more emotionally aware, he realized that his physical symptoms were caused by his social anxiety. Who would they meet on their walk? What would these people want to talk about? What he was going to say? These were the thoughts that raced through his mind, spiked his anxiety, and escalated his heart rate and caused his palms to sweat.

He began using deep breathing—prolonged inhales and exhales— as he begun to feel his heart rate going up. Once Levi began to get his physical sensations under control and understand that this was his social anxiety acting up, he was able to say to Tia, "I am feeling very anxious right now. What if we meet Mrs. T on our way out, what am I going to say to her?" Knowing how he felt, helped Tia to assist him by giving him a script to have handy in case they did run into Mrs. T, their elderly landlady.

Levi learnt to label his social anxiety and slow down and truly observe his physiological sensations. He realized that he was less anxious if he prepared himself by having a list of topics to talk about, no matter what social setting he found himself in. He began to exercise more in order to reduce his day-to-day stress. He invested his time in a chanting practice that he'd been interested in for a while. He would use the chant he learnt in times of distress as an immediate self-soothing mechanism.

Levi also learnt to notice his positive physiological sensations. He realized that every time Tia walked in the door, he felt like he was seeing her anew. He felt a mild sexual arousal, combined with a feeling of "refreshment" for his whole being. He gradually came to express how he felt to Tia who was surprised to learn that she had such a positive effect on him. He had never before had words for how he felt when he saw her, and he certainly hadn't revealed these feelings to her.

Levi began expressing his positive feelings of being happy when he saw Tia by telling her she looked beautiful. As part of their greeting, he also incorporated a habit of giving her a hug that lasted a minimum of 30 seconds. The hug was topped by a kiss on Tia's forehead. All of which made Tia feel really good. Levi committed to long-term couples counseling "until we die" as he jokingly put it because he felt like he needed the accountability, encouragement, and new strategies that counseling provided.

Building Empathy and Relational Consciousness

The partner with ASD typically finds it challenging to notice emotional or physical distress in his partner. In these moments, he may struggle to express concern for his partner. Due to the apparent aloofness and detachment that he may display, his partner may think that he is lacking in empathy. He may, however, be able to train himself to anticipate the needs of his NS partner, even if it is in minute increments and "baby steps." With repeated effort, he may be able to learn to express concern in a way that feels comfortable and satisfactory to his partner. Working on expressing empathy can dramatically improve his marriage.

Learning about his partner's distress signals and a few options on how to respond to her can be a good starting point. At first, this might seem like a lot of work and may actually cause more conflict in the relationship. He may feel like he is being pushed beyond his limits. It's important to remember that learning any new skill comes with significant discomfort, false starts, and trial and error.

Even with a lot of training and skill building for the partner with ASD, the NS partner would still need to accept that her partner is neurologically different. He may never fully understand her needs and be able to step in to meet them at the crucial moment. She may find that she would still need to verbally express her distress, and any specific requests that she has for him during these times.

♥ AUDREY AND JACOB'S STORY: PART 2 ♥

Audrey realized that she needed to work on expanding her EI—her TOM, empathy, and relational consciousness. She needed to begin looking at the big picture, instead of perseverating on the negative details in her interactions with people. Audrey learnt that she had a tendency to magnify the negative. She always went back in time, to events that happened in the past, and admitted to having a hard time letting go.

Audrey realized that she needed to avoid speaking about certain topics that triggered her. For example, with her neighbor, she needed to stop speaking about astrology. She realized that hers wasn't the only perspective. Just because she had a strong view on something, that didn't mean that it was the ultimate truth. Even if it was, it wasn't her place to go about correcting people around her.

Audrey decided to visit her psychiatrist whom she hadn't seen in two years, about getting back on her anti-anxiety medications. She reported that she was better able to manage her relationship when she wasn't so anxious all the time due to her work pressures.

Jacob began working on changing some of his behaviors with her. He learnt that Audrey behaved better when he prepared her for his mother's visits ahead of time, and when she had planned breaks from being around her mother-in-law and his friends. Jacob learnt more about ASD and began to understand Audrey's need for solitude and structure. He worked on being direct and clear in his communications with her. He explained to her in detail over the course of several couples counseling sessions that his mother's unexpected jabs at her were due to his mother's own insecurity, need for attention, vulnerability at getting older, and living so far away from him. With Jacob's help, Audrey began problem-solving the social situations that were confusing to her. Jacob realized that Audrey had a softer, kinder, and optimistic side to her.

Jacob also worked on his own coping strategies. He decided to seek out his own individual counseling in order to work on his gambling issues. He suggested that they meet with a financial planner to reduce Audrey's anxiety about their economic situation. Jacob realized that if he wanted Audrey to change, he would have to work on his own issues as well.

They both made *The Appreciation and Gratitude Exercise*™ a daily habit, along with *The Walking in Your Partner's Shoes Practice*™. With a lot of hard work, self-work, and applying ASD-specific strategies, Jacob and Audrey were able to improve their marriage.

Chapter 7

COPING WITH SENSORY OVERLOAD AND AVOIDING MELTDOWNS

*Have a heart that never hardens, and a temper
that never tires, and a touch that never hurts.*

CHARLES DICKENS

Sensory Sensitivity

According to a research study, 95 percent of children with an ASD were found to struggle with some degree of sensory integration (Tomchek and Dunn, 2007). Sensory processing or sensory integration problems in individuals with ASD exist because the nervous system isn't able to adequately process sensory signals received from the individual's five senses: taste, touch, smell, sound, and sight—and output them into appropriate motor and behavioral responses (SPD Foundation, n.d.). The individual with ASD either receives too much sensory input (hypersensitivity), leaving them overwhelmed, or not enough sensory stimulation (hyposensitivity), leading them to engage in sensation-seeking behavior.

Some examples of being overwhelmed with sensory input are: a startle response to touch, extreme sensitivity to light, an aversion to the taste or texture of certain foods, trouble filtering out background noise, or feeling nauseous from particular smells. Fluorescent lighting can induce an immediate migraine in some people. The noise at a train station, or too many people talking at once at a party, can feel like the loud clanking of metal on metal. Smells at the grocery store can induce overwhelming feelings of nausea. Not having enough sensory stimulation or hyposensitivity can include: a high pain threshold, a lack of awareness of extreme hot or cold temperatures, or a diminished sense of smell or taste.

Many of the married individuals I see in my practice learn about ASD in adulthood, and have not received any occupational or sensory integration therapy to help them manage sensory issues. While some adults outgrow some of their sensory issues, many others continue to struggle with these all their lives. When sensory issues go unrecognized and if the partner with ASD lacks effective coping mechanisms, sensory issues can lead to behavioral and sexual problems, anxiety, depression, and meltdowns. In a neurodiverse marriage, these issues can cause significant distress for both partners.

Self-Awareness of Sensory Issues

The partner with ASD might not be fully aware of his sensory issues. For example, Barry, an NS partner in a same-sex marriage once reported that his partner, Don, had no idea why he didn't like spending time outdoors. Once Don received an ASD diagnosis, he was able to realize that he had a sensitivity to sunlight. He invested in a good pair of sunglasses and a wide-brimmed hat, and was able to enjoy outdoor activities with his husband.

Adam, a young man with an ASD, is another example of someone who was unaware of his sensory issues. He came to my office complaining about his new job. At first, he couldn't explain why. He felt it might have to do with the fact that his co-workers were loud and didn't speak English as their first language. After some discussion, I learnt that his new office had open cubicles.

The sound of people talking or rustling papers in the neighboring cubicles was amplified a hundred-fold to Adam's ears. We were able to unravel that it was his sensitivity to sound that was making it impossible for him to work. Once he realized what was causing his distress, he decided to speak to his manager about using noise-canceling headphones. With this simple accommodation, he was able to stay at his job, without being so miserable.

Sensitivity to Smells

Sensitivity to smells can sometimes cause significant problems in a marriage. Many adults with ASD are highly sensitive to their partner's body odor, so it can be important to negotiate fresh showers before cuddling or sex. It's important that the NS partner truly understand that this is a neurological trait and that her partner with ASD isn't just trying to be difficult. On the other hand, some individuals with ASD can have a poor sense of smell and not realize when they need to use deodorant or take a shower.

♥ AYLA AND BRAD'S STORY ♥

Ayla lived in Turkey, where she had been diagnosed with ASD. Brad lived in America. They met in an Internet chat-room. After an international romance ensued, they were married, and Ayla moved to Boston. While Brad had been privy to Ayla's ASD diagnosis, he had no idea that she had a highly acute sense of smell and strong reactions to particular odors. His aftershave, deodorant, bath products, and even the laundry detergent were overwhelming for Ayla and frequently made her nauseous.

Not understanding the reason for his wife's olfactory sensitivities, Brad thought that she was exaggerating her experience. "Every time we are together, she complains that I smell bad. What am I supposed to think?" He began to take her reactions personally and would walk away feeling hurt and upset. If he was in a better mood, he would tease her for "having the nose of a dog." Ayla struggled to fully explain her sensitivities to him, and became upset that he couldn't accommodate her.

Ayla began to physically withdraw from Brad. He assumed that her withdrawal was based on her unhappiness with him and the marriage in general. He continued to tease Ayla, thus multiplying the distress that she felt. She became afraid of Brad approaching her at all.

When they came to see me for couples counseling, Brad complained that the sex had all but disappeared in their marriage. He seemed defeated and angry. I explained to Brad about ASD and the sensory issues that came with it. Even though he had heard the same thing from Ayla before, in hearing it from a clinician, he finally realized how serious Ayla's sensory issues were. He threw out all the chemical products he was using and switched to a fragrance-free brand.

Visual Sensitivity

Many individuals with ASD are hypersensitive to certain kinds of light, and may find visually cluttered environments intolerably distracting. Strategies can include lights with dimmers, light-blocking curtains, hats, visors, and sunglasses.

Many individuals with an ASD are visually gifted. They may have artistic talent or a strong aesthetic sense. While their visual abilities can make them successful in certain professions, it's not great when they criticize their partner's appearance or fashion choices.

♥ ANNIE AND MARK'S STORY ♥

Annie complained that her boyfriend Mark insisted on going shopping with her and picking out her clothes. Moreover, he only wanted her to wear form-fitting mini-dresses in order to accentuate her petite figure. If Annie wore clothes that were loose or free flowing, he told her that "she was drowning in her outfit" and that her clothes weren't proportionate to her five-foot frame.

While Mark might have been right in his assessment of Annie's clothes, she found his behavior controlling.

"It's not your place to monitor my clothes."

"When you wear clothes that are disproportionate, it hurts my brain."

Once Annie understood the reason behind Mark's comments, she was able to not take his comments personally. She also realized that she could use his aesthetic talents to her advantage. She came to rely on his aesthetic sense. Mark also realized that he had to reduce his comments on Annie's clothing and pay her more compliments.

While Annie and Mark's story illustrates a case of how a partner with an ASD can be hypersensitive to his partner's appearance, it's also important to note that the vast majority of partners with ASD can be very accepting of their partner's appearance and physical flaws, which is a real strength in relationships.

Sound Sensitivity

Some individuals with ASD are hypersensitive to loud noises. Others may detect even the subtlest of sound frequencies, such as the sound of electricity running through the wiring in the house. Some may have perfect pitch, and off-key singing may be grating to their ears. Those with sound sensitivity might want to try noise-canceling headphones, earplugs, or have sound machines while working or sleeping. Taking periodic breaks when visiting noisy places can also be tremendously beneficial.

♥ YOLLY AND SVEN'S STORY ♥

Sven and Yolly had been married for six years. In the last two years, Yolly had joined an amateur klezmer band. She reported that Sven—who has sensory issues and possibly ASD—never wanted to accompany her to any of her concerts. Whenever she invited him to one of her performances, he would make some excuse or the other. After she confronted him, he told her that he really "couldn't stand listening to that noise!" Yolly was dumbfounded and very hurt. Participating in the band was very meaningful to her as part of her heritage as a Jewish woman.

After reading up on ASD sensory issues, she realized that the sounds in certain types of music were difficult for her husband to hear. Nevertheless, she wanted Sven to come to an understanding of how important her music was and how much it would mean to her if he came to her concerts to show his support for her work. Once he was able to acknowledge her feelings and apologize, they worked out a compromise. Sven would drop her off and stay for the beginning of the concert. Then he would take a break, walking around the neighborhood, returning towards the end of the performance. He also decided to wear earplugs so that the really high-pitched tones wouldn't hurt his ears so much.

Note: Another issue related to sound sensitivity is auditory processing disorder. Many individuals with ASD may have trouble processing words and sound over the phone. In a group situation, they may have trouble following the conversation. This may lead them to avoid speaking on the phone altogether, or feel anxious in social situations. It's important that the NS partner understands why her husband avoids talking on the phone, and has a meltdown after a party. While not every individual with ASD has auditory processing disorder, it can be a factor complicating a couple's communication.

Sensory Issues with Touch

Individuals with ASD can have tactile sensitivities, which cause them to feel very uncomfortable wearing certain kinds of clothing, or being touched in certain ways by another person. The individual may find a woolen sweater intolerably scratchy or may cut off labels from all of his shirts. When it comes to touch, he may prefer deep pressure. Too light a touch may feel like tickling and be irritating, while a deep massage might feel pleasurable. Obviously, this can sometimes pose a challenge for physical affection and intimacy.

The NS partner might feel frustrated, confused, and depressed over the physical disconnect with her husband.

It's important that the NS partner not shame or blame her partner for being hypersensitive, and not view her partner's discomfort to touch as a rejection of her love and affection. Each partner might need to be clear and explicit about his/her needs and touch preferences, in order to find the types of touch that they both enjoy.

Taste and Texture Sensitivity

The individual with ASD can be excessively sensitive to certain tastes or textures of food. He may be a fussy eater, need to control everything he eats, or want to eat the same thing every day. Not surprisingly, his taste and texture sensitivities may mean that he does not enjoy giving oral sex or kissing his wife. The couple might have to negotiate how to meet each other's needs in the bedroom. (See Chapter 8, "Meeting Each Other's Sexual Needs".)

Hyposensitivity Issues

In addition to hypersensitivity, the individual with ASD can also have hyposensitivity, low sensitivity to stimuli as we have seen. Hyposensitivity may result in sensory-seeking behaviors. For example, the partner with ASD may ask his wife to scratch his scalp or skin really vigorously, just so that he can "feel something." Sleeping with a weighted blanket, or being in a tight wetsuit may feel good to him. The pressure on his skin, from the weighted blanket or wetsuit can provide him with sensory feedback in his muscles and joints, and can induce feelings of comfort and relaxation. For this reason, he may also enjoy a vigorous run or intense yoga. A woman with ASD once reported to me, "Yoga helps me get back into my body."

For the NS partner who's never heard of or encountered such behavior, such idiosyncrasies in her husband might seem strange. It's important to speak to an ASD-specific counselor if the couple finds themselves struggling with sensory issues. Knowing, understanding, and making accommodations for sensory issues is important so that both partners feel understood, accepted, safe, and comfortable in the relationship.

Avoiding Meltdowns

For the partner with ASD, unwelcome or sudden sensory overload is a factor that can trigger explosive, emotional outbursts known as meltdowns. However, he can cultivate awareness of his various sensory sensitivities and needs and develop coping strategies to stave off meltdowns.

♥ ISABELLE'S STORY ♥

Isabelle didn't have a formal diagnosis of ASD, but she was convinced of her diagnosis after reading numerous articles and books on the subject. She joined my Women's ASD Support Group. She reported that almost everything that the other women in the group said about their experience resonated with her.

Isabelle had an intense sensitivity to smells and sounds, and a "sort of driving dyslexia" as she put it. She explained that she often lost her way despite the Global Positioning System (GPS) tracking device in the car.

Once her company hosted a conference 25 miles away from her home. A number of her colleagues asked if they could carpool with her. Isabelle felt uncomfortable saying no, and reluctantly agreed to drive three of her colleagues to the conference center. It was a hot, summer day. As soon as her colleagues piled into her modest car, she became hypersensitive to her co-workers' body odors. Then her co-workers began talking amongst themselves, and the laugh of one of her co-workers really began to grate on her ears. Add to that her anxiety over getting lost while driving a long distance to an unfamiliar location!

By the time Isabelle arrived at the conference center, she was a complete wreck. She had no choice but to pretend that everything was all right, so that nobody would suspect that anything was amiss. After the day-long conference, Isabelle had to drive her colleagues home again!

At the end of the day, when she entered her house and encountered her husband Manuel, she exploded at him. She complained about how hard she had to work because he wasn't making enough money. Manuel was completely blindsided by her anger. He in turn became upset with her and Isabelle's meltdown resulted in a huge fight.

It was only the next day, in her counseling session that she was able to trace the steps that had led to the fight with her husband. She realized how the cumulative effect of her sensory issues had led to her meltdown. By learning more about her sensory sensitivities, Isabelle realized that she had to monitor her mental and physical state. She couldn't always extend herself on behalf of other people; she needed to prioritize her own well being. She had to train herself to say no to certain requests that might cause her distress. She learnt to rate her anxiety on a numbers scale when she was escalating towards a meltdown. She also realized that she had to have better ways of coping with her stress, rather than exploding at her husband. Isabelle began using *The Sensation-Emotion Awareness Chart*™ in order to tune into physical manifestations of her distress and implement coping skills.

Understanding the causes and learning coping behaviors can lessen the frequency and intensity of meltdowns. As the partner with ASD becomes more self-aware, she can begin recognizing the early signs of a sensory overload and promptly implement coping strategies. The NS partner can also learn to assist her by bringing her awareness to her rising stress levels and remind her to use a calming technique such as deep breathing or counting from 1000 backwards.

CHAPTER 8

MEETING EACH OTHER'S SEXUAL NEEDS

Wherever you go, go with all your heart.

CONFUCIUS

♥ GLEN AND ROBIN'S STORY ♥

Glen and Robin met while they were both married to other people. They felt an instant attraction to each other. After a few months of struggling with their feelings for each other, they decided to end their marriages, and be together. Neither of them had children from their first marriage.

Unbeknownst to them, both had ASD. In the beginning, being together seemed just what they needed. They had each felt stifled in their previous relationships and that their spouses didn't understand them. The sex was great! While the quality and frequency of sex, for many couples, can diminish over time, but for Glen and Robin, the sex went downhill fast. They were together for about three months when as Glen put it, "Robin decided to close shop!"

"We just don't have sex anymore."

"That's not true!" Robin countered, "We have sex about twice a week."

"Once a month. It's because she has sensory issues. She doesn't like being touched."

"It's not that I don't like it, it hurts to be touched."

"Is it all types of touch?" I asked.

"No, I just don't like light touch, but Glen likes to sit on the couch and run his fingers over me as a way of stimming. At first, we didn't know why it felt so familiar to be with each other. When my niece was diagnosed with ASD last year, I read up about ASD and realized that it described both Glen and me perfectly."

"Yes, very much so."

"Anyway, we learnt all these Aspie terms like stimming and such. He likes to stim by caressing me, but every time he runs his fingers up and down my arms, I feel like I'm on fire. It makes me flinch and avoid any touching. Even the sex we have once a month is not something I am too excited about. I might have a low drive I guess. My ex-husband was really frustrated with me, but I didn't like sex with him. I don't mind it so much with Glen." She smiled at Glen and held his hand.

"He's really good in bed too! In the beginning, we had a lot of sex. I guess not having sex with my ex for many years had caused a build up for me. Now that Glen and I are living together, it's harder for me to be sexually available to him. The other issue is that I think Glen uses sex to manage his anxiety. So, he wants to have sex all the time. We don't know how to reconcile this problem."

While the above story is about an ASD-ASD couple, the NS-ASD dynamic can be similar. While sex can vary considerably in all marriages, difficulties with sexual interaction are probably more prevalent in relationships where one or both partners have ASD. This can be due to: sensory issues, differences in sex drive, low energy levels, stress, lack of emotional connection, delayed psychosexual maturity, and lack of imaginative play.

Sensory Issues in the Bedroom

The most common barrier to the neurodiverse couple's sex life are the sensory issues of the partner with ASD. Sensory issues can affect foreplay. For the partner with ASD, who is often hypersensitive to touch, the light caresses of foreplay can feel uncomfortable. Caressing can cause her to feel tickled, induce a startle response, or feel downright painful. She might begin to feel anxious, and push her partner away.

Even if she had initially tolerated her partner touching her, as she settles into the relationship she might divulge that she has difficulties tolerating him touching her. This revelation can often be confusing and upsetting for her NS partner. Further discussion may reveal that she prefers deep pressure and firm touch instead of light caresses. Her boyfriend may then have to change how he touches her.

Kissing can be a challenge if the partner with ASD has taste or texture issues. She might find kissing to be "too wet" and dislike the taste of her partner's mouth. These challenges might diminish over time, or the couple might have to compensate by kissing other body parts. Many men with ASD in particular tend to dislike oral sex due to taste, texture, and smell sensitivities. In such cases, his partner may have to use creative strategies to get him to participate in oral sex. For example, she might agree to shower prior to sex, or she might prepare him by requesting oral sex ahead of time. A husband with ASD once revealed in a session, "I'm more likely to be in the mood for oral sex if I receive advance warning. If she lets me know on my way home from work that she's in the mood for it, I can prepare myself. Then, I don't mind it so much, and I know it makes her happy because it's me showing her extra love that day."

While such strategies may at first feel strange and awkward to the NS partner, she may find that planning for and creating accommodations around sensory issues can improve her sexual experience with her husband. If she doesn't understand the sensory issues of her partner, she may not realize the sensory basis for some of the refusals in the bedroom. When the partner with ASD is unaware of his sensory issues, problems can arise due to his silence or limited communication. Even if he is aware of his sensory issues, he might feel ashamed and vulnerable. He may think that he will lose his partner's love if he reveals "his secrets." However, communicating sensory issues and sexual needs honestly can ensure that sex is not only satisfactory, but safe for both partners. Conversations around sexuality can often be a challenging, and an ASD-specific couples counselor can sometimes be valuable in such a situation.

Differences in Sex Drive

A High Drive

While sexual desire varies from person to person, many individuals with ASD either have a very high or a very low sex drive. The NS partner often reports that her husband with ASD wants sex daily, or even multiple times a day. This high drive may be based on his hyper-arousal, or he may view sex as a way to beat anxiety and regulate his mood.

Similar to a teenage boy, even just sitting next to his wife might cause him to become immediately aroused, which can sometimes be off-putting to her. She might feel upset that her husband has a one-track mind, but the reality may be that her husband can't really help how his body reacts to her. He might seek to either masturbate or have sex every time this happens, sometimes as a way to relieve sexual tension and other times to prevent embarrassing himself in public. For the NS wife, it's necessary to realize that her husband doesn't necessarily just see her as a sex object, but that he has limited control over his physiological reactions.

Sex can not only provide a sense of security and closeness to one's partner, it can also be a way to beat stress. Sex can provide a temporary relief from anxiety and depression as it hits the neurological reset button. Neurotransmitters such as norepinephrine, dopamine, and serotonin surge into the brain during sex, particularly during orgasm, and can dramatically improve an individual's mood (Romero, 2002). Even though sex can be a source of emotional regulation and feeling good, it's important that the partner with ASD have other coping strategies as well.

In some cases, the partner with ASD might not know when it is inappropriate to request sex. For example, there might have been a death in the family, and not being able to read his partner's somber mood, he might approach her for sex. He may become confused and upset when his partner turns him down. She might have to explain that sex will need to wait for a few days or weeks until she's ready again.

A Low Drive

On the other end of the sexual spectrum, some individuals with ASD can have a low sex drive, and they may not need or desire sex at all. Psychotropic medications or hormonal issues can often affect libido, so it's important to rule out medical issues by consulting with the appropriate specialist. In many cases, the partner with ASD may not know that his low sexual drive is unusual. He may accuse his wife of wanting too much sex. In some cases, the low-libido partner with ASD might even have a premise—self-created or taken from the media—to go with the fact that he doesn't want or need sex. For example, he may say, "People over the age of forty shouldn't be having sex. It's wrong to have sex once our children are grown up."

Understanding that low sexual desire in the partner with ASD is often a physiological or neurological issue can take away the stigma of shame and rejection for both partners. There are hormone and drug-based treatments that can be very effective for individuals with low libido. Couples can seek advice from a doctor for the best way to correct the problem. Maintaining a healthy body weight and a regular exercise routine can also enhance an individual's sex drive.

Low Energy

Another cause of infrequent sex can be the low energy of the partner with ASD. He might find that most of his energy is spent at work and on the evening commute. By the time he walks into the front door, he may feel extremely drained. After dinner, he may doze off on the couch while watching TV. The very idea and perceived demand for sex might feel beyond what he can handle in an average work day.

He might struggle with executive functioning issues or OCD tendencies. He might not know how to organize a task efficiently, or he may obsess over perfectly accomplishing it. He might spend relatively more energy than his NS partner on cleaning dishes, ironing clothes, and fixing the house, leaving less energy for sex. He might need guidance from his wife to prioritize tasks, and need to follow the "good enough" rule so that he doesn't spend hours obsessing over mundane tasks. Doing so can immediately increase the time and energy available to him for sex with his partner.

The lack of energy (or even the low sex drive) of the partner with ASD may inadvertently impose an unnegotiated sexual routine on the relationship. For example, with no discussion or mutual agreement, the NS partner may realize that her partner only initiates sex every two weeks. If the couple are in a long-distance relationship during the dating phase, this routine may work well, and may well go unnoticed by the NS partner. However, once the couple is married and living together, the two-week intervals may seem rigid and not enough for her. The husband with ASD might turn down his wife initiating sex, before the two-week mark, thereby causing her to feel rejected and unloved.

Putting sex on *The Relationship Schedule*™ can take out the surprise element, and regulate sex for both partners. The couple might discuss and schedule who initiates sex, on what day and time, and for how long. Doing so may allow both partners to feel more secure about their sex life. The partner with ASD can "budget" his energy for the day and week so that he has some left to have sex.

The NS partner can come to rely on the sex schedule so that she's not left wondering when the next time she's going to have sex with her husband will be. Scheduled sex can be just as beneficial as sex that is spontaneously initiated.

Stress

Stress can impact every couple's sex life. In a neurodiverse marriage, stress for the partner with ASD can sometimes mean a lot more sex, or a complete withdrawal and a dry spell for the NS partner. Stress can cause exhaustion, and deplete the energy level of the partner with ASD even faster. "Quickies" or sex without foreplay can become the norm during such times. When this is the case, it's important that the couple acknowledge the situation, and make time for a more prolonged sex session before too much time goes by. Sex without foreplay and emotional reciprocity can leave the NS partner feeling disconnected, objectified, used, and even depressed.

It's not always possible to know about upcoming stressful events or periods in one's life. However, if both partners try their best to anticipate difficult situations and discuss them ahead of time, they might be able to come up with stress-management techniques and coping strategies.

For example, if Diane, a partner with ASD, had a particularly stressful day at work, she had a ritual of taking a long shower immediately after coming home. She and her husband had learnt to communicate over text message about her need to "cool down" prior to interacting with him. Her "cool down" ritual included taking a long hot shower with her favorite music blasting in the bathroom to help her shake off her day. She was then able to switch gears for a romantic evening with her husband. The "cool down" period was very helpful to Diane; she could minimize the impact of stress on her marriage. Diane increased her antidepressant and anti-anxiety doses during a more recent company merger due to the increased amounts of work stress.

Stress can add to sensory sensitivity or overload. The higher the stress, the more acute or raw the senses can be. Stress can also affect individuals with ASD more severely and disproportionately. Understanding this as an aspect of ASD, both partners can be vigilant about stressful times. They can adjust their expectations of sex during stressful periods and do their best to comfort and support each other.

Lack of Emotional Connection

Many individuals with ASD are not as attuned to their feelings and they may often not see the connection between emotions and sex. For example, after a fight, the partner with ASD might not realize that his partner does not want to have sex that night. Or, he may say something insensitive one moment, and in the very next, be ready to jump into bed. He may be clueless as to how hurt her partner was by his remark and be confused about her refusal to be intimate.

The hurt and pain that the NS partner feels from the harsh words, can cause deep-seated resentment to the point where they may eventually stop feeling sexual towards her partner. Many neurodiverse couples can go months and even years without physical affection and sex. Both partners can feel frustrated and stuck not knowing how to move forward.

After learning about ASD, the NS partner might become more forgiving or find it easier to let go of upset and anger. Upon discovering the connection between emotion and sex, the partner with ASD can begin apologizing for the past, and become more mindful of his actions and speech going forward. Dialogue and understanding can heal even the deepest rifts.

Another reason for sexual distance in the neurodiverse marriage can be the weak emotional intelligence of the partner with ASD who might not have much emotional awareness (EI), or be inexpressive about feelings towards his partner. For example, a man with ASD might not tell his partner that he thinks about her, misses her, or loves her, nor does he bring her flowers or presents for any occasion. He may not understand the thread of emotional connection that needs to be maintained between partners on a day-to-day basis, as we have seen. The partner with ASD may have to learn to express his emotions and demonstrate his love to his partner in ways that are meaningful to her. For example, Jack discovered how much his wife liked it when he rubbed her shoulders every night after their children went to bed, so he got into a habit of doing so. His wife, Janet really appreciated both the massage and the effort he made to show his affection for her. Their sex life that had diminished gradually returned as Jack discovered more ways of emotionally nurturing Janet.

Understanding each other's "love language" as described by Gary Chapman (2010) in his book *The Five Love Languages*, can also be a useful tool to help partners meet each other's emotional needs.

Delayed Psychosexual Maturity

Many individuals with ASD can be slow to develop and mature. This lack of maturity can often play out in the bedroom. The partner with ASD may engage in behavior that is highly inappropriate without meaning to. For example, he may try to fondle his wife in public or expose his genitals at inopportune moments. His wife may often feel put off by such behavior and she may lose sexual interest in him.

She might not say anything for fear of hurting his feelings, but she might need to tactfully discuss with him why such behavior is inappropriate and "not sexy." Even bringing it up in couples counseling can feel embarrassing. I would advise meeting with the couples counselor one-on-one in order to have full disclosure of the situation if necessary.

Lack of Imaginative Play

ASD is characterized by a lack of imaginative play. In the bedroom, this can mean that the partner with ASD may not put any effort into creating an ambiance for foreplay and sex. He may be robotic without paying attention to his partner's need for emotional connection. An NS partner once described her husband thus, "It's like in figure skating. Technically he's a ten, but he's a three in charm and playfulness. I wish he would loosen up a bit."

With cues from his wife, the partner with ASD could learn to improve his charm in the bedroom. She might want to breakdown the sequence of foreplay and sexual acts in a step-by-step "sexual storyboard" or choreography to give her husband a clear idea of what she wants. The couple may benefit from using sex-education videos to learn new techniques and expand their repertoire of sexual interactions. Once he has some ideas, he may want to try them out and ask his wife for feedback.

Communicating sexual needs and desires and finding creative ways in which to satisfy each other can rejuvenate a couple's sex life. Individuals with ASD can be good at thinking outside the box and there's no reason why this skill cannot be employed in the bedroom! A couple's sex life can therefore be as interesting and dynamic as they both want it to be.

CHAPTER 9

BRIDGING PARALLEL PLAY

*Do the difficult things while they are easy and do
the great things while they are small. A journey of
a thousand miles must begin with a single step.*

LAO TZU

♥ NICO AND ZOEY'S STORY ♥

Nico, an electrician and Zoey, an art-school professor had been married for 11 months. When they came to see me, Zoey said, "The moment we got married, everything changed! Nico used to write me poems and plan these wonderful romantic dates for us. Practically the day after we got married, he stopped everything. We were basically fighting on our honeymoon because he wanted to play video games in the hotel room instead of spending time with me. Ever since, it's only gotten worse. Every evening, he comes home and either goes straight to his computer, or works on his lamps…he restores antique lamps on the side… He won't even say hello to me."

"Well, she's always complaining, so now I just try to avoid her. It's true that we used to spend more time together doing fun things, but then we didn't live together, so I could go home after and relax. In fact, I used to play a lot more video games and have a bigger lamp business. It's just that she wasn't there to see me."

"I admit that it might feel like I'm nagging him, but the truth is," she turned to look at Nico, "you just sit there and ignore me if I don't say anything. If it were up to you, we wouldn't spend any time together at all, nor would you talk to me. What am I to do? I feel so lonely."

"But we do spend time together. I like it when you're painting and I'm fixing my lamps…"

"That's not us spending time together; that's us working in parallel!"

Even though many married NS couples struggle to spend quality time together, in a neurodiverse marriage, being together can be a real challenge. The partner with ASD often struggles with initiating and sustaining social-emotional reciprocity. She or he can also have a preoccupation with a special interest, and challenges with Theory of Mind, alexithymia and executive functioning— all ASD traits that can lead to spending a lot of time alone—or engaged in parallel play.

Parallel Play

Parallel play is a term I borrowed from child development literature, and Tim Page's book *Parallel Play: Growing Up with Undiagnosed Asperger's* (2009), to describe neurodiverse partners who spend time engaged in individual activities rather than spending time together. They might work in the same house in separate spaces, or share the same working space without much interaction with each other. The partner with ASD can inadvertently initiate the culture of parallel play, as he often tends to spend a lot of time working, and not initiating conversation, touch or dates with his wife.

When the partner with ASD thus engages in parallel play, the female NS partner might try different ways to get his attention. She might drop hints about spending more time together, buy new lingerie, and plan special dates and outings. More often than not, he has difficulty interpreting these behaviors, and might tell his wife that he is uncomfortable with lingerie, going out in public, or he may just continue to spend time on his special interest. She might then try verbally expressing her desire for closeness and connection, which her husband often interprets as criticism. Not knowing why his wife is complaining when he's perfectly happy in the marriage, he might either lash out at her, or continue to withdraw.

While the NS partner might initially be motivated to initiate dates and activities with his partner, if his efforts aren't met with success, he can become resentful. If the couple has children, he might build a life around family and community, while still continuing to make efforts to connect with his wife. Children and community often provide a much needed distraction and support for the NS partner. He may design a life with a career, activities, and his own special interests. Seeing her partner preoccupied with his own life, the wife with ASD might now feel freer than ever before to focus on her own special interests. Both partners involved in their own interests, may go days, weeks, and even months engaged in parallel play, without spending time with each other. Parallel play can easily become a pattern in the neurodiverse relationship. While not the ideal marital arrangement, parallel play may work for a few couples when their children are young; however, as the children become more independent or leave home for college, the NS partner may begin to experience a void in his life. Many couples in my private practice fit this profile.

When the NS partner's need for emotional reciprocity and closeness go unmet, he might lose sexual interest in his partner, become very unhappy and often want out of the marriage. Parallel play can have serious repercussions for the neurodiverse marriage. Once both partners understand parallel play and strategies to bridge it, they can learn to plan activities and relationship time more easily.

Reasons for Parallel Play

The reasons for parallel play are important to understand, so that neither partner blames the other for the disconnection between them.

A Very Special Interest

Individuals with ASD often have intense interests in one or more subjects—scholarly, professional, or purely entertainment—to the point of being obsessive (APA, 2013). For example, a seven-year-old boy with ASD I once met had a highly motivated interest in the obscure subject of airmail carrier routes before World War II. While some adults with ASD might also have similar idiosyncratic preoccupations, most are interested in mainstream topics like history, science, technology, medicine, music, art, or engineering. The only difference is that their interests tend to be more extreme in nature compared to their NS counterparts which often lead to highly successful careers in these areas. Being well accomplished and often possessing a high income and status, they can be highly sought after as life partners.

In the initial stages of a relationship, or during the courtship phase, the individual with ASD might temporarily shift focus from his existing interest to making his partner his *special* interest. His special interest in her may mean that he intensively sets out to gather information about his partner's life—her past, present, likes and dislikes—and go to great lengths to woo her. He may write poetry and music, or orchestrate exciting activities and make elaborate travel plans in order to win over his lady love. However, after marriage, he will tend to revert to his original special interest, leaving his wife feeling abandoned, disappointed, and lonely.

A mutual special interest also brings many ASD-NS partners together. For example, I once worked with a couple that shared a special interest in outer space and NASA. Over the the course of their marriage, they had made trips to see numerous space shuttle launches, and had many exciting stories of chasing space shuttles. They could complete each other's sentences when it came to speaking about NASA! Other couples might enjoy activities such as playing music together, travelling, hiking, rowing, attending gaming conventions, or studying an esoteric subject like Egyptology. After marriage, often due to the pressures of having children or the demands of their professional lives, the couple may struggle to engage in these common activities and special interests. Extra effort might be needed to rekindle and continue scheduling and spending time on shared interests.

Lack of Initiation and Reciprocity

The individual with ASD can struggle with social initiation and reciprocity, which means that in a relationship she may not always reach out to connect with her partner on a regular basis. Going hours, days, and weeks without any social contact with her partner might be normal for her. Even after her partner tells her that he needs more contact from her, she might find it challenging to text, email, or call. Even if her partner initiates contact, she may not reciprocate.

Theory of Mind (TOM)

A weak Theory of Mind (TOM), or challenges in reading his partner's thinking-feeling state is why the partner with ASD isn't always able to understand his partner wanting to spend time together. He might struggle to understand that his partner needs to fulfill her basic need for emotional connection by spending time with him. His lack of understanding might lead him to blame or shame his partner for being needy, insecure or demanding, which can leave his NS partner questioning herself. Not understanding his NS partner and her needs can also make him paranoid and suspicious about her behavior. For example, he might think that his partner's purchase of lingerie is because she is hypersexual, whereas she might have done so to create intimacy in order to reduce the parallel play in their marriage.

It is important that the partner with ASD is told and made to understand that NS individuals, including his partner, need social-emotional interaction and connection as one needs food—on a daily basis. He will need to realize that his partner is neurologically different from him in her needs and that she isn't being needy, insecure, or demanding when she asks him to spend time with him. He has to understand that her sense of comfort, belonging, and happiness is contingent on the emotional feedback she receives from her partner and loved ones.

Alexithymia

Alexithymia or a weakness in understanding and expressing emotions in the partner with ASD can also mean a reduced need for emotional connection. The partner with ASD often struggles to be aware of his emotions and thus has trouble verbally expressing love and affection to his partner. The combination of low TOM and alexithymia can be a potent mix making the partner with ASD likely to be emotionally absent, unreciprocal, and rigid. The NS partner's perception of her partner's aloofness can often result in her creating and perpetuating the distance in her marriage both emotionally and physically.

Executive Functioning

Executive functioning or organizational and planning challenges for the partner with ASD can also contribute to parallel play in the neurodiverse relationship. Many times, the partner with ASD is motivated to spend time with her partner, but has trouble figuring out which activity to pick and the steps that go into planning it. Trying to sort out the various options and organizing around the particular activity could be so overwhelming, that she might abandon the task altogether. "She knows what I like to do and where I'd like to go on a date, she just doesn't do it," is a common complaint of the NS partner.

In such cases, if the NS partner doesn't understand his partner's executive functioning issues, he may take her lack of initiative in planning dates or activities to mean that his partner does not love or care for him. Executive functioning challenges can be managed by using *The Relationship Schedule*™, and the NS partner's assistance.

Bridging Parallel Play

Even if the partner with ASD intellectually understands that spending quality time with his partner is important, he might find it difficult to put his intentions into action. Therefore bridging parallel play isn't always an easy task. It requires both partners working together. The partner with ASD has to learn to value the need for emotional connection, and the NS partner might have to realize that her partner "just won't do it" unless there are certain strategies and compensatory tools in place such as a *The Relationship Schedule*™. Balancing alone time and share time as a couple is also a must. For many couples discovering a shared mission can result in a newfound intimacy and meaning for their lives and relationship. Engaging in novel and exciting activities is another strategy to keep things fresh and invigorating in the neurodiverse relationship.

Valuing Time Spent Together

Many times, the partner with ASD doesn't realize the value of spending time together, therefore he must deeply understand that spending one-on-one time with his wife in conversation, cuddling, talking a stroll and even just listening to her is a necessary and non-negotiable part of the relationship. Internalizing his wife's NS values of emotional expression and connection is crucial to him making any lasting changes in his behavior.

There is also research to suggest that the couple that plays together stays together (Aron *et al.*, 2000). "The more you invest in fun and friendship and being there for your partner, the happier the relationship will get over time," says Howard Markman, a marriage researcher of the Center for Marital and Family Studies at the University of Denver (Jayson, 2008). "Time spent playing together," explains Markman, "is an investment in the relationship" (Jayson, 2008). The activity doesn't have to be anything elaborate or costly. Exercising together, window shopping at the mall, or watching a classic movie can help bring a couple closer. Scheduling a weekly "date night" is essential (Noles Jr., n.d.).

Research data indicated a direct correlation between couples engaging in fun activities together and marital happiness (Aron *et al.*, 2000). While couples in the research study weren't classified as NS or neurodiverse, the findings are clear that playing together—participating in joint leisure activities—can help bridge the physical/emotional distance between couples. With emotional connection being a major hurdle in neurodiverse relationships, ASD-NS partners can bridge this gap by cultivating mutual hobbies and engaging in activities together.

Enjoying activities together can improve the mental and physical health of both partners. Engaging in mutual special interests can even help a couple find a new passion and life mission. By enjoying quality time together, a couple can create new memories, deepen their relational bonds, and greatly improve their quality of life. In addition to weekly and monthly leisure activities, some couples might also want to plan yearly active vacations such as a trek in the Himalayas, scuba diving in Belize, or learning Italian in Rome as a way to invigorate and refresh their marriage.

Relationship Schedule™

Refer to Chapter 10 on *The Relationship Schedule*™ for more information on this strategy. In order to bridge parallel play, using *The Relationship Schedule*™, both partners might start by making a short list of preferred activities. It's important to note that in many cases even if the NS partner makes a list of activities that interest him, and hands it to his partner hoping that she'll pick one and schedule it, she might not. She might get overwhelmed by the list and not do anything at all. This is particularly true if there's a history of her picking an activity that her partner didn't like. She might mistakenly think, "He didn't like the play the last time I took him to the theater, so why bother…" Due to her black and white thinking, she might give up trying to please her partner altogether.

Therefore, the couple might need to sit together and pick a few activities to put on their *Relationship Schedule*™. Adding reminders leading up to the day of the activity might be necessary for the partner with ASD as she might easily forget the upcoming event, or she might have to prepare herself for an event if it involves social interactions such as being at a fundraising walk, or a dinner party. Scheduling a weekly time—an hour to plan, schedule, and evaluate upcoming activities and dates—would also ensure that events don't simply stay on the calendar, but actually happen.

Calendaring on a weekly and monthly basis is important so that the partner with ASD knows what to expect and how to ration her energy for the romantic dates. Many individuals with ASD also prefer having a lot of structure to their life, and having an itinerary of upcoming dates can help them feel more in control.

Care should be taken so that the responsibility for initiating, planning, and implementing the activities doesn't always fall to the NS partner. If the couple experience this pattern, they might want to work with a couples counselor, or even an organizational coach to come up with even more creative strategies to bridge parallel play. Also, many times a couple might struggle to agree upon a shared activity, and a counseling session to discuss the issue can be very helpful.

Balancing Shared Time with Alone Time

As much as it's important for couples to spend time together, it's important to keep in mind that many individuals with ASD tend to need a lot of solitude and alone time to recharge their batteries and relax. The couple might need to negotiate how much shared time versus alone time is reasonable. A little bit of give and take, dialogue, and flexibility can go a long way. It is also best to have set times for alone time and date nights. Thus both partners can experience a sense of security and comfort knowing that their needs will be met.

Another situation worth mentioning is when the NS partner is more extroverted in temperament and needs to engage in more social activities than his ASD partner is comfortable with. Often the partner with ASD might be an introvert and can feel drained after social interactions. The NS partner might need to meet part of his social needs outside his marriage with friends, family, neighbors, colleagues, clubs, volunteering, or a religious community.

Discovering a Shared Mission

Many individuals with ASD have a highly developed sense of social justice and tend to be very active in animal rights, social advocacy, cultural and educational causes, and world-peace issues. In most neurodiverse couples, these are shared values. Engaging in values-based activities and causes can give meaning and direction for their lives as a couple and as individuals. Both partners feel motivated to create social or environmental change, and they may find their relationship infused with a newfound happiness. For example, Mitzy and Brenden found a creative way to bond with each other by participating in their local town politics. They not only found a way to make a positive contribution to their community, but also discovered that they loved working together and uniting their different way of thinking to problem-solve various issues.

Rita and Ron, another couple in a neurodiverse marriage, share a deep commitment towards conservation. Their passionate commitment towards the environment has enabled them to protect the shoreline of their small New England town against development and commercialization. Their shared work keeps them focused on their united mission in life. They both report that this shared mission has helped them to overcome many of the difficulties in their marriage.

Keep it Fresh, Novel and Exciting!

Long walks, movies, window shopping, boat rides, hikes, travel, dance or exercise classes, attending lectures, spiritual retreats, deep-sea dives, mountain summits, musical concerts, fairs, community events, parties, fundraising and social justice events— there are numerous opportunities for the neurodiverse couple to spend time together to create a lasting and happy relationship. Having rituals and activities that the couple can rotate through in order to keep parallel play at bay is crucial.

Research on couples playing together also indicates that engaging in novel and exciting activities resulted in increased happiness and a deeper bonding of partners (Aron *et al.*, 2000). Couples experienced an increase in romance and the feeling of being in love. Again, the research doesn't identify any of these couples as being neurodiverse, but it seems that these would apply to all couples irrespective of their neurological makeup. The researchers believe that these passionate and loving feelings after engaging in the novel and stimulating activities for couples are based on the theory of self-expansion (Aron *et al.*, 2000).

The theory of self-expansion asserts that an individual enters into relationships as a means to expand herself by experiencing the life of her partner (Aron and Aron, 1996). Individual growth and development can never be achieved in solitude; therefore, relationships are necessary vehicles to take us out of our comfort zones and stimulate a positive inner transformation. When couples expose themselves to novel and arousing activities, they might feel refreshed and energized about their relationship because these activities result in an expansion of themselves (Aron *et al.*, 2000). Couples thus need to seek and create new opportunities to enrich their lives both as individuals and as a couple.

CHAPTER 10

CREATING A
RELATIONSHIP SCHEDULE™

Start by doing what's necessary; then do what's
possible; and suddenly you are doing the impossible.

FRANCIS OF ASSISI

In the fast-paced modern world, every couple probably needs a calendar to keep track of important weekly, monthly, and yearly events such as holidays, birthdays, anniversaries, as well as family visits, doctors' appointments, children's school and extracurricular activities, and social events. Similarly, a *Relationship Schedule*™ creates a scaffolding to support the efforts of the ASD partner to meet his partner's need for emotional connection. Establishing and implementing a *Relationship Schedule*™ is helpful not only for the NS partner, but the partner with ASD can also use it to include his own need for breaks, alone time, and solitary activities.

What is a *Relationship Schedule*™?

A *Relationship Schedule*™ is a tool to help the couple ensure that they make time for the behaviors and activities that they enjoy, and that help them stay connected and keep their relationship healthy and thriving. The schedule should include short daily conversations (uninterrupted by screen time), and physical and verbal expressions of love and affection (cuddling, sex, compliments), weekly dates (movies, walks, playing games, concerts, hiking) and bi-monthly getaways.

The Relationship Schedule™ can help any couple. However, it is crucial to the neurodiverse couple, because the partner with ASD often struggles with initiating and expressing affection, spontaneous sharing, and social-emotional reciprocity. The NS partner might find that even if she gives her husband explicit and concrete directions of how he can meet her needs, he still might not be able to carry out these requests unless the actions are put into their *Relationship Schedule*™.

The Need for Creating a *Relationship Schedule*™

Many individuals with ASD can be creatures of habit and tend to do well with established patterns and routines. *The Relationship Schedule*™ can act as a compensatory tool for typical ASD traits such as executive functioning challenges, a preference for structure and routine, and a preference for processing information visually. The schedule reduces confusion and anxiety by demystifying what the NS partner expects from the relationship and how the ASD partner can provide it. Creating a *Relationship Schedule*™ and sticking to it, can truly transform the neurodiverse relationship. Here's how:

Scheduling Intimacy-Building "To Dos"

Due to his challenges with executive functioning (organizing, planning, strategizing) the partner with ASD might find it difficult to plan, remember, and actually go out on dates with his wife. Even though his executive functioning weakness is neurologically based—it's not that he doesn't care—the wife may feel that her husband habitually neglects her. When her legitimate need for affection and emotional connection go unmet, she may develop symptoms of Affective Deprivation Disorder and question the worthwhileness of the relationship. She may also express her unhappiness to her husband. He may then experience his wife as being demanding, unreasonable, and needy. He may feel confused, overwhelmed, frustrated, and at a loss about what to do.

To improve the chances of the wife getting what she needs, the couple should put the emotional and intimacy-building "to dos" on *The Relationship Schedule*™. The couple can openly discuss and decide upon acts of love that the NS partner would appreciate from her partner. For example, they could include scheduled time for short, daily conversations, gestures of affection such as a shoulder rub, bringing her coffee every Sunday morning, drawing her bath on Friday evenings, or going on a date to the new restaurant in town. When acts of affection are scheduled on a regular basis, the partner with ASD can feel better prepared to carry them out. By making it more possible for her husband to attend to her needs, *The Relationship Schedule*™ improves the couples chances of long-term marital success.

Planning Reduces Anxiety

Often the partner with ASD has a sense that he's not fulfilling his partner's needs and that she's deeply unhappy. Especially if he's experienced failed relationships in the past, he might be insecure about his ability to sustain this relationship, and be afraid that she may leave him. Not understanding the basis for his partner's unhappiness, he may become increasingly anxious, and even experience panic attacks. Some partners with ASD might even come up with some bizarre, paranoid explanations for their marital woes.

For the partner with ASD, *The Relationship Schedule*™ can provide reassurance. Knowing what the NS partner expects and being able to do the things she or he wants, can give a sense of security. A man with ASD no longer has to wonder if he's paying his wife enough compliments, or if he should be spending more time with her.

Visual Processing

In some cases, the partner with ASD might not know what to do to provide for his wife's emotional needs. In others, his wife may repeatedly tell him orally what she needs, but the information just doesn't register. Many individuals with ASD process information more efficiently when it is presented in visual form. Therefore, the visual format of *The Relationship Schedule*™ makes it more likely for him to understand, remember, and perform the actions that will create and sustain emotional connectedness.

Couples may want to experiment to see what works best for them: to use a paper, white board or online calendar for their *Relationship Schedule*™.

Checking-In

It's advisable to set aside time for a weekly check-in (preferably at the same time each week so that it becomes a ritual) during which the couple can evaluate how well *The Relationship Schedule*™ is working for them. It is a good idea to designate a space in the home, preferably not in the bedroom, to sit down and discuss *The Relationship Schedule*™. Did they stick to the schedule? Did they enjoy their shared experiences? Is there anything they would like to change?

This would be a good time for the NS partner to thank his ASD partner for the effort she's made. He can give her lots of encouragement and praise for the kind things she's done for him. When *The Relationship Schedule*™ starts working, the NS partner might be tempted to request several changes and additions; however, he should remember that change and trying new things could be difficult for his partner. His partner is more likely to respond positively if he introduces changes more gradually.

If the partner with ASD feels overwhelmed, she might want to use the check-in to ask her partner to ease up a bit. For example, she might admit, "Last week, we had conversation time scheduled for twenty minutes and you went over by forty. That really exhausted me and I had trouble focusing at work the next day. Would it be possible to stick to twenty minutes like our couples counselor suggested? Perhaps we can set a timer."

Through the check-in process, both partners will discover what works in their relationship and what doesn't. If the couple start getting upset with each other during the check-in, they could agree to continue the discussion in their next session with their ASD-specific couples counselor.

Meeting the Needs of Both Partners

Here's a story that illustrates how both partners in a neurodiverse marriage used *The Relationship Schedule*™ to get their needs met.

♥ TONY AND TONI'S STORY ♥

Tony and Toni had the same name, but the uncanny commonalities didn't end there. They shared the same birth date, had the same curly mop of hair, and worked in the same creative field of graphic design. They sometimes spoke in unison, and claimed that they had the exact same taste in esthetics, music, and food. Nevertheless, they were struggling with their emotional relationship. Tony, the partner with ASD, complained that he wasn't getting enough sex, and Toni, the NS partner, complained that she wasn't getting what she needed in order to feel emotionally connected.

"It's like being with a robot."

"I'm not a robot! I'm always there for you when you need me. I drop everything whenever you need me, no matter how often. How can you say that I'm a robot?"

"Because you never share what you're feeling with me. It's like I don't even exist."

"What?! We spend every spare moment together."

After listening to both of them go on like this for a few more minutes, I asked Toni if she would be willing to break down what she needed from Tony on a day-to-day basis.

"Well, I'd like for us to cuddle a little extra in the mornings when we wake up, before he jumps on me for sex!"

"And?"

"And, I would like for him to text me during his lunch hour to see how I'm doing. And I'd like for him to say, 'I love you' at least once a day and when I get home, and give me a proper hug! Not a pat on my bottom!"

I asked Tony if he would be willing to implement these behaviors for Toni on a daily basis.

"I want to, but I'm afraid I'll forget."

I asked him, "what would make things easier?"

"Putting things on my Google calendar would definitely help, but I'd also like some kind of reward in exchange if I'm going to put all this effort in. Can Toni send me a selfie whenever I want? And how about my favorite breakfast of omelette and chocolate chip pancakes every Sunday in return for extra cuddling on the weekends?"

After some surprised laughter, they agreed on a sort of barter system so that they both got what they wanted out of their relationship. Tony got all excited about this "exchange of services" as he called it, and they began to enjoy a more fulfilling relationship where both their needs were met.

Over time, they worked on a detailed *Relationship Schedule*™ that included both of their individual requests. They programmed this into their online calendars that synced with their smartphones; each received notifications to remind them of the task that they needed to perform. Tony found that his tasks became habitual, easier, and even enjoyable for him over time. Now if Toni is travelling for business over the weekend, it was *he* who misses the Sunday morning cuddle.

Both Partners Need to Take Ownership
of *The Relationship Schedule*™

It's important that both partners take ownership of *The Relationship Schedule*™. The schedule and the check-in offer the partner with ASD opportunities to participate with their NS partner in creating a high-quality family life. With a working *Relationship Schedule*™, the NS partner no longer needs to feel that they have sole responsibility for the emotional life of the relationship. Seeing their ASD partner making tangible efforts to meet their needs lets the NS partner recognize that they care.

The Relationship Schedule™

Examples # 1 and # 2 are examples of what *The Relationship Schedule*™ could look like. Please note that each *Relationship Schedule*™ needs to reflect the desires, lifestyle and personalities of the specific couple. There is no one-size-fits-all; each couple has to negotiate what they need. *The Relationship Schedule*™ will also have to be adjusted during transitions and life changes.

Example # 3 of *The Relationship Schedule*™ is a monthly calendar and it is less detailed. Couples might find it useful to combine the weekly and monthly schedules create a more comprehensive template for their relationship.

Example # 1 of *The Relationship Schedule*™

TIME	MONDAY	TUESDAY	WEDNESDAY	THURSDAY	FRIDAY	SATURDAY	SUNDAY
6:00 a.m.	Extra long cuddle in bed	Cheerful "good morning" and cuddle	Extra long cuddle in bed			Sleep in	Sleep in
7:30 a.m.	Goodbye hug and kiss	Compliment: "You smell so good." Goodbye hug and kiss	Goodbye hug and kiss	Goodbye hug and kiss	Compliment: "You look good today!" Goodbye hug and kiss	Cuddle and sex	Cuddle and watching Sunday TV
Noon	Text message, "thinking of you"	Email: "Looking forward to seeing you later. It's date night."	Text message, "thinking of you"	Text message, "thinking of you"	Text message, "thinking of you"	Alone time	Go grocery shopping together
3:00 p.m. Text message, "I'll be home by 6:00 tonight" Text message, "Only a few hours more until our date!" Text message, "I'll be home by 7:30 tonight" Text message, "I'll be home by 8:00 tonight"					Text message, "I'll be home by 6:00 tonight"	Alone time	Alone time
5:00 p.m.	Phone call to say, "I'm heading home now. Do you need anything from the grocery store?"	Phone call, "See you at the restaurant in 30 minutes. Where do you want to eat?"	Phone call to say, "I'm heading home now. I did have a rough day at work, might need to relax before we hang out."	Phone call to say, "I'm heading home now."	Phone call to say, "I'm heading home now."	Alone time	

cont.

Example # 1 of *The Relationship Schedule*™ (*cont.*)

TIME	MONDAY	TUESDAY	WEDNESDAY	THURSDAY	FRIDAY	SATURDAY	SUNDAY
6:00 p.m.	Seek out wife, say "hello" with a hug and kiss	Seek out wife, say "hello" with a hug and kiss	Seek out wife, say "hello" with a hug and kiss	Seek out wife, say "hello" with a hug and kiss	Seek out wife, say "hello" with a hug and kiss	Alone time	Dinner and TV together
8:30 p.m.	Half an hour "Conversation Time"	Alone time		Half an hour "Conversation Time"		Alone time	Half an hour "Conversation Time"
10:30 p.m.	Cuddling and sex	Smooch goodnight	Cuddling and appreciation	Cuddling and appreciation	Cuddling and appreciation	Cuddling and compliment	Smooch and goodnight

Example # 2 of *The Relationship Schedule*™

TIME	MONDAY	TUESDAY	WEDNESDAY	THURSDAY	FRIDAY	SATURDAY	SUNDAY
7:00 a.m.	Spooning in bed for 10 minutes	Spooning in bed for 10 minutes	Spooning in bed for 10 minutes	Spooning in bed for 10 minutes	Spooning in bed for 10 minutes	Spooning for longer	Spooning and sex
9:30 a.m.	A 6-second hug and 2-second kiss goodbye	Compliment: "You look great!" A 6-second hug and 2-second kiss goodbye	A 6-second hug and 2-second kiss goodbye	A 6-second hug and 2-second kiss goodbye	Compliment: "You're so beautiful!" A 6-second hug and 2-second kiss goodbye	Go out to breakfast and play a game of Uno at Starbucks after	Cook a leisurley breakfast together.
1 p.m.	Text message, "Work busy today, might be late tonight. Miss you"	Text message, "thinking of you... having lunch"	Text message, "thinking of you... having lunch"	Text message, "thinking of you... having lunch"	Email: "Looking forward to seeing you later. It's date night!"	Pick an afternoon activity to do after lunch	Give each other a massage
6:00 p.m.	Phone call to say, "Going swimming after work, see you soon."	Phone call to say, "See you soon, leaving for the train now."	Phone call to say, "Rough day at work, going swimming, see you soon."	Phone call to say, "See you soon, leaving for the train now."	Phone call to say, "See you at the restaurant, leaving for the train now."	Alone time	Alone time
8:00 p.m.	Seek out wife and give her the 6-second hug and 2-second kiss	Seek out wife and give her the 6-second hug and 2-second kiss	Seek out wife and give her the 6-second hug and 2-second kiss	Seek out wife and give her the 6-second hug and 2-second kiss	Seek out wife and give her the 6-second hug and 2-second kiss	Cook dinner together	Alone time
10:00 p.m.	Reading to each other in bed	Alone time	Listening to music together in bed	Alone time	Reading to each other in bed	Alone time	Alone time
11:00 p.m.	Cuddling and express one sentence of appreciation	Cuddling and express one sentence of appreciation	Cuddling and express one sentence of appreciation	Cuddling and express one sentence of appreciation and sex	Cuddling and express one sentence of appreciation	Cuddling and express one sentence of appreciation	Cuddling and express one sentence of appreciation

Example # 3 of *The Relationship Schedule*™

FEBRUARY

SUNDAY	MONDAY	TUESDAY	WEDNESDAY	THURSDAY	FRIDAY	SATURDAY
1 Hiking in the Blue Hills	2	3 Conversation, dinner, and movie night	4	5	6 Date night at the Red Tent Restaurant	7 Dinner with new neighbors
8 Reading two chapters of the Asperger book to each other	9	10	11 Date night at the Museum of Fine Arts	12	13	14 *Valentine's Day* Gift: necklace with geometric pendant. Ski weekend
15 Ski weekend	16	17 Conversation, dinner, and movie night	18	19	20 Date night at Stella's Restaurant	21 Reading two chapters of the Asperger book to each other
22 Concert at the BSO	23	24	25 Conversation, dinner, and movie night	26	27 Conversation, dinner and movie night	28 Date: Arts and crafts fair

CHAPTER 11

IMPROVING COMMUNICATION

Raise your words, not voice. It is rain
that grows flowers, not thunder.

RUMI

Communication is difficult even for non-neurodiverse couples. People find that they have to work at their communication skills on a daily basis. Within a neurodiverse marriage, improving communication skills is an even greater necessity. The partner with ASD often has an usual style of communication, one that is different from what the NS partner expects. This mismatch in communication styles can leave both partners feeling surprised, confused, and frustrated at times.

Many individuals with ASD struggle to know what to say and how to say it. Often they may not think before they speak, and may say things that are reactive and hurtful to their partners. They may also not be as adept at verbalizing their thoughts at crucial moments to avoid and smooth over conflicts. Not knowing what to say can often exacerbate relational problems in the neurodiverse marriage. For the NS partner, it's important to understand that their partner's silence or inability to speak up at crucial moments in the relationship is an ASD trait, and that her partner's not choosing to be difficult, rude, or reactive. However, many partners with ASD can also deliberately exhibit such behavior.

While individuals with ASD have inherent communication challenges, they can also have certain strengths: they can be honest, open, forthright, and transparent in what they say; there won't be any double meanings or subtexts; and they can often be very good listeners. Nevertheless, ASD primarily is a social-communication difference and individuals with ASD can struggle with communication in a variety of ways.

Eye contact and Body Language

Studies show that up to 80 percent of human interaction is based on nonverbal cues and body language (Mehrabian, 1972). The NS partner instinctively uses nonverbal cues and body language to communicate, and supplement verbal communication, adding context, irony, humor, and feelings. Often the partner with ASD not does pick up these facial cues, vocal intonations, and body language, and misunderstanding can ensue. Thus, the partner with ASD can miss out on a significant amount of nuanced information that is a vital part of interpersonal communication.

In particular, NS individuals communicate a lot of information through their eyes and the muscles around them. The partner with ASD can fail to receive that information because she might struggle with eye contact. She may find eye contact painful or intrusive. She may not be able to simultaneously hold eye contact and attend to a conversation.

People with ASD can learn to make approximate eye contact by looking at the other person's nose, forehead, or earrings. Some may be able to progress to glancing briefly into the person's eyes. Some people with ASD report that they are better able to tolerate eye contact as they mature.

However, even if the partner with ASD learns to make eye contact, she may remain generally uncomfortable with it, and may be inconsistent in how she holds her partner's gaze. Sometimes she may stare at her partner because she finds it comforting, pleasing, and soothing to her eye. During the courting phase, her NS partner might interpret this intense gaze as an expression of passionate love or longing, when in fact she's just receiving a sort of visual boost to her brain from watching her partner. Looking at her partner can be a form of positive sensory stimulation.

It's important for both partners to bear in mind the neurological differences around eye contact. The NS partner has to realize that his partner with ASD is probably not picking up the subtle information he is expressing through eye contact and body language. The partner with ASD needs to realize that her NS partner is probably communicating more information than she is receiving. She may need to ask him for verbal clarification, especially if she feels that the communication is going awry. This strategy can help prevent misunderstandings.

Informing Versus Connecting

Generally people with ASD do not engage in small talk or banter; they use communication to impart information, whereas NS individuals also communicate in order to build rapport and feel connected. The NS wife often reports that her husband isn't interested in talking about feelings or anything related to emotions. He's comfortable discussing factual and concrete subjects. "He only wants to talk about his special interest—the business we own together. I don't mind talking about the business, but it seems like that's all he wants to talk about! When I try to ask him how he feels about me or our relationship, he doesn't seem to have anything to say."

The husband needs to understand that his NS wife has an emotional need for communication that involves an expression of feelings. He would do well to pay attention even if the things she wants to discuss seem trivial or mundane. It's important that he learns to listen and show an interest in what his partner has to say, even if he has to fake it. The NS partner has to understand that emotional conversations are challenging and exhausting for the partner with ASD.

Differences in Perception and Memory

Individuals with ASD tend to perceive information differently from their NS partners. Therefore, many times, couples come into a session to see me, and they have completely different views of the same event.

For example, once a couple came in for a counseling session on a day when there was a heavy rainstorm predicted. I asked the couple, "I've been indoors all day, what's it like out there?"

The NS spouse responded, "The sun is still out, so who knows, maybe it won't rain after all." Her husband contradicted, "That's not true, the sky is dark and cloudy, it's probably going to rain any minute now!" How could two people have such contrasting views of the same weather system? They focused on different details, and drew different conclusions.

Due to their different experiences and memories, partners argue and insist that the other person is wrong. They may even accuse each other of lying. So, it's important that both partners understand that there is a difference between NS and ASD perception and memory. Both partners need to recognize, appreciate and be curious regarding the other person's perspective. Avoid jumping to a negative judgment about the other partner's intentions and voracity. As a wise person once said about relationships, "You can either chose to be happy or to be right."

Slower Processing Speed

Individuals with ASD are sometimes slower to process information. For example, the NS partner might want to analyze a fight the couple had while visiting her parents over the Christmas holidays. She might ask her husband questions about what happened, and how they could have better handled the situation. The wife is full of feelings and has a lot to say. Her husband with ASD might get overwhelmed by the amount and speed of information coming his way, and quickly shut down.

He may become silent as his wife continues to speak because he hasn't yet figured out what to say. By the time he is done processing the first thing his partner said, she's already said two more. When he does not immediately respond, the wife continues to talk further overloading him with additional information and complaints. The argument that started out over the family visit for the holidays may have moved on to include unrelated issues such as laundry, or childcare. This type of conversational pacing can be difficult to keep up with for most people, regardless of neurology, but especially so for individuals with ASD.

Sometimes, the partner with ASD may ask for more time to think about it and get back to his wife at a later time. However, she may never get a response from him, or it might take him days, weeks, and months to process something that she can process in minutes. This difference in processing speed can create a lot of frustration for her.

A good strategy for her would be to focus on one issue at a time, and to give him time to respond, without filling in the silences. If necessary, I recommend that couples designate a weekly time to have regular conversations. See the previous chapter on *The Relationship Schedule*™ for more details.

♥ KATE AND ADAM'S STORY ♥

Kate and Adam were a couple in their mid-thirties. Together they ran a technology startup company. They had met at a party a few years ago. It was love at first sight for both, and their common interest in technology cemented their relationship. Kate had ADHD; Adam didn't have a formal diagnosis, but self-identified with ASD. Kate said that they came to see me because Adam was being rigid and inflexible about having children. Kate wanted to start trying to get pregnant, but Adam felt that they weren't ready.

Kate said, "I've been telling Adam that now is a good time to have our first child, but he says that we need to get more funding for our company and hire more staff in order to have time to focus on a family. I don't understand this. We'll *always* be working crazy hours, but my biological clock is ticking and I really want to have children while I'm still young enough. He only thinks about himself!"

Adam deliberated for a while on what he wanted to say. "That's not true. It's not that I'm opposed to having children right now. Yes, it's true that I want the company to have more of a financial cushion before we start trying for children. That will probably happen in the next few months."

"I really don't see how we'll get the funding we need in that short of a period of time. The last time we raised money, it took almost a year."

"The company is in a better place and is attracting bigger investors this time around. We're getting press coverage and our client base is stronger. We're being valued at more. So the investments will come sooner."

"Adam, we've been through this before. We keep having the same conversation. It took us a whole year to even begin dating! I'm tired of your slow processing. Whether we grow or not, things are good enough with the company. I think it's time we try to have a baby. There's never a good time."

Adam sighed. "I want to get married before we have children, but Kate doesn't want to marry me. Plus, I truly question her wanting to have children. This desire to have children is very new."

Kate seemed truly shocked by Adam's revelations. "What?! That's the first time I'm hearing anything about marriage. And my desire to have children is new? I've *always* wanted to have children. This is so typical of Adam and his distortion of facts. Once again, I have no idea what he's referring to."

"You told me once that you never wanted to get married or have children."

"I don't remember saying any such thing."

"You did. We were watching a movie and you said, 'Remind me never to get married or have children!'"

"What are you talking about? I'm sure I'd remember if I said something like that."

"We were watching a movie when you said it. And you said it again when we were at Marcelo's wedding. There were children crying and you said it again. You seemed so sure when you said it. So for a while, I thought you didn't want to get married *or* have children. Then all of a sudden, you said you wanted to have children."

Kate was truly at a loss for words. Adam continued, "I'm also worried that if we have a child, the kid will have autism. You keep telling me how life with me is so hard because I have autism. I'm really not sure it's a good idea for us to have children. And we would have to move to a larger place. I don't want to live in the suburbs. I would hate that."

Clearly there was a lot that Adam hadn't revealed to Kate. The conversation turned out to be very revealing for Kate. She realized that she might have been insensitive to Adam about his ASD. After giving it some thought, she realized that perhaps she had casually mentioned to Adam that marriage didn't seem as important as having children. The selective manner in which Adam processed and communicated information led him to harbor his own version of what she had said to him. Kate became aware for the first time of just how anxious and afraid he was to have children. Adam had a slower processing time and it took him a long time to clarify and express how he really felt.

Initiating and Sustaining Conversations

In some cases, the disconnect in a neurodiverse marriage is due to the fact that the partner with ASD has great difficulty initiating and sustaining conversations. In the beginning of the relationship, the NS partner might initiate most of the conversations whether or not she's aware of it. During the courtship phase, the partner with ASD might also exert extra effort and go outside their comfort zone to have more conversations. However, as time passes, her partner's lack of initiation might begin to get to her. If the NS spouse doesn't understand his ASD, she may think that his lack of initiation means that he's fallen out of love with her. As for the partner with ASD, the more comfortable and close he feels to his partner, the less he feels a need to initiate conversations. Once he is married, he may relax, revert to his comfort zone, and rarely initiate conversations.

Although it may not come naturally to him, the partner with ASD can learn strategies for initiating and sustaining conversations so that the burden of doing so doesn't fall entirely on the NS partner. The partner with ASD can work on initiating contact by scheduling specific times when they email, text, call, or seek out their partner for a conversation.

Some individuals with ASD talk too much and others are very quiet. A helpful guideline for the partner with ASD to moderate his conversations would be to not say more than three to five sentences at once, and to use *The Listen, Validate, and Compliment Strategy*™.

The Listen, Validate, and Compliment Strategy™

Convey the following three points during your conversational turn. Use no more than three to five sentences for each point.

1. *Listen* to your partner, and paraphrase what you've heard her say to show her that you've been listening: "I heard you say that you had a frustrating day at work. You said that you've been doing the work of two accountants for almost six months. Is that right?"

2. *Validate* your partner: "That sounds an awful lot of extra work. That must be challenging."

3. *Compliment* your partner: "It sounds like you are doing all you can to do the work of two people. You're such a hard worker."

The NS partner too can facilitate positive communication with the ASD partner. She might provide him with a script to give him an idea of what to say. For example, she might tell her husband to support her by saying, "I would like for us to have a conversation about how rough my week at work has been. I don't need you to solve my work problems, I just want you to listen, validate, and compliment me by saying something like, 'I'm sorry that work is hard. You're a hard worker and your company is lucky to have you.'"

Emotional Expression

The partner with ASD is often not aware of his feelings and is even less able to express them. He might show his love for his wife by doing things for her; he might assume that his actions speak louder than words. Even though the NS partner might intellectually understand that her partner cares about her, she still needs to hear words and gestures of affection. When she expresses this to her partner, he might feel unappreciated for all the things he already does for her to show her his love. He might not understand why his partner needs him to tell her that he cares about her. Both partners can thus feel frustrated.

Receiving regular emotional feedback from her partner is something the NS partner needs on a daily basis, just as one needs food. Just because we eat one day, doesn't mean that we don't need food anymore. In the same way, the NS partner needs, "emotional food" or reinforcement on a daily basis or she can experience symptoms of Affective Deprivation Disorder. The couple can add saying "I love you" to their daily *Relationship Schedule*™. Even if the partner with ASD might feel that the behavior is contrived, or that he's being fake when he says this to his wife, she will not only appreciate the effort he has made, but she will also feel emotionally nourished.

A Battle of Logic

The partner with ASD tends to have a hyper analytical mind. He is most comfortable when using logic, and may take this approach to all of life's challenges. He might have a tendency to use logic as a weapon. He might get into long drawn out arguments and come across as aggressive and arrogant. He may not realize how much distress this can cause his partner. She might feel attacked by her partner's cutting logic, whereas the partner with ASD is baffled by her reaction. Such exchanges can bring the neurodiverse marriage to a crisis point.

It is important to set ground rules for compassionate, non-violent dialogue to replace the slicing and dicing of cutting logic. Keeping conversations short and to the point can be helpful. Sometimes, even short conversations can trigger the couple and the only solution is to abort the conversation as soon as either partner realizes that it is escalating. The couple can create ways to safely end the conversation with a pre-established hand-signal, such as a football referee's time out, or a code phrase such as, "gremlin!"

Tone of Voice and Volume

A lot of individuals with ASD are unaware of how others perceive their tone of voice and volume. The NS partner will say that his wife with ASD is "always angry." To which she may respond, "I'm not! I'm not an angry person. You're just overreacting!" The NS husband will then report that his wife always speaks in an angry tone, even to their four-year-old daughter. The partner with ASD often doesn't realize that her volume is increasing, and that her tone might be getting sharper. Simply put, she may not realize that she sounds angry and that her partner feels intimidated, attacked, or even traumatized.

Once partners understand and accept that tone and volume is an issue in their communication, they can use some strategies to address it. They can work with a numeric rating scale for the volume. For example, the NS partner might say, "Honey, your voice is at a seven now. Is this conversation making you upset?" The wife with ASD might then be able to become more aware of her voice and gauge her level of agitation. She might then count to ten out loud or in her head and say, "Yes, I'm sorry I seem to be getting worked up. I guess I'm more anxious today than I realized. The meeting I had with my boss really depleted my energy. Let's talk about this some other time."

Visual Communication

Temple Grandin describes how she thinks in images rather than words (Grandin and Panek, 2013). Similar to Temple, many individuals with ASD are visual thinkers and learners: they communicate and learn better through visuals such as pictures, videos, photographs, and even reading rather than hearing instructions. Therefore, many neurodiverse couples find it helpful to communicate via emails, text messages, drawings, cards, or hand-written notes.

♥ SYRA AND JOHN ♥

Syra and John had only been engaged for a few weeks, but already they had been running into misunderstandings related to planning their wedding. John had received an ASD diagnosis and counseling while he was in college, which he thought had really helped him. Since the engagement, John and his fiancee got into a few tiffs that both suspected had to do with his ASD. That was when John suggested that they come and see me for premarital counseling.

"John and I are having some issues around planning our wedding. I want to have the wedding at my parent's beach house. I thought John had agreed to it, but he says he didn't."

"I don't remember actually agreeing to the wedding venue. I thought we were going to look at the place my mother recommended. Once we see both, we can make up our minds."

"But you've seen my parent's beach house. You liked being there. You've seen how it is."

"It's nice, but it's a beach house, not a wedding venue."

"We'll set up a gazebo in the garden where we'll have the ceremony and mom said we might even look into putting up a tent."

"I don't know. I can't imagine it. We're inviting almost a hundred people."

I asked John if it would help him to see a sketch or photograph of a similar space in order to imagine what the beach house would look like converted into the wedding venue.

"Yes, I think that would at least give me something to start with."

Syra called a friend who had a background in art, and together they sketched out a plan for how her parent's beach house would look once it was set up for their summer wedding. Immediately John was able to see her vision and embrace it.

CHAPTER 12

CO-PARENTING
STRATEGIES

Let parents bequeath to their children not
riches, but the spirit of reverence.

PLATO

Raising children, however joyful, exciting, and rewarding, is hard work, even in NS marriages. Having children radically changes the lives of the parents, and the relationship between them. For a neurodiverse couple, having a child tests the marriage bond: it shakes up or overturns their routines, and alters the partners' expectations of one another. Adjusting to their altered lives, with a child in the equation, partners can feel jealous, abandoned, stressed, or tense.

In a neurodiverse marriage, the typical stress of marriage and raising children can often be multiplied. Due to his ASD traits such as susceptibility to stress, executive functioning issues, and social-communication challenges, an ASD father may have enough on his plate just managing his other responsibilities, such as holding down a job and keeping himself on an even keel.

In my experience, in many neurodiverse marriages, the majority of the child-rearing responsibilities can fall on the NS wife. Despite the challenges of raising children, the husband with ASD can be a really good parent and can often provide a loyal, accepting, supportive, and steady presence for his children. Even though the ASD partner might struggle with certain aspects of raising children, with the appropriate coaching and guidance, he can develop skills that help him become a better parenting partner.

A Child with Special Needs

Due to the genetic nature of ASD, many couples in a neurodiverse marriage may have one or more children with ASD, ASD traits, social anxiety, or related neurological conditions such as ADD/ADHD or NVLD. Whether the parents have ASD or not, the special needs of a child can often be overwhelming. If parents suspect that a child might have ASD, it's important that they understand her traits and that she receives the appropriate interventions. It may be important for parents to learn about ASD and to get professional help when needed. Joining parenting support groups for ASD and working with ASD-specialists can provide useful solutions and resources.

The NS child

Having a neurodiverse family can also mean that the child might not have ASD. The NS child can often have the experience of having both a parent and a sibling with ASD. He might need help understanding that there is something different about his mother or father and that he isn't to blame for the conflict that can sometimes be a part of neurodiverse families. The NS child might need help in relating to his parent with ASD. Learning about ASD and family counseling could be a good way for him to learn how to connect with his parent and/or sibling with ASD.

A List of Concrete Tasks

The parent with ASD can be very good at concrete tasks such as helping the children with homework, teaching them sports skills, tinkering with toys, and taking them on adventures. When there are predictable and concrete responsibilities, such as picking up the children from school or helping teenagers with college applications, they might even become the parent in charge of these tasks. Not every individual with ASD struggles with executive functioning issues and the ASD partner might even be more efficient at certain tasks than their NS partner such as laundry and cleaning.

When the partner with ASD is unable to intuit or recognize what needs to be done for the children, it's best for the NS partner to provide a concrete list for them to work from. Knowing what's expected would take away the anxiety of not knowing what to do.

The NS partner can often be frustrated with the ASD partner if she feels like her husband is not being able to intuit and recognize their children's needs or if he takes too long to attend to them. It's important that they both realize that many aspects of parenting do not come naturally to the ASD partner. In order for both partners to have a clear understanding of shared responsibilities, it's important that child-rearing duties are discussed before they are expected to be fulfilled.

Relationship Schedule™ with the Children

Scheduling, organizing, and using a calendar can be useful to manage school and recreational activities with children. Often many fathers in general, in traditionally structured families, ASD or not, tend to not be aware of their children's day-to-day schedule. It's important for families to share calendars and set a time to sit down and discuss all the upcoming events in the week or month. Just as the couple in the neurodiverse marriage might need a *Relationship Schedule*™, having a schedule for spending quality time with the child can be necessary in some neurodiverse families. The parallel play phenomenon discussed in relation to the ASD-NS couple, can also be a problem for the ASD parent–child relationship. Many times, it's not that the ASD parent doesn't want to spend time with the children, it's just that he can get hyperfocused on his special interest and work in the garage all weekend, or clean the house to perfection rather than seeking out the children and playing with them.

The NS parent might sometimes have to facilitate opportunities for the children to spend time with her husband. For example, one wife reported that she helped her husband set up a weekly spring and summer ritual with their six-year-old, twin daughters. Every Sunday from May to October, her husband took the twins to a local animal farm to visit the sheep and their newborn lambs. This exciting weekly activity provided the wife with a needed respite from the children. She used this time to attend an exercise class, while allowing for an enjoyable experience for her husband and children.

Below is an of examples of what *The Relationship Schedule*™ could look like for the parent with ASD.

Example # 4 of *The Relationship Schedule*™—for parents

TIME	MONDAY	TUESDAY	WEDNESDAY	THURSDAY	FRIDAY	SATURDAY	SUNDAY
7:10 a.m.	Good morning to the kids	Good morning to the kids	Good morning to the kids	Good morning to the kids	Good morning to the kids	Good morning to the kids	Good morning to the kids
7:30	Emotional expression: "I love you!" A 6-second hug and 2-second kiss goodbye. School drop off!	Compliment: "Good job on the science project last night!" A 6-second hug and 2-second kiss goodbye. School drop off!	Emotional expression: "I love you!" A 6-second hug and 2-second kiss goodbye. School drop off!	Emotional expression: "I love you!" A 6-second hug and 2-second kiss goodbye. School drop off!	Emotional expression: "I love you!" A 6-second hug and 2-second kiss goodbye. School drop off!	Set the table together with the kids for a family breakfast	Read the children a story in bed
2:30 p.m.			School pick up. 6-second hug and 2-second kiss			Take the kids to the local park	Trip to the dog park
4:00 p.m.			Help the kids with homework			Help the kids with homework	Drive to football practice
6:30 p.m.	Seek out the kids and give them the 6-second hug and 2-second kiss	Seek out the kids and give them the 6-second hug and 2-second kiss	Seek out the kids and give them the 6-second hug and 2-second kiss	Seek out the kids and give them the 6-second hug and 2-second kiss	Seek out the kids and give them the 6-second hug and 2-second kiss	Family board game night	Family movie night
6:45 p.m.	Family dinner	Family dinner	Family dinner	Family dinner	Family dinner	Family dinner	Family dinner
8:30 p.m.	Hug and kiss. Emotional expression: "I love you."	Read the kids a bedtime story. Hug and kiss. Emotional express on: "I love you."	Hug and kiss. Emotional expression: "I love you."	Read the kids a bedtime story. Hug and kiss. Emotional expression: "I love you."	Hug and kiss. Emotional expression: "I love you."	Read the kids a bedtime story. Hug and kiss. Emotional expression: "I love you."	Read the kids a bedtime story. Hug and kiss. Emotional expression: "I love you."

Undistracted, Quality Time

Distracted parenting is increasingly becoming the norm amongst parents as a result of their constant use of smartphones while spending time with their children. When parents are on their phones, their children are naturally more prone to acting out; parents miss out on their children's facial cues and subtle moments of interactions that developing brains are programmed to learn from (Radesky *et al.,* 2014).

For both parents, it would probably be good to create and set rules on the use of screen time, so that the children don't lose out on having the foundational connections that they so need. This might mean that all devices and screens are turned off during family dinners, and that parents limit their phone usage when spending time with their children. Scheduling one-on-one, undistracted, quality time with each of the children as well as the entire family on a daily and weekly basis is very important for the children's healthy physical and psychological development.

Emotional Needs of Children

Many parents with ASD struggle to emotionally connect with or understand their children's emotional needs. The mother with ASD can be blind to the developmental stages of children. She might expect adult behavior from her children and may speak to them in a raised voice and sharp tone that can crush a child's delicate self-esteem. If the mother has anger issues, it's really important that these are addressed and treated with both counseling and medication if appropriate. Having an explosive mother can be detrimental to any child and issues of anger management must be taken seriously in any family.

Even though the mother with ASD might struggle to emotionally connect with her children, she can be ready and willing to learn what to say and how to behave with her children. Her NS husband may have to inform and cue her on the emotional states of their child. For example, if their son is feeling down after losing a basketball tournament, the NS husband might have to inform his partner with ASD about what happened and how specifically to soothe their son—what to say and how to say it. She might learn to say, "I'm sorry your team lost the game today. I know how hard all of you worked in the last few weeks. I'm really proud of you." Additionally, the mother might have her own way of soothing her son with his favorite food that evening or buying him tickets to see his favorite artist in concert.

Many individuals with ASD lean towards pessimism and they can be negative in how they speak to their children. The partner with ASD might not realize how valuable it is for her children that their mother praise and compliment them. With some coaching and well-timed cues from her NS husband, she can learn to be more positive and encouraging towards them.

In most cases, the children of parents with ASD learn to accommodate their parent's personality and quirks. They are able to establish their own unique relationship and can come to enjoy a strong bond with their neurodiverse parent.

Family, Community, and Professional help

Families, neurodiverse or not, always benefit from multiple sources of child-rearing help. The proverbial village that assisted parents in raising children a long time ago, isn't right outside our doorstep anymore. In modern times, the village is something that often needs to be created. In a neurodiverse marriage, due to the special needs of the entire family, it is advisable for the village to include, both sets of the extended family (when possible), the community (neighbors, friends, spiritual organizations), and professional help such as nannies, housekeepers, organizational coaches, and ASD-specialists. Having family, friends, and babysitters help with child-rearing can provide both partners in the marriage much needed support and respite from the constant demands of raising a family.

Becoming a Parental Unit

Many parents struggle to unite and work together as a parental unit to raise their children. The partner's ASD traits such as rigidity, black and white thinking, and a hyperlogical mind, can create an impasse on parenting decisions. The father or mother with ASD can be extreme in disciplining and rule setting for children. Unable to understand children's developmental stages, they may try to enforce adult rules on them. Or they may either be extremely lackadaisical in their approach or think that the NS partner is too strict and is overreacting to her children's behaviors. They may lack boundaries and share inappropriate information with their children.

For example, an adult child of a parent with ASD once revealed to me how her father with ASD would reveal details about his marital struggles to her when she was 10 years old. Years later, she was able to identify her father's ASD and put into perspective the issues that were so confusing and painful for her growing up. Once she learnt ASD affected her father–daughter dynamic, she was able to slowly rebuild her connection to him.

Parenting classes, workshops, and working with an ASD-specific counselor can help the neurodiverse couple understand each other's parenting values and perspectives. The counselor can help them agree upon certain parenting strategies and action steps to work together as a parental unit.

♥ MARY AND LANI'S STORY ♥

Mary and Lani were a longtime married, professional lesbian couple. They had two adopted children from Guatemala, a boy aged 12, and a girl aged 14. Lani was a lawyer and Mary was a physician. Mary wasn't officially diagnosed with ASD, but Lani strongly suspected that Mary had Asperger's Syndrome. They came to couples counseling because they were having challenges with their 14-year-old daughter, Sara, and couldn't agree on how to parent her. The disagreements over their rebelling daughter were escalating the conflicts in their household.

Lani said that there were two main issues that they were struggling with Sara on, and Mary wasn't able to understand or support her.

"The first issue is that Sara has been staying out late one or two nights a week and then lying about her whereabouts. And the other thing is that she has not been doing her schoolwork. When I speak to Sara about her behaviors, if Mary is around, she gets stuck on a technicality and sides with Sara. She'll say, 'Sara didn't lie, she just forgot to call us.' She then looks at Sara and shares a chuckle. Sara of course loves to create these 'logical loopholes' knowing that Mary will see her point of view."

Not only was Mary not being a parenting ally to Lani, but she was also undermining her authority as a parent. Lani was at her wit's end as to how to co-parent with Mary. With two demanding careers, their live-in nanny did much of the raising of the children in the early years. However, in the past four years Lani had cut back on her work to be with the kids, and she really wanted to get Mary on board with co-parenting.

"Here's another example: when I ask Sara to do her homework, she responds by saying, 'The teacher is stupid and I'll pass the class even if I don't turn in my homework. When I tried to explain to Sara that that wasn't true, Mary interrupted me saying, 'Yah, I know all about stupid teachers! Lani, she's a straight A student anyway, what does it matter if she doesn't do her homework?!' At that point, I just lost it and I think I must have yelled at both of them. It's so frustrating when Mary acts like that."

In the couples counseling session, I had to interpret and explain Lani's deeper intent to Mary in terms of instilling in their daughter the value of being diligent about schoolwork, the risks of a 14-year-old staying out late at night, and the need for respect towards her mothers.

Mary had to be told that Sara was taking advantage of the fact that Mary got stuck on the "logical loopholes" in order to avoid listening to her mother. The need for presenting a united front to the children as a parenting strategy was also discussed and agreed upon in the session. Lani began to give Mary words to say as they learnt to take turns speaking when disciplining Sara. Mary needed coaching and building of her self-confidence to be able to discipline Sara in a manner that wasn't too harsh or too lenient in shaping her positive behavior.

Having Children

Given the complexity and challenges of a neurodiverse marriage, many couples choose not to have children. Couples who want to have children should become aware of ASD and carefully consider the decision to become parents. They should assess the strength of their economic, physical, and emotional resources, the level of their support networks—the proverbial village consisting of extended family, friends, or professional resources. For many neurodiverse couples, the bulk of the parenting responsibilities can fall on the NS partner's shoulders. A lot of NS partners may find this to be acceptable, especially if the ASD partner is the primary breadwinner of the family.

ASD traits and mental health issues vary from person to person. It's important for both partners to understand the strengths and limitations of their marriage, as they approach the decision to have children. Where some individuals with ASD thrive and truly enjoy parenthood, there are those who struggle and feel stretched to capacity.

As much as individuals with ASD struggle in some aspects of the relationship, they can and do make good parents, even exceptional parents in some cases. The same sense of loyalty that first attracted the NS partner to their ASD partner is also sensed and seen by their children. Even though the ASD parent can unintentionally say hurtful things to their children, they can be unparalleled in the unconditional loyalty and steady, secure presence that they provide for the children. They might demonstrate their love and affection through acts of service and with the appropriate guidance can often transform into an exceptional parent.

CHAPTER 13

PRIORITIZING SELF-CARE FOR THE NS PARTNER

You, yourself, as much as anybody in the entire
universe, deserve your love and affection.

GAUTAMA BUDDHA

David Finch, author of *The Journal of Best Practices,* a married man
with ASD said it best, an individual married to someone with special
needs has special needs too (Finch and Finch, 2012). It's important
that the special needs of the NS partner are acknowledged and
understood, and that they make it a priority to take care of
themselves. The well being of her neurodiverse marriage depends
upon it; this chapter is therefore focused on self-care strategies for
the NS partner.

The partner with ASD has social-communication-emotional
challenges and may struggle to understand his partner's emotions
and needs, as we've seen. They might be more susceptible to stress,
and their NS partner in turn can be exposed to this stress. Executive
functioning issues can mean that the NS partner might have to
compensate for this weakness and have to shoulder the lion's share
of the household responsibilities.

One such challenge is that the NS partner may have to meet
their need for emotional connection and social interactions outside
the marriage as we saw in previous chapters. Many NS partners

report struggling with depression, anxiety, health issues, addictions, and even infidelity as a result of having unmet needs. Therefore, it's imperative that the NS partner acknowledges their own needs. They need to prioritize their own self-care—socially, emotionally, and even physically. They have to manage their stress, in order to avoid burn out.

In any relationship, the welfare of one partner depends upon the other, and the partner with ASD would be wise to support their NS partner in this. Thus, the self-care of the NS partner cannot be underscored enough.

Self-Care is Not Selfish

Self-care is a necessity rather than a luxury. NS partners, especially those with kids, may often feel like their needs come last. However, the airplane analogy of putting on one's own oxygen mask before helping others put on theirs is a good lesson for the NS partner. If they don't take care of themselves, their partner and marriage will most definitely suffer. If they are not healthy and happy themselves, they might find it all the more challenging to cope with the challenges of being in a neurodiverse marriage.

Social-Communication Self-Care

The partner with ASD typically enjoys solitude, and may avoid socializing if he deems it unnecessary. In some cases, he might not want to socialize at all outside the family. He may in fact be happier being on his own or just with his immediate family. His NS partner might then adjust her own social life to accommodate her husband's preference.

However, if she goes too long without having social interactions such as a dinner party, a girls' night out, a cocktail party, or even tea with a close friend, she can begin to feel sad and out of sorts. For many NS individuals socializing can feel very nourishing and satisfying, much in the same way that being alone can feel refreshing for the partner with ASD. Spending time with other NS individuals can help restore her sense of self and ground her in the NS culture.

While it can be important that her partner accompany her to social events when he can, it might be necessary for her to socialize on her own as needed. It is also critical that she have a support system and identity separate from her partner.

Emotional Self-Care

The NS partner often reports feeling unloved and emotionally drained due to his wife's low emotional intelligence quotient and Theory of Mind. The lack of emotional reciprocity from his partner can cause him to experience Affective Deprivation Disorder (AfDD). Especially when his partner's ASD remains undiagnosed or unacknowledged, it can create an atmosphere of confusion, anger, and despair. His symptoms of AfDD, which are similar to Seasonal Affectation Disorder (SAD), and unmet emotional needs can put him at risk for using alcohol or medication to cope. In some cases, he might even be susceptible to an extra-marital affair.

He may also feel energetically drained due to his partner's alexithymia or lack of emotional expression. If his partner has anger issues, her lack of empathy and the unpredictable nature of her meltdowns can wear him down and even cause him to have anxiety and symptoms of PTSD. With no help and being unaware of his partner's ASD, the NS spouse can begin to doubt his own sanity and perception of reality. With no one to believe and validate his experience, he can sink into despair (Marshack, n.d.). It's therefore important for the NS partner to find the appropriate help for his struggles in the context of ASD and the neurodiverse marriage.

He might need to spend time with friends, family, or see an ASD-specific counselor who understands adult ASD and neurodiverse relationships. Receiving emotional feedback and solace from friends can really uplift him. Friendships and community can increase resilience to stress and give a sense that one is not alone in one's struggles. Participating in a Spouse and Partner's Support Group can provide the NS partner with understanding, insights, and validation. Similarly, investing in a hobby or class, a spiritual community, or a non-profit collaborative can be equally enriching.

If the NS partner finds that he is experiencing AfDD, depression, anxiety, and PTSD he may benefit from seeking help with psychotropic medications. Regular exercise both aerobic and restorative, dance, as well as meditation and yoga can aid in regulating his mental health. He may find that having a pet dog or cat can also provide emotional support and companionship.

Mental Self-Care

Prior to viewing her marriage through the ASD framework, an NS spouse could for years on end live in a state of mental confusion. She may have formed her own set of theories and notions for her partner's behavior. She might blame his upbringing or his culture. Not knowing the NS-ASD neurological difference, she might have tried to apply her own explanations and approach to her partner's ASD traits. She may feel responsible for the emotional-communication disconnect in the marriage, or shift the blame to her partner.

Once she learns about ASD and regardless of whether her partner pursues a diagnosis or not, she has to make a paradigm shift in her whole way of thinking. She will often need the knowledge and assistance of a ASD-specific couples counselor, or she can read books and articles in order to make sense of her neurodiverse marriage. An important aspect of the NS partner's self-care is that by understanding her partner's ASD traits, she might be able to get more of what she wants from her partner. Once her understanding of ASD grows, she might be able to see things from her partner's perspective and improve her communication with him.

From years of being in a difficult relationship and not receiving the appropriate help for her marriage, many NS partners can be unhappy and feel badly about themselves. Working with a counselor, reading self-help books, and strengthening her spiritual life can help a NS spouse or partner develop more self-confidence.

Physical Self-Care

Sometimes, the partner with ASD has sensory issues that can include a touch aversion. Even if he doesn't mind being physically close to his partner, he might not be good at initiating physical affection. In the beginning of the relationship, the NS wife here might actively seek out her partner's physical attention, but if her attempts have been repeatedly rebuffed, she might give up. While the sexual relationship of the couple might manage to stay somewhat regular, the small touches of spontaneous affection that she craves such as a hug, a pat on the shoulder, a grab around the waist, or a quick peck on the cheek may be all but absent in many neurodiverse marriages. Touch deprivation is a factor in AfDD symptoms.

As part of their self-care and to supplement the lack of touch in her neurodiverse marriage, the NS partner might want to invest in regular massages, facials, manicures-pedicures, spa visits, and spending time cuddling with children and pets. In addition touch, listening to music, taking a luxurious bath, aromatherapy, and engaging in tactile art projects can feel very replenishing for the NS partner.

Stress Management

Many NS partners find that they need strategies to beat stress on a daily basis. Being in a neurodiverse relationship with a partner who can be more susceptible to stress than average, the NS partner is often also stressed. They may find that they have to focus on keeping their own stress levels at bay. A balanced diet, a proper sleep schedule, and regular exercise are all ways in which the NS partner can alleviate stress. The investment in healthy living that the NS partner makes benefits her partner as well. Being happy and relaxed allows them to take time to have more fun togther.

For example, Joni, an NS woman married to Nathan, a man with ASD used *The Relationship Schedule*™ to plan "fun days" with Nathan and their two children. Their fun days were scheduled once a month. Fun days meant that they would all engage in a new activity, such as horseback riding for about half a day. They would often invite friends to join them. Even if it was playing with hula-hoops in their backyard for half a day, that's what they did for fun.

Nathan often needed breaks from all the sensory stimulation, but he enjoyed seeing his family have such a good time. For Joni, it provided the physical stimulation she needed, and the quality time spent with her children and with their neighbors helped her better manage her stress.

Life Mission as Self-Care

Another important aspect of self-care for the NS partner is exploring their own life mission and purpose. Many NS partners feel like they've lost themselves in the neurodiverse marriage. Most of the loss felt may be due to the fact that the NS partner may have given up on their own hobbies and social life. They might have to develop their own interests, invest in education, and explore a new career, or spiritual practice in order to discover their unique mission. This can create opportunities and open doors that they may never have thought possible. Full of hope and with a life that is propelling forward, they experience a whole new phase in their life.

♥ MING'S STORY ♥

Ming, a 50-year-old Chinese woman had been married for over 25 years to her husband, Chen. Chen was a scientist, and the CEO of a pharmaceutical company in Boston. They had one daughter who was away at college. After she discovered her husband's ASD, she realized why she had been confused and depressed for so long. All the pain and suffering that she endured began to have meaning.

Ming began to see me once a week for counseling and started attending workshops and reading about neurodiverse marriages. As she discovered more about her husband and marriage, she realized that she really needed to start rebuilding her own life. For most of her marriage, Ming had been a stay-at-home mother and had given up all the things she enjoyed in hopes of having a better marriage. "I've been the CEO of my marriage for so long that I haven't done anything else. I need to change."

"I've started teaching Tai Chi again!" she announced the next week.

Two months later, "I've started taking ballroom dancing lessons!"

Then, "I'm going to a yoga retreat in Costa Rica."

Ming thus began to take care of herself emotionally, mentally, and physically, and doing things that made her happy.

Over the course of two years, by learning about ASD and rebuilding her life, she eventually got Chen to enter into couples counseling. With a lot of understanding, self-awareness, and hard work things were beginning to feel easier with him.

She expressed, "Now, that things are slightly better at home, I want to change my life at a deeper level. Even though I know that I married my husband for love, I know that I also married him because he was rich and had status. I come from a humble background. We met at university. The prospect of marrying someone who was so successful blinded me to the occasional disrespect he showed me. I need to achieve something myself."

Ming decided that she was going to go back to school to pursue her Master's in Fine Arts. She had always been interested in sculpture, so she applied to an art school, and was immediately admitted. She thrived in her program and at the time of her graduation, was working on a sculpture commission for her local library. Her work was being well received and Ming felt like she was coming into her own.

In addition to sculpting, Ming also began actively building connections in the community. She was on a mission to pursue her dreams and expand her life. Her dramatic transformation from a depressed housewife to an up and coming artist was inspiring to her husband and daughter. She felt like she had finally earned her husband's respect. Finding out about her husband's ASD and using her talents to live out her mission changed Ming's life. She revealed, "No matter what happens, and even if my marriage were to end, I don't care. I've found the inner peace that I'd been looking for. I'm happy."

CHAPTER 14

ORGANIZING, PLANNING, AND OUTSOURCING

*He who every morning plans the transactions of that
day and follows that plan carries a thread that will guide
him through the labyrinth of the most busy life.*

VICTOR HUGO

Many individuals with ASD struggle with executive functioning. Challenges in executive functioning, caused by differences in the brain's prefrontal cortex, often include struggles in planning, organizing, decision-making, disinhibited behaviors, trouble with shifting focus, and making coherent judgments (Elliot, 2003).

The severity of executive functioning issues varies from individual to individual. For example, for one individual it might mean that he has trouble figuring how to boil an egg, or do laundry, while in another it may mean that she can never keep her appointments on time, and responds to only half of the emails she receives. However, there are also individuals with ASD who can be organized to the point of being obsessive compulsive. Nevertheless, executive functioning issues can pose obstacles in the neurodiverse relationship. The NS spouse can often take on the role of being a housekeeper and personal organizer of their ASD partner, which can leave them feeling frustrated and exhausted.

Therefore, it is advisable that the partner with ASD develops compensatory skills and finds tools to plan ahead, stay organized, manage time and space, make decisions, set goals, and plan for the future. When needed, the couple might invest in outside help for house cleaning, maintenance projects, financial planning, and childcare.

Planning Ahead for Events and Situations

Individuals with ASD typically find new situations, change, and transitions difficult. To quote Anita Lesko, an adult with ASD, "We like to be able to predict what is coming next... When that comfort is removed we get unhinged. Everything becomes magnified. Anxiety then skyrockets. This can manifest itself in numerous ways such as withdrawing, getting flustered, decompensating" (Attwood, Evans and Lesko, 2014, p.58). The couple can reduce a significant amount of anxiety and stress by sitting down together each week (preferably at the same day and time, for example, Sunday mornings from 9 to 10 a.m.) with a family calendar to process and get ready for upcoming events.

They can discuss new situations, voice any concerns they might have, and plan for contingencies. If the NS partner is more skilled at handling a particular situation, such as their child's birthday party, they can coach their ASD partner on a few social skills beforehand and be an ally during the event. Calendaring and checking the schedule on a regular basis takes out the element of surprise for the partner with ASD. Over time, both partners will see patterns in the types of situations that are challenging and be ready to problem-solve them.

Organizational Skills and Tools
Using Calendars and Smartphones

In order to help with the day-to-day tasks, the partner with ASD can greatly benefit from using a day planner either in the form of a paper diary, a white board hanging in her home and office, an online calendars and using smartphone applications (apps). Many adults with ASD are visual and kinesthetic learners, so typing into the phone, computer, tablet, or writing things down in a diary or on a whiteboard can help them better visualize and internalize the schedule.

A smartphone can act as a personal organizer and send push notifications to alert them when a bill needs to be paid, for example. A daily, weekly, monthly, and yearly calendar schedule that is updated and revisited each week can help them keep on top of all tasks and duties. Completing tasks can make them feel more in charge and happy to be accomplishing their goals, no matter how small. Calendars and electronic devices can also help them become less reliant on their NS partner.

Dividing Tasks into Mini Chunks

Individuals with ASD often struggle to complete certain tasks. For example, Jenny, a 40-year-old woman with ASD had so much trouble organizing herself that she hadn't paid her taxes in several years. Not paying her taxes had all but crippled her life and she hadn't been on vacation or a date in several years. Jenny was self-employed as an occupational therapist and filing for her taxes included gathering receipts, keeping track of expenses and income, and numerous business transactions. Things had gotten so out of control in her life that even the thought of doing her taxes overwhelmed her. Instead, she would go online and watch hours of anime videos.

Eventually, Jenny began counseling, an ASD support group, and attended a tax workshop for those independently employed. There she learnt to break down a big task into manageable chunks and lots of mini goals. She also put checkmarks next to each goal and told herself to accomplish one goal a day. With a little help from her sister, in six months, she was able to pay off all her past due taxes. She felt such a huge weight lifted from her shoulders; she went on a singles cruise for vacation, and even began dating again.

Breaking down tasks into manageable units, adding them to a daily To Do List and being accountable to someone such as a family member, friend, or professional can make a huge difference in assisting the individual with ASD to complete tasks.

Managing Time

Individuals with ASD are either extremely time-bound or not very mindful of time at all. Individuals with ASD who are not conscious of time report that their perception of time is different than it is for NS individuals. The partner with ASD may report that time moves differently for him. He may say that for him time is nonlinear, has no dimension, and that he often feels like he is "floating in time." If working on his special interest, or something that really interests him, computer coding, for example, he may be able to work on it for hours on end, without pausing for water or food. Likewise, if he is working on a mundane chore like vacuuming the house, he may get distracted by a text on his phone and never get back to the vacuuming; or, he may take two hours to vacuum the house instead of 30 minutes.

The fluidity of time for the partner with ASD can also remove the urgency of getting a task done. For example, if his partner asks him to fold the laundry, he might finish the task a week later, instead of the same evening. His internal alarm clock might not exist or be slow to operate. To stay focused and finish a task in a timely manner, it can thus be helpful to have external tools such as clocks, timers, and alarms. Having a stimulus such as music or television in the background while folding clothes might also help. The partner with ASD might also need assistance in gauging how much time a given task will take, and allocating sufficient time. Visually plotting timelines on a graph or chart could also help create more of a concept of time.

Managing Space

Some individuals with ASD can have OCD tendencies that result in them having very neat spaces and an obsession with cleaning. However, the other extreme is also true and many individuals with ASD can have extremely messy homes and offices bordering on hoarding. An NS partner once reported, "My fiancé makes neat piles of papers on every surface available in the house. Even the kitchen counters! And our two-car garage is packed from floor to ceiling with stuff." In short, managing space for the partner with ASD can be a struggle due to his executive functioning issues. He might not be able to decide what is important to keep, and what can be thrown away. He may lack fluency in sorting items in his possession, make impulsive purchases, and have an unusually sentimental attachment to objects.

In the case of the partner with ASD who has OCD tendencies, the NS partner might feel exhausted from having to adhere to his strict standard of cleanliness. In the case of the partner who is messy or has hoarding issues, she might constantly have to clean up after him. Depending on the severity of the issue in either direction, professional intervention might be needed if the whole household is on edge from having to constantly clean up, or if the clutter in the house is causing the NS partner to be stressed out. Hoarding Disorder is now included in the DSM-5 as a diagnosis. If there is a suspicion that the partner with ASD meets the criteria for it, then it's important to receive appropriate treatment and intervention.

Decision-Making

The NS partner may also find that the partner with ASD is slow to make decisions, or doesn't actually make pertinent decisions. For example, they may go months "researching" a new car, house, or even what type of coffee maker to purchase, without ever actually buying anything. Executive functioning issues can also affect the individual's ability to make decisions easily and efficiently. They might say, "I'm researching the absolute best deal on the car. I've to make sure it has everything on our list of features for what we want in the car." While in the beginning, such detailed efforts at finding the best car can feel like a good way to go about things, the NS partner can soon feel impatient and frustrated at their lack of decision and ability to move forward.

They may need a new car for safety reasons, or because there's a baby on the way, so after a reasonable time for "research" has passed, the NS partner might have to make an executive decision. The ASD partner may feel upset and at first resist the change, but eventually come to accept it. If decision-making begins to cause tensions in the relationship, it can be wise to seek the counsel of an ASD-specific couples counselor. The partner with ASD might have to learn that it's important to make timely decisions in order to prioritize safety and comfort, rather than spending months arriving at the most accurate decision.

ASD-Specific Organizational Coaching

Very often, I'll find that a couple is in my office due to the stress, frustration, and conflict resulting from executive functioning issues. The following narrative can sum up the NS partner's experience: "I have been the one who pays the bills and balances the checkbook. I budget our finances, cook, clean, and take care of everything related to the children. Their doctor's appointments, their school plays, their football practice, and parent-teacher conferences. I'm always tired and feel really stressed out." Working with an organizational life coach can help the partner with ASD learn new skills to begin assisting with some of the household, financial, or childcare duties.

Sometimes, the partner with ASD might also struggle with finding employment due to executive functioning issues. At such times, the stress on the marriage might increase. Organizational and career coaches can assist the partner with ASD in job hunting tasks such as creating a resume, filling out job applications, making phone calls and sending emails, preparing for interviews, and social skills training after securing the position.

Outsourcing Tasks and Chores
Household Help

Hiring help and receiving professional assistance when necessary can be a huge help for any marriage, but can be life-saving for the neurodiverse marriage. If the couple can afford to hire help for house cleaning, gardening, and home assistants, even occasionally, both partners may feel less stressed and be able to spend more time doing fun things with each other. Alternately, a couple I know of use the Roomba, a self-operating robot-vacuum cleaner that cleans floors even when the couple isn't home. Having a robot do the job of cleaning the floors helped both partners feel less pressured about doing cleaning and both were very satisfied with this easy solution.

Do It Yourself (DIY) or Not to Do It Yourself Projects

A lot of individuals with ASD can be very handy around the house. For example, Doug, a 55-year-old mechanical engineer by trade always fixed everything around the house, from the kitchen pipes and cabinets to the tiles in the bathroom. Due to his executive functioning issues and a recent diagnosis of rheumatoid arthritis, the project to refinish the roof over his garage got very delayed. Even though it was hard for him to admit that he needed to hire professional help, he eventually did so that his project didn't drag on for months more. It is important to evaluate whether a task is better handled by hiring a professional versus doing it yourself. Many times deciding on grounds of safety and comfort can be more important than the satisfaction of doing the job yourself or saving money.

Childcare

When the neurodiverse couple have children, it is important to have reliable childcare in the form of family members, neighbors, friends, and professional babysitters, so that both partners get a break.

Financial Planners and Helpers

"Couples in successful marriages…set guidelines and boundaries for their financial decisions…respecting that [they both] have equal rights and responsibilities" (Washburn and Christensen, 2008, para. 1). The partner with ASD is often extremely good at planning for the future with meticulous retirement plans, financial investments, and conservative spending; however, they might also be very rigid and controlling when it comes to money. The neurodiverse couple might have to work with an ASD-specific counselor or a financial planner to arrive at a compromise at how they want to manage their money.

The other type of partner with ASD is the one who does not think ahead or plan for the future at all. Discussions to set goals and ensure long-term financial security may feel highly tense and quickly escalate because they may have trouble seeing the big picture, and may not see the point in planning ahead. They may withdraw or try to ignore the issue, which in turn can make the NS partner anxious. In such cases, the couple might need to speak to a financial planner, life coach, a knowledgeable family member or friend who might be willing to help. Working with a professional can really help the couple to get unstuck and move ahead with their plans for the future.

The partner with ASD may also have trouble balancing a checkbook, budgeting, and planning the family finances due to his executive functioning issues. Working with a professional accountant or using money-tracking software applications can help him manage money better. Scheduling joint monthly reviews of the family budget and accounts can also help the couple feel more in control of their financial well being.

♥ ANIL AND PRIYA'S STORY ♥

Anil and Priya were an American-East Indian couple in their mid-thirties. They'd been married for three years. Priya, Anil's wife, was now ready to buy a house and start having a family. However, Anil, who

Priya suspected to have Asperger's Syndrome, was being rigid about not having enough money saved up to buy a house or to have a child. Priya found this to be ridiculous as she felt like they had good jobs and more than enough to cover the down payment for the house. She just couldn't understand why Anil felt the way he did. Any amount of her cajoling or convincing wasn't working, and that's why they sought couples counseling.

In the counseling session, Anil narrated how he grew up in a house with financial struggles and how his father had filed for bankruptcy just three years ago. For the past three years, he'd been helping his family with their living expenses. He felt that if Priya and he started their own family, he would feel like he couldn't contribute to his family anymore. Priya voiced her perspective that since they made enough money to cover a house mortgage and childcare, that they would be fine. Anil then spoke of the startup that he worked for and revealed how he felt anxious about losing his job, if his company were to fail. Anil had a high level of anxiety and was truly adamant about accumulating more savings before he was going to relent to have a child. He said that he had a five-year plan leading up to home ownership and having a child. Priya felt very distraught at his five-year timeline and was beginning to lose her patience. She was beginning to wonder if this was the marriage or life partner for her.

I recommended that Anil and Priya sit down and work with a spreadsheet to map out their finances in detail, as well as involve a professional financial planner. Once they followed both recommendations, they were able to view their finances from a more objective point of view. They spoke to the financial specialist about preparing for contingencies such as Anil losing his job and Priya working part-time. With a lot of calculations, projections, and a detailed savings plan that felt comfortable to both partners, Anil and Priya concluded that they needed to wait for another year to buy a house and have their first child.

In this case, even though Priya felt like Anil had been needlessly worrying about their financial situation, she was able to see the wisdom in having a concrete plan before they embarked on homeownership and childrearing. Anil too reevaluated his five-year saving plan and realized that he was closer to his goal than he thought.

Division of Labor According to Strengths

Many couples come up with a system of exchanging services based on each other's expertize. For example, if the partner with ASD is good with money, they handle the household finances. If the NS partner is better at being the primary breadwinner, the couple might prioritize their career, while the ASD partner can do a larger share of the household chores. Working from their individual strengths, both partners can work as a very successful team.

CHAPTER 15

SUSPENDING JUDGMENTS AND MANAGING EXPECTATIONS

Everyone complains of his memory, and
no one complains of his judgment.

FRANÇOIS DE LA ROCHEFOUCAULD

Due to the nature of the NS-ASD differences in perspectives, it can be easy for both partners to assume the worst, draw conclusions that aren't true, and create an atmosphere of disappointments. Due to the pervasive nature of ASD, both partners can find it difficult to bridge their differences.

If the NS partner doesn't understand her partner's ASD, she might be confused by her partner's lack of emotional reciprocity. She can ascribe meaning to his actions without asking him what he is thinking or feeling and falsely assume that he doesn't care or love her. She may label her partner cold, arrogant, and unfeeling, deepening the misunderstanding between them.

For the partner with ASD, he might expect his partner to speak in logical terms and might get frustrated when their partner cannot speak "his language". They might not understand why his NS partner is upset over something he said or did. Not understanding his partner's way of thinking, he can falsely assume that his partner is overreacting, being irrational, and overly sensitive. Furthermore, he might try to debate with them in an attempt to get her to succumb to seeing his point of view.

Making assumptions and judgments can escalate conflicts between partners and drive them apart. They can easily become discouraged by setbacks and begin to catastrophize or think the worse of their partner or relationship. It is beneficial when couples stop the blame, slow down, seek more information, and assume the best of each other.

Due to the differences in neurology, both partners may also have to manage their expectations of each other. Each partner has to work to understand his/her partner's personality, neurology, and life. Knowing what to expect from one's partner can only come from a deep and thorough understanding of them and is important in order to expand one's own capacity for patience, acceptance, and caring.

Blame and Responsibility

Many times, one or both partners believe that the difficulties in the relationship are solely due to the other partner. This type of thinking can result in defensiveness, stonewalling, criticism, and contempt. Behaviors that marriage researcher, John Gottman, calls the "Four Horsemen of the Apocalypse," the most significant predictors of divorce (Gottman, 1995). Defensiveness, stonewalling, criticism, and contempt can propel the marriage headlong into divorce.

I believe the basis for the "Four Horsemen" can be traced to making judgments and blaming one's partner. Therefore, it's important to become self-aware and be cognizant about one's thinking process and avoid making judgments and blaming one's partner. A better strategy is to take full responsibility for one's own actions, and make what cognitive and behavioral modifications one can. Individuals often choose partners based on their own personalities and lives. Instead of pointing the finger, it is always more productive to focus on one's own areas for improvement, no matter how small they might seem relative to one's partner's flaws.

Practicing Curiosity

To avoid judging one's partner, one needs to deeply understand them. Practicing curiosity by engaging in dialogue with one's partner is the only way to prevent the "Four Horsemen" from taking over. Being curious means trying to figure out the reason behind one's partner's thoughts and behavior.

Due to their different styles in processing information, the NS partner may have to ask their partner the same question in different ways (preferably on different days) until she receives a satisfactory answer. The partner with ASD may feel frustrated if they think their partner is interrogating them or not believing their responses. They need to understand that their partner is just trying to get a better sense of their thoughts and behavior. They might not realize that their behavior is unusual and that their partner is trying to understand. They will need to exercise patience, curiosity, and understanding with their NS partner.

In any dialogue, it's important that both partners watch their tone of voice, and the manner in which they phrase their questions. There is also a time and place to ask questions. When the tension is high and anxiety is escalated for either or both partners, it's probably best to pause the discussion and pick it up at another time when the partners are more at ease.

Curiosity and dialogue facilitate understanding. There are no shortcuts to the process of understanding one's partner. In order to have the mindset to practice curiosity, it's important that both partners prioritize self-care and work on their individual self-growth.

♥ MANDY AND ALEKSY ♥

Mandy, an American and Aleksy, originally from Poland, were a newly married couple. They were both physicians. Mandy had initiated the couples counseling sessions with me because she had suspected that Aleksy had a lot of ASD traits. They had been seeing me for two months.

Both of them walked into the counseling session visibly upset with each other. "We had a fight on our way here," began Aleksy.

"We did," said Mandy, "and you won't believe us when we tell you what the fight was about."

"On our way here," Alesky continued, "we stopped by a farmer's market. Mandy began examining some turnips at a stall. I don't like turnips, and she knows this, so I reminded her, 'I don't like turnips.' She immediately got really upset and glared at me right in front of the vendor. She then started walking towards the car. I am completely confused and upset at her reaction. As we drove home, she kept telling me how I'm selfish and self-absorbed and that I couldn't care less about what she wants. When the truth is that we live in a town she had her heart set on, even though it doubled my work commute. We bought a car that she liked even though it's not the one I would have preferred. And, we come here to therapy even though I'm not really sure about this whole Asperger's thing."

"What did you mean when you said that you didn't like turnips, Aleksy?" I asked.

"I meant exactly that—that I don't like turnips. But Mandy turned that into what a selfish person I am!"

"It's not that you just innocently said that you don't like turnips, you said it with such gusto and a really mean tone! Sometimes, I don't think you realize just how mean and angry you sound when you speak."

"Aleksy, Mandy has mentioned your tone of voice before and we've talked about you becoming more aware of how you sound."

"Yes, I'm aware of that. It's just not that easy to focus on how I sound. I need to constantly remind myself. But I'm working on it, am I not?" he asked Mandy.

"Yes, it's true. You're working on it, but you're not progressing fast enough! You're rude half the time you speak."

"Ok, let's focus back on the turnip example," I reminded them. "You said you don't like turnips. What did you mean by that?"

"Nothing!" Aleksy exclaimed, "I guess it was just something that popped into my mind and I said it. I didn't mean that Mandy shouldn't buy them, cook them, or eat them. In fact, I wouldn't mind eating them. Sure, I don't like them. They're not my favorite. Who likes turnips anyway?! But I definitely didn't imply that Mandy should only cook vegetables I like. And honestly, there aren't even that many that I like anyway. Do I eat them? Yes."

"So, you were just mentioning the fact that you didn't like turnips because that's a detail about yourself that popped into your mind when you saw the turnips? You weren't implying that Mandy not buy them." I reiterated.

"Yes." Aleksy agreed. He had now visibly calmed down; so had Mandy.

"I guess I just have to learn to not take every little thing he says seriously or jump to conclusions. I really need to not get triggered by the things he says. It's hard not to though." Mandy concluded.

"I need to edit what I say too. And my tone can be very abrasive. I can sound angry without meaning to. I'm sorry baby."

The partner with ASD often thinks and communicates in a literal and factual manner, without being aware of how his words and actions are affecting others. He can speak in a sharp tone with a lot of force and authority which can sound intimidating, belittling, and dismissive. He therefore has to learn better communication skills and manage his sudden explosions. The NS partner can easily misunderstand what her husband says. She might have to slow down her reactions and avoid forming conclusions until she gathers more information.

Managing Expectations
♥ NICK AND ELLEN'S STORY ♥

Nick, a software programmer, was married to Ellen, a clinical psychologist, for over 25 years. They were both in their mid-fifties and Ellen had just discovered that Nick might have ASD. They had 18-year-old twin girls, both of whom had recently left for college.

"I feel so stupid now when I look at our life through the prism of ASD. Nick here thinks that because I was always so focused on our cultural differences, that I failed to see some of his quirks and idiosyncrasies." Nick, a quiet and mild-mannered man, just smiled at what his wife was saying.

"You know, when we got married, I just thought that Nick was different because he was from California. And then, for many years his mother lived with us. She was a widow, so she came to stay with us about two years into our marriage. She bought the house next to us, and was a big emotional support to me. She looked after the children as Nick and I pursued our careers. She died almost two years ago."

Nick added, "My mother would often say that I was odd. I guess she always knew," as he looked towards Ellen for confirmation.

"That's true," Ellen agreed, "She used to say that she had to teach him to make eye contact as a child. And she was a social worker, so she knew about child psychology. I think in our marriage, she filled in the social-communication gap that Nick has. Now that she's gone and the girls are gone, all of a sudden, I feel like I don't even know who my husband is. I feel so confused about our relationship. Nick took the online ASD quiz and he came out ASD. I know those quizzes aren't entirely accurate, but he related to almost all of the traits listed," she paused to look at him.

Nick shifted in his seat sensing that Ellen wanted him to say something, but it seemed like his processing speed wasn't cooperating.

"See?" she gave him an impatient look, "He doesn't talk."

"I've just never been one to talk a lot." Nick said smiling nervously. "Plus, I find that I don't have a lot to say."

"I've been really trying to get Nick to talk to me more, but it's so hard for him. As a psychologist, I'm a little familiar with Asperger's myself, but I don't know how much I can expect him to change? I've been trying to get him to express himself and talk to me more, but it's not easy. Can he ever change?"

Ellen's question is a common one. Many NS partners want to know what they can expect, and how much their partner with ASD is capable of changing.

Change and growth is a slow and painful process for any couple or individual wanting to improve their marriage and this is particularly true in a neurodiverse marriage. For the NS partner, managing expectations is particularly important. In order to gauge what to expect from her partner, it is important that she understand the fundamental differences between the ASD and NS mind. Typically, after finding out about ASD, she can begin to feel a lot of hope, because she now has a diagnosis and can finally understand her marital struggles. She might assume that her partner will learn all kinds of new social and relationship skills and turn over a new leaf.

ASD is a broad spectrum and traits vary greatly from person to person. Some individuals with ASD might have better emotional intelligence than others. Others have anger issues or are shy and gentle. Many who read this book will be interested in applying the strategies listed. Others might not see that they need to change anything about their behavior or understand why these strategies are important. Others will be open to trying out the strategies, but find it extremely hard to be consistent.

Based on her husband's strengths and weaknesses, the NS partner may have to manage her expectations around what kind of progress she can expect from him. Even when the husband is self-aware and is willing to learn new skills, making lasting changes can be extremely challenging. For every step forward, there are often two backwards. Progress can seem painstakingly slow, but it important to recognize and acknowledge even the slightest bit of forward movement. Change has to be measured over weeks, months, and even years. Using a marital satisfaction scale to do so can be a useful strategy.

The Marital Satisfaction Scale

1	2	3	4	5	6	7	8	9	10

Calling the divorce lawyer   *Completely happy in the marriage*

I ask each partner to use a 1 to 10 scale to rate their satisfaction in the marriage. 1 being that they are about to *call the divorce lawyer* and 10 being that they are *completely happy in the marriage*. Using the marital satisfaction scale both partners can become more aware of the state of their marriage. Giving their feelings a concrete number can also prove to them if the strategies are actually working. If the partner with ASD feels like their partner is never happy no matter how hard they try, they can ask them to use the scale to gauge how they are really feeling. Many times the scale is useful to the NS partner too; they can remain more in touch with their own feelings about the marriage.

ASD is Pervasive

ASD differences are pervasive and can affect almost every aspect of a couple's life. Emotional intelligence, anger, processing speed, sensory issues, depression—each of these traits can affect almost every aspect of the couple's life. While applying new strategies, it's important to prioritize the most important changes that need to occur. The NS partner might have to adjust expectations of their partner keeping in mind that ASD is pervasive. Making changes takes a monumental effort and lots of accountability. However, if expectations are too low, or let go of altogether, the NS partner may feel like they're settling for an unhappy relationship. Even though change is slow, individuals with ASD can and do show improvement over time.

Often it is the NS partner who tends to make the bigger adjustment in the marriage. It's not that the partner with ASD cannot learn new skills and strategies, but based on his unique cluster of ASD traits, it might just take him a long time. Due to the neurological nature of ASD, change is often painstaking and hard. Some traits are easier to work with than others; it's important to not compare any two individuals with ASD.

The Model of the Neurodiverse Relationship Can Be Atypical

The model of the neurodiverse relationship is often unusual compared to NS relationships. For example, neurodiverse relationships tend not to progress at the same speed as NS relationships. They can take relatively longer to build and establish. Even progressing from a dating relationship to a marriage can be complicated and fraught with setbacks. Once married, the couple may need a lot of outside assistance with household management, and relationship maintenance with a couples counselor.

As it is, each marriage is different from another. Having the same expectations from the neurodiverse marriage as one would from a NS marriage might be unrealistic. If they want to be in the neurodiverse marriage, they might have to understand, accept and build the marriage they have.

Strategies, Patience, and Acceptance

Striking a constant balance between trying out strategies, exercising patience, and accepting one's partner can be a challenging feat.

Strategies

Children with ASD receive interventions and work on strategies for social-communication-emotional educational differences on a daily basis, often for many hours a day. The majority of adults in neurodiverse relationships learn about ASD in adulthood, and are introduced to the idea of interventions for the first time in couples counseling. Some partners with ASD might have experience with psychotherapy, yoga, and meditation practices. They may also have ex-partners that have helped them become more self-aware. In such cases, the partner with ASD might have more skills to build on than someone who's never received any type of psychological assistance or is a stranger to self-contemplation. Individuals who are given to self-reflection and are motivated to grow will obviously be able to do better than those who are resistant. That said, even if it's only the NS partner who utilizes the strategies outlined in this book, there will likely be a visible shift in the relationship. If one partner changes, the other is soon to follow.

Patience and Acceptance

The NS partner can often think to herself, "If he loved me, he would do it!" The truth is her partner with ASD can't just make changes by deciding to do so. Each day he has to work against his natural impulses, whilst exercising patience with his partner. Understanding the slow pace of progress can wear down the NS partner. In addition to patience, she has to work on understanding and accepting her partner just as he is with all his traits. Working with the delicate balance of strategies, patience and acceptance can often result in a happy relationship. Setbacks are common and should be expected. These are par for the course; it is by overcoming obstacles that a couple can build a truly harmonious relationship. Both partners must be wise about when to apply strategies versus patience and acceptance. Acting from a place of wisdom, courage and compassion in the marriage requires a daily commitment to inner growth and transformation.

CHAPTER 16

STAYING MOTIVATED

The two most powerful warriors are patience and time.

LEO TOLSTOY

Couples are motivated to work on the neurodiverse relationship due to the loyal nature of both partners, and because the marriage continues to provide value to each of them. However, the neurodiverse relationship can be challenging, especially for the NS partner. Staying resilient and motivated can be an important strategy for a lasting neurodiverse relationship.

♥ ALISHA AND KEVIN'S STORY: PART 1 ♥

Alisha and Kevin were an engaged couple in their mid-thirties. They lived in Maine and had been driving to Boston for almost eight months for their counseling appointments. They wanted to learn strategies and skills to strengthen their relationship prior to their wedding the following summer. They had broken up five different times and didn't want to keep repeating this pattern. They once drove down to see me the day after Kevin had a meltdown at a dinner with Alisha's family. Alisha was very angry with Kevin.

"I've had it with him!" she said. "I'm beginning to have second thoughts about marrying him. I can't take this anymore. It's too much. When is he going to learn that he can't just argue about things without considering the feelings of those around him?! I'm done."

"Can you tell me what happened?"

"He made such a fuss over my father's new motorboat. My father just retired and my parents just bought a tiny little motorboat for their lake house. Kevin was so rude. You know how he cares about the environment and how that's his pet subject. Well, the moment he heard that my parents bought a motorboat, he started going on about how motorboats are loud, noisy, and bad for the wildlife. My parents hadn't experienced this side of him before. They were completely shocked. He was so rude."

"I said I'm sorry," Kevin said, "I spent the entire weekend apologizing. I was on edge the whole time I was at your parents. Even before we went, you know I was stressed about work and you still insisted that I go with you to your parents house."

"Is that true?" I asked.

"Yes, work has been busier than usual and stressful for about a month now. I thought going away for the weekend at my parent's lake house would cheer him up. I probably should have let him stay at home and play video games to relax. But, I wanted to spend time with him. What about my needs? Sometimes, I wonder if this is all worth it."

"You've broken up with me five times before. If you don't want to be with me, just tell me."

"See? This is what he does. He takes things literally. I get angry sometimes and lose patience. That's when I say things like 'I wonder if this is worth it,' but the truth is after I calm down, I do look at all the ways in which he's really good to me."

"You do?!" Kevin asked surprise.

"Of course, why else do you think I *made up* with you *five* times?" She paused, "But it's not easy to be with you, honey. You can drive anybody nuts."

"I'm sorry. I've been neglecting you lately."

"I just need to think of the positives when I'm down I suppose. And look at all the ways in which you have changed."

"You've come a long way since we first began working together," I acknowledged.

"Well, I do have a right to be angry with him when he behaves badly, like he did with my parents. But, I probably should cut him some slack and remember the progress we've made. It's been hard not seeing you though honey."

"I agree. It's been hard for me too. I could also use some help on how to detach from work once I get home. Do you have any thoughts on that?" he asked me.

Once Alisha's feelings of anger and anxiety settled down, she realized that she truly loved Kevin despite his many shortcomings, and that he in turn accepted many of her issues. Taking stock of the improvements they'd made since learning about ASD helped Alisha stay motivated in her relationship despite the challenges.

To Stay or Leave

The NS partner often vacillates between leaving and staying. This back and forth is rather common in the neurodiverse relationship. In some cases, the vacillating is because the NS partner is slowly working her way out of the relationship, and she is still struggling with her decision. In others, the NS partner uses the ultimatum as a tool to try and get her partner with ASD to change. If she's just threatening to leave, she has to be very careful when she expresses this to her partner. Her partner with ASD is most likely a literal thinker and he will assume that the relationship is over. He may become confused when his partner apologies and wants to reconcile. Therefore, using the threat of leaving the relationship is not a good relational strategy.

It helps when the NS partner is clear on what their objective is. If they act out when they're struggling with emotions of hurt, fear, and anger, they are likely to lash out at their partner and even end the relationship. It's better that they make decisions about the relationship only after they've had time to calm down and reflect.

Clarity and Motivation for the Partner with ASD

When the NS partner voices discontent and says, "You're never going to change! I'm so unhappy in this relationship," the partner with ASD can become discouraged and lose the motivation to work on the relationship. If the NS partner says things like they want to leave the relationship, it's important that the ASD partner understand that their true intentions might not be to leave and that they're just venting their frustrations.

However, it's important that the ASD partner take their NS partner's concerns seriously as the threat to leave may often mean that if things continue to stay the way they are, they're definitely on their way out. The marital satisfaction scale is a good tool to use in such situations. A five on the scale could mean that if an ASD partner does nothing to improve the score in the next few days or weeks, the NS partner's satisfaction will further decline eventually leading them to file for divorce.

It's important for the partner with ASD to clarify where they stand with their partner so that they know where to focus their efforts in order to bring the relationship back on course. Just as the NS partner needs strategies to refresh their determination to continue in the relationship, the partner with ASD may also need to seek the wisdom and motivation they need to stay the course.

Finding the Right Support and Encouragement

A positive and supportive circle of friends, family members, ASD-focused support groups, individual and couples counselors is crucial to the longevity of a neurodiverse couple. The NS partner often reports that friends and family members do not understand the experience of being in a neurodiverse relationship and are often unable to relate to her struggles. If they seek support and guidance from family members, they might feel alarmed that the NS partner is suffering and might advise them to file for divorce. The NS partner might also burn out friends and family members with the high degree of stress that can come from being with a partner with ASD.

Even though friends or family members might not understand the situation, the NS partner will still need positive feedback and encouragement. In order not to burn out or overburden their support system, a lot NS partners seek counseling.

Individual and Couples Counseling

I work with many NS partners who see me for individual counseling. Even though the partner with ASD might not be ready for counseling yet, they can begin receiving support and strategies around the neurodiverse relationship.

An ASD-specific couples counselor can be a lifeline for both partners. A good counselor can explain and interpret the differences in neurology, processing, and the ASD-NS culture. She can teach the couple new skills, encourage, and help them feel hopeful in their darkest moments. She can provide perspective and help the couple see the progress they've made. They can learn where they need to focus their efforts in order to achieve the next success phase in their relationship. A counselor can act as a cheerleader and coach, thus helping the couple stay motivated and accountable.

Support Groups

The Couple's and Spouse Support Groups, and an ASD-community can be crucial in helping the neurodiverse couple stay motivated. Group and community support can help normalize being in a neurodiverse relationship and remind both partners that they are not alone in their struggles.

Seeking New Strategies

Maintaining a strong determination and remaining motivated in the neurodiverse marriage can come from seeking new strategies. As both partners seek new strategies for their relationship, they can feel more positive and optimistic about their life. Such a couple will naturally develop resilience and a resourcefulness to help themselves.

Rather than feeling like a victim, taking full responsibility for his or her life and relationship will automatically have the partners thinking in terms of solutions. Striving towards solutions can help a couple feel like a team and that can refresh their motivation to go on in the relationship.

A Long-Term Vision

Successful marriages and lasting relationships require that both partners take a long-term view. Having a long-term vision helps a couple not to get swayed by temporary or circumstantial hurdles. Breakthroughs often come after overcoming major obstacles or challenges. Having a long-term view can often motivate couples to exert themselves and strive their hardest when things are at their most difficult in a marriage.

A Marriage that is Mission-Based

Having a joint mission can keep a neurodiverse couple together. Being focused on the same goal or life mission can often help the couple weather the ups and downs of their relationship. Collaborating and supporting one another on a life mission, a cause for the greater good, something that is bigger than themselves, can often push both partners to problem-solve their issues rather than give up. For many happy couples, the commitment to support each other in achieving each other's own unique mission in the world is the glue that keeps them together. A marriage that is mission-based is perhaps one of the most important strategies of a successful marriage and a lasting relationship.

♥ ALISHA AND KEVIN'S STORY: PART 2 ♥

In Alisha and Kevin's case, one of the many things that kept bringing them back together was the fact that they inspired each other. They both worked as historic preservation and restoration architects at a small company and their collaboration had resulted in many successful projects. Their synergy transferred into their personal relationship and they had a lot of fun together. They encouraged each other when things got difficult at work and really stood by each other. Their loyalty towards each other was very strong.

They reported that even when things got difficult for them and even in the times when the future of their relationship was doubtful, they believed in their shared mission. Their values around work and standing up for the greater good seemed to bind them. In addition to the historical architecture, both of them had other causes that they were dedicated to. Alisha was very keen on community building and Kevin mentored first-generation students going to college.

"He just has such a good heart, you know," Alisha once said, describing Kevin, "He does not have a selfish bone in his body. No matter what I tell him, and how outrageous my plan may seem, he listens to me and goes along with it. He's also very good with these kids. I've never met anyone so altruistically inclined. He's even helped one or two students with their tuition fees. Of course, it means that he cannot be trusted when it comes to making financial decisions!" she smiled. "It's a good thing we share the same values. And he does make me laugh. If I have a setback at work, he's very optimistic and encouraging. So, that's a good thing, right?"

She continued, "I often think of our future together and what we're going to achieve in five or ten or even twenty years. Having a long-term vision of our life together does keep me on track. That's what brings me back to him. Seeing him work so hard inspires me to forge on even when things get difficult. I've been following your advice about thinking about all the things that I'm grateful for about Kevin on a daily basis. Doing that has helped me a lot."

"We're a good team. She's fun." Kevin summed up about his relationship with Alisha. "She's good. She's forgiving of me and puts up with my family. My family is crazy. My mother is probably an Aspie too, but Alisha has a really nice way with her. She's a keeper."

"That's Kevin's new phrase," Alisha said affectionately, "'She's a keeper.' I think he heard it on some TV show. See? He cracks me up!" Reiterating each other's positive characteristics and ways in which they inspired each other lit up their eyes.

Motivated couples can make remarkable changes and experience tremendous growth in their relationships.

Chapter 17

NEURODIVERSE COUPLES COUNSELING

> The world is the great gymnasium where
> we come to make ourselves strong.
>
> SWAMI VIVEKANANDA

To solve problems and reset negative behavioral patterns, it's necessary to introduce a fresh perspective. For couples entrenched in negative cycles of interaction, a couples counselor can provide that fresh perspective, thus opening up the door to the insights and solutions they seek.

Relationship issues are almost universal. However, the average couple is distressed for six years before seeking professional help (Weil, 2012). For couples in a neurodiverse relationship, ASD is pervasive. It affects everything; their communication, social and emotional life, sex, economy, and parenting. As Jim Sinclair (1993, para. 5), an autism advocate confirms, "[for a person with ASD], it colors every experience, every sensation, perception, thought, emotion, and encounter, every aspect of existence." Therefore, couples counseling or some form of awareness and accommodations within the ASD framework seems to be a necessity, and well before the six-year mark.

The longevity or even the very survival of many neurodiverse marriages depends in my view on finding an appropriate couples counselor. A couples counselor who is experienced with NS-ASD relationships can provide both partners with information about ASD, help them understand each other's perspectives, create a space where both partners can feel safe, help the partners create and implement strategies, and provide accountability, motivation, and support to move the couple in a positive direction.

ASD-Specific Couples Counseling

Even among therapists, couples counseling is considered to be challenging work. A couples counselor has to manage conflicts, moderate both personalities, reframe perspectives, and assign action steps for partners to work on between sessions (Weil, 2012). As family therapist and author Terry Real (Weil, 2012) puts it, to be an effective couples counselor, "You have to like action. To manage marital combat, a therapist needs to get in there, mix it up with the client, be a ninja. This is intimidating." Therefore, a couple seeking help needs to see someone whose practice is in couples counseling, rather than individual work.

In addition, it's important to seek counseling with an ASD-specific couples counselor (Aston, 2001; Myhill and Jekel, 2008). Counselors who are not familiar with ASD often tend to ascribe a neurodiverse couple's conflicts and challenges to "personality clashes," or family of origin issues. Uninformed counselors may unintentionally fall into the trap of blaming one partner or the other. They may either see the partner with ASD as the villain, or the NS partner as too needy and emotionally demanding.

When a counselor misunderstands the root of the marital issues, and is thus unable to provide the appropriate treatment, the couple often feels even more frustrated and discouraged. Therapy that fails to address the ASD issues not only perpetuates a couple's unhappiness, it can even bring about the demise of the relationship.

An untrained couples counselor may not fully take into account the pervasive nature of ASD. The counselor may focus on just one or two traits such as the anxiety or anger of the partner with ASD. The counselor may then try to treat these two traits, without realizing that the anxiety may stem from sensory issues, or that the anger may be a result of taking everything their NS partner says literally. All in all, a non-ASD specialist may just not get the full picture of the individual with ASD and the neurodiverse marriage. Many couples that I see report having previously seen other counselors who did not understand the neurodiverse aspect of their relationship. Some couples say things like, "We've been in couples counseling for eight out of the fourteen years we've been married, but our issues never really got resolved." It's common for me to be the fourth or fifth counselor that the couple has seen either individually or as a couple.

An ASD-specific couples counselor is better able to handle the mindset and communication style of the partner with ASD. The ASD partner's logical view and ability to "litigate" in counseling can challenge even the most skilled couples counselor. Like a ninja, the couples counselor must be prepared to manage anger issues, and often strong personalities.

Understanding and working within the context of the ASD framework is key to successfully counseling neurodiverse couples. A couples counselor who has a good grasp on ASD will be able to connect with both spouses—especially, to the spouse with ASD—in a manner that motivates the person to make positive changes. For the rest of the chapter, when I say counselor assume that I'm referring to an ASD-specific couples counselor.

The Couple's Responsibility

Although, the right counselor can help a struggling couple to progress, it is even more crucial that each partner be ready and motivated to work on their issues and take responsibility for implementing the strategies that are discussed in counseling. It's hard to make progress if either partner persists in believing that the other partner is solely responsible for the problems in the relationship. "If we continually blame...our partner, without reflecting on ourselves and striving to carry out our own [inner transformation], we will never break through our situation" (Ikeda, 2014, p.44). A couples counselor can act as a transformational coach and cheerlead the couple as they go through their process of implementing changes, growing, and syncing up to each other. Nevertheless, the determination to change and improve the quality of one's life and relationship has to come from within each partner.

The Partner with ASD

Often an individual with ASD will have his own perception and theory about his partner and their relationship, which may or may not correspond to reality. Unlike his NS counterparts, he may not discuss these ideas or perceptions with his partner, his family or his friends. Therefore, he may become more rigidly entrenched in his own ideas.

Initiating conversations and processing relational matters can be highly challenging for those with ASD. Counseling provides a much-needed forum for the couple to share their thoughts and experiences with each other. It's easier for the individual with ASD to hear information or suggestions from the counselor whom he sees as a more unbiased, objective person, than his partner. The counselor can speak his language and get through to him. Instead of feeling stuck and hopeless, now the couple can share information and see new possibilities for resolving their issues. Therefore, even a few couples counseling sessions can make a world of difference.

Psychoeducation

The counselor can wear many hats while assisting the neurodiverse couple; one of those is the psychoeducator hat. The counselor can educate and inform the couple by providing them with books and articles on ASD. It's helpful to realize that other couples share their struggles with ASD. The counselor can educate both partners about the other person's neurology. Thus the NS partner learns how her partner's mindset differs from hers, based on their neurological differences, and vice versa. Rather than blame or shame each other, they can learn how to better accommodate the other's behavior and needs.

Psychoeducation about ASD can also help the NS partner to manage her expectations. Psychoeducation is thus a critical part of ASD-specific couples counseling, and can provide much needed understanding and insight.

Interpreting and Providing Perspective

When neurodiverse partners come to counseling, they each report their own version of events. If you were a fly on the wall in my office, you would think they were describing two completely different marriages! The counselor needs to speak the language of both partners and act as a translator when necessary. The counselor also needs to understand the very different perspective the partners may have, and be able to explain each partner's perspective to the other.

♥ NEAL AND THERESA'S STORY ♥

Neal, Theresa, and their five-year-old daughter went on a week long vacation to his family reunion. The NS partner, Neal had a great time reconnecting with many of his friends and family whom he hadn't seen for a long time. He assumed that his wife also enjoyed the vacation.

For Theresa, the partner with the ASD, the vacation was terrible. She hardly got a night's sleep due to her sensitive hearing. She felt anxious the whole time, because their daughter had fallen sick on the second day of their vacation, and had needed almost constant care. Her husband's family didn't hold to any type of schedule, and she felt lost and discombobulated amid the chaos. Out of concern for her husband, she had chosen to suffer silently, and had to increase her anti-anxiety pill dosage to cope. Once or twice she almost had a meltdown, but thankfully had the strategies to cope. While her husband spent time with family members, she took time to be alone in order to calm herself down.

Theresa only expressed her feelings about the vacation on their long drive home. Neal was very surprised to hear about Theresa's version of events, and had no idea why she was so upset. Why was she making such a big deal about these minor inconveniences?

I explained to Neal that Theresa needed to operate on a schedule, and to know how each day would unfold. Neal's spontaneous and flexible style with regard to schedules increased his wife's stress level. He needed to adapt to his wife's style a little more, and plan for more structure and predictability in their life.

Creating Safe Space

When the counselor conveys respect and caring for both partners, based on a thorough understanding of ASD and neurodiversity, the counselor's very presence can serve as a catalyst that inspires the couple to remain engaged in the arduous work of couples counseling.

The counselor needs to create a safe space: a neutral, non-judgmental environment where the couple can discuss their issues. Many times partners are afraid to speak freely to each other about their concerns. Even though the husband may instinctively know the resolution to their problems, he may feel unsafe in speaking to his wife by himself. A counselor can facilitate an open dialogue and make sure that there continues to be an equal power balance and that the space remains calm, neutral, and positive.

When on the car ride home, Theresa found that Neal was not receptive to her feelings, she shut down. In couples counseling however, she felt comfortable enough to continue the conversation. In the past, when she had tried to speak to Neal about her need for routine and structure, he had dismissed her saying, "You need to loosen up and relax." He didn't appreciate her concerns, and how vital predictability was to her well being.

Strategy Creation and Implementation

Each individual with ASD, and each neurodiverse couple is unique. Even though the steps and strategies discussed in this book are relevant to most neurodiverse relationships, the solution must be tailored to each couple. With the counselor, the couple can brainstorm creative ways to resolve their differences. Once the couple decides on a strategy, it is up to them to implement it. However, adapting new behaviors is easier said than done, and may take a lot longer than people expect.

Accountability

For most couples, working on a relationship and changing habitual behaviors doesn't come naturally—change may be especially hard for the partner with ASD. Despite repeated discussions about the NS partner's unmet needs, the partner with ASD might be very slow to actually change his behavior. Meanwhile, the NS partner may feel increasingly neglected and frustrated, or may even despair. Then the partner with ASD may feel like he can't do anything right, and that his partner is never satisfied.

While it's important to acknowledge the challenges of the partner with ASD, it's still important for him to make an effort to do his best to make changes that will benefit his partner. The weekly or bi-weekly meetings of couples counseling over a period of weeks and months can truly influence the thinking and behavioral patterns of the partner with ASD. Even for the NS partner, accountability can be important. When couples know that they are scheduled to see the counselor in a few days time, they are more likely to implement the strategies and solutions that were discussed in the previous session. Just knowing that they'll be seeing the counselor can help a couple feel more motivated and follow-through on their commitments.

Motivational Coach

A counselor also acts as a motivational coach and cheerleader for the couple. When couples are in the thick of their own problems, they lose sight of all the progress they've made. At times when couples are facing their most difficult issues and reach their lowest point of suffering and pain, they can feel truly hopeless. At such times, the couples counselor can be the one who holds the flame of hope alive.

For example, in Neal and Theresa's case, after months of working to accommodate each other's needs, and making good progress, they had a major setback. Theresa had a big meltdown after Neal unexpectedly brought his friends over one evening after work, expecting her to cook an impromptu meal for them. Neal felt blindsided by her anger. He felt as if she never made an sacrifices for him and he seemed at his wit's end.

In counseling, we were able to reevaluate all the changes they had been making as a couple and how their relationship had improved tremendously in just a couple of months of counseling. I told them that it was to be expected that they would run into setbacks given that both partners had been making so many behavioral changes. In this instance, it also seemed that Neal, the NS partner had been inconsiderate about his wife's ability to cook and entertain his friends without any notice. Neal admitted that he'd felt strange about the fact that they had not had any conflicts in a while, and felt like he could indulge his spontaneous nature.

In the beginning, couples that are trying to improve their marriage may see rapid gains, but after a while progress can plateau—or life may throw the couple a curveball. When the positive trajectory is interrupted, one or both partners may become discouraged. The counselor can step in at such a critical juncture, and remind the couple of the bigger picture and the progress they have made so far. Motivational coaching remains appropriate as long as the partners maintain their intention to stay together and work on their relationship. If the couple decides to separate, the counselor may have to provide a different kind of support.

Conscious Uncoupling

In some cases, couples can make enough progress to significantly reduce their conflicts. Each partner finds enough reward in the relationship that they stay together. However, eventually some couples may find that the NS-ASD gap is too hard to bridge. The NS wife may feel that the husband either will not or cannot meet her emotional needs. The husband with ASD may realize that he cannot or does not wish to continue trying to meet his wife's needs or expectations and that it's just too hard. One or both partners may conclude that their needs are not compatible, and decide to part. Counseling may help the couple estimate if they will be happier uncoupling or staying together.

Even if a couple decides to divorce, they may still benefit from the counseling process. Counseling during the separation and divorce can provide the couple with a safe space to process issues around the split. The work they do to improve their understanding of one another may lead to a healthier, more civil parting, or perhaps even a lasting friendship. One or both partners may decide to continue counseling to receive support around building a new life after divorce.

If there are children in the marriage, then discussing co-parenting strategies in counseling can be an important part of the family transition. Having to manage the children's schedules, the back and forth between two households and the psychological and emotional impact of divorce on the whole family is best handled with a lot of thought and care.

What if Only One Partner is Interested in Counseling?

Even one partner working to reset negative patterns of interaction can dramatically shift the dynamic in the neurodiverse relationship. I've worked with both the NS partner and the partner with ASD in individual counseling focused on relationship issues.

Sometimes, the partner with ASD may know what annoys his NS partner. For example, one of my clients with ASD had been assigned the task of emptying out the diaper pail in their daughter's room on a daily basis, by his NS partner. His not doing so made her life as a new mother more difficult on a daily basis. Once he revealed this in individual counseling, we were able to work out how he could make emptying the diaper pail a non-negotiable part of his daily routine. Little by little, he was able to take on more chores, becoming a stronger co-parent.

It is even more common for the NS partner to seek individual counseling, because it provides the emotional support and understanding that they may not be getting from the marriage, or other family and friends. As a result of the individual counseling, their better understanding of their partner's ASD traits, their more ASD-friendly communication, and developing new strategies can dramatically improve the relationship.

The Value of Couples Counseling

Not attending to relationship issues while married can often lead to divorce, and the price tag is high. The generally accepted figure for the cost of divorce in the United States, estimated in 2013, is anywhere from $15,000 to $20,000... Basically, "it costs as much to get unmarried as it does to get married" (Seldon, 2013, para. 3). If there are children involved, there is a decade or two of child support payments for the primary earner in the relationship, which can be about 30 percent of one's income.

Financial costs aside, the end of a marriage can take a significant emotional toll on the couple and their children.

Couples who stay together, but are unhappy in their marriages and don't seek couples counseling can also pay a high price. Neglecting their relationship can often lead to stress, unhappiness, and physical and mental health problems. When partners are unhappy in their marriage, it can affect their job performance and ability to succeed and progress at work (Knerr, n.d.). If the conflict-ridden couple is raising children, negative emotions from the marriage can seep into the children, with potential long-term psychological repercussions. It's important to weigh the cost of couples counseling in terms of money and time against the very lives of the couples and their children.

How Long Can Couples Expect to Be in Counseling?

I often say to couples that watching a marriage improve is like watching a tree grow. We are unable to see a seed sprouting into a plant. However, a time-release camera that took a picture of the growing sapling every day, would enable us to see each millimeter of progress. Over the course of a year, we would also see a grown tree.

How long does it take for the average neurodiverse couple to get their marriage back on track? This truly depends on each individual couple. I've seen couples who've flown from out of state to see me for several sessions over a weekend, and who've reported being able to turn a corner over days. The suitability of short-term counseling may further be influenced by the fact that the couple have young children and childcare is hard to coordinate, or the couples' location and the lack of ASD-specific counseling available in their area. The more common span of time that couples typically spend in couples counseling is eight months to a year. The process of resolving their marriage can take regular weekly or bi-weekly sessions over several months. Patterns of interaction formed over years take time to reset.

And there are other couples who come indefinitely, with no timeframe in mind. Long-term couples counseling gives many couples the accountability, motivation, and space for marital connectedness. Though even long-term couples can eventually settle on coming once a month for maintenance. Other couples taper off regular sessions and come on an as-needed basis during a particular life-stressor or event.

Support Groups

To further build on their knowledge of ASD, both partners may also want to join support groups that are available to them. Learning about ASD in a group setting and exchanging experiences on the neurodiverse marriage can be a rich and rewarding experience. Many of these groups focus on educating both partners about ASD. Being with other spouses or couples can also normalize some of the neurodiverse relationship challenges. Groups can also reveal the range and variety in these relationships. They can also provide much needed validation, solace, and support to both partners.

All the book knowledge and television programs cannot compare to the connection that individuals both NS and ASD can form with each other in person.

Counseling Strategies that Work for the Neurodiverse Relationship

Identifying ASD traits that are contributing to problems in the marriage is key. Untangling the NS partner's own issues from their partner's ASD is also important. Couples counseling for neurodiverse couples is most useful when concrete, action steps, and "to-do" strategies are implemented within the ASD framework. It is important that counseling be clear, direct, nonjudgmental, and collaborative (Cully and Teten, 2008) in creating solutions in your marriage.

Using Cognitive Behavioral Therapy (CBT) to identify distortions in thinking for both partners is helpful, as we've seen. For example, a particular NS partner might have a tendency to hyperfocus on their partner's issues rather than their own areas of growth. Or the partner with ASD, because of their high anxiety around money, may paint a completely dismal picture of their financial situation, when the truth may be far from it. While listening to and validating both partners' concerns, fears, and experiences, it's necessary that the couples counselor is able to discern the true depth and reality of the couple's situation.

It is also important that conflicts arising in sessions are well managed by the therapist (Weil, 2012). Moderating both personalities, reframing perspectives, and assigning action steps to work on between sessions is a necessary part of the couple's interventions (Weil, 2012).

What to Expect from Couples Counseling?

Let's look at a session between Chris and Ginny to get a better idea.

♥ CHRIS AND GINNY'S STORY ♥

When they first came to me for counseling about a year ago, Chris and Ginny were both unsure about what to expect from counseling. They had been to couples counseling before, as well as individual counseling to figure out the issues in their marriage. It was Ginny who had recently heard a program on the radio about ASD, and her suspicions about Chris having ASD had resurfaced.

In our first session, Chris was open to hearing about ASD, but he was not convinced he fit the bill. Ginny on the other hand, was eager to see me and instantly enumerated all the issues in their marriage.

"We've been married for two years and in that time Chris has changed into a completely different person. He is constantly on-edge, stressed out and flies off the handle at the smallest thing. I don't know where the man who had courted me with flowers and weekend getaways has gone. No matter what I talk about, he becomes irritated. But he's most upset when I talk about my boss at work. I'm hurt and exhausted from the constant fighting."

Due to the unhappiness that couples feel, they bring a sense of urgency to the counseling sessions, hoping to address all their relationship challenges in one go. While it is natural to want to solve everything at once, it is important to focus on one or two pressing issues in each session.

In Chris and Ginny's case, the problem that Ginny was struggling with the most was that Chris would have meltdowns over the smallest things. I asked Chris what his perception of the issue was.

"Every time Ginny talks about her boss, she goes on about how the company she works for is sexist. Then she adds how the world is unfair and women have it so bad. And I get defensive when she goes on about how the men at work are out to get her. I'm a man, of course I get defensive."

Both Ginny and Chris had their own perspective on this particular exchange. However, hearing each other in counseling made them both reflect on their own behavior.

"I guess I didn't realize that I sound like a man-hater when I vent about my frustrations at work."

"Man-hater! That's funny. I just don't know how to help you when you come home every day complaining. I've told you that maybe you should leave your job. And sometimes you do sound like you hate men."

"I don't need you to tell me what to do. I am already looking for a new job. What upsets me the most is when you shut down when I begin to tell you anything. You get uptight. You fold your arms, you get a glazed look in your eyes, and then you say that things like, 'But what are you doing to help yourself?' That sounds insensitive and like you're blaming me for my problems."

"Ginny, can you tell Chris what an appropriate response to you would be? Many times a husband might not know how exactly to respond to his wife's frustrations about her job."

"Maybe he can start by appearing to be interested. Have a more receptive body language and then say something like, "I hear you. That's a difficult situation." Anything, but 'What are you doing about it?' He sounds so dismissive and arrogant when he says that."

Chris realized that he would have to work on his body language and slowing down his response time. He would have to pause and think before he said anything. For adults with ASD, who tell me that they just don't know what to say or how to react to a particular situation, I experiment with scripts, role-playing, and behavioral sequences to use for different situations.

Learning more about ASD helped Ginny to not take many of the things he said seriously. She was able to more easily recover from Chris's insensitive comments. Despite some backslides, over several months of couples counseling, Chris and Ginny have been able to improve their communication patterns.

Marriage and Lasting Relationships with ASD

Couples counseling can contribute to the growth and development of both partners, helping them create happier, more mutually satisfying, and lasting relationships. Some of the stories illustrated in this book may seem overly optimistic to some people working with and in neurodiverse relationships. That's partly due to the incredible variations in neurodiverse relationships, but also due to the ASD-specific strategies that I've outlined in this book. And though couples counseling can help address and problem-solve emotional and practical issues in the neurodiverse marriage, in the end, it is the hard work and tenacity of the couples in facing and overcoming obstacles on a day-to-day basis that make their marriages work.

CHAPTER 18

EVERY NEURODIVERSE MARRIAGE IS UNIQUE

We know what we are, but know not what we may be.

WILLIAM SHAKESPEARE

When he says "If you've met one person with Asperger's Syndrome, you've met one person with Asperger's Syndrome" (Shore, 2015) Stephen Shore, autism advocate, professor, and an author with ASD makes an important point. While many of the challenges that couples face in neurodiverse relationships are similar, every individual with ASD is unique, which makes each neurodiverse relationship unique. Some individuals with ASD are rigid and uncompromising; others self-aware and motivated to want to work on their relationships. There are those who makes notes in therapy sessions, read books, and make use of the strategies listed in this book, and those who might resist them at first.

These differences extend to the NS partner as well. Their traits, family background, and personality affect the dynamic of the neurodiverse relationship. It is valuable to understand and apply solutions to the relationship based on the traits, personality, temperament, family of origin, trauma issues if any, and cultural backgrounds of both partners.

Personality and Temperament

Each individual with ASD has a unique personality and temperament. There are those who are extroverted and affectionate, and those who are reticent and aloof. While most individuals with ASD are honest, transparent, and loyal, in some cases, they can be manipulative, secretive, and deliberately hurtful. There are those with ASD who are painfully aware of their traits and challenges, while there are individuals who aren't self-aware regarding their anger and tendency to hurt others. The latter type of individual with ASD can resemble someone with a personality disorder. And many individuals with ASD might even fit DSM criteria for personality disorders. It's important to understand the complex nature of individuals with ASD.

Not only do individuals with ASD vary. Each NS partner is different too, thus creating truly unique configurations in neurodiverse relationships. For example, a gentle and sweet tempered individual with ASD can be found to be paired with a partner who may have a difficult personality. She can be quick to point the finger at her partner, hold grudges and be unforgiving. This finger-pointing and resentment is mirrored by her partner as well. In such cases, it can be harder to start sorting and working through the marital issues. However, even if the partners are only slightly open and willing to self-examine and compromise they can start building a more stable relationship.

Family of Origin

The family of origin of each partner in the neurodiverse relationship can also influence how couples interact with each other. An individual with ASD raised in a stable and loving household may be better adjusted and have more self-awareness, than one raised in a dysfunctional family. Families that harbor secrets and perpetuate anger and abuse can often produce deeply wounded individuals.

Due to the genetic nature of ASD, it's common for individuals with ASD to be raised by other undiagnosed and untreated adults with ASD. If the parents, one or both, had ASD or mental health issues themselves, the individual with ASD can grow up with a distorted view of relationships. If anger was the norm in her family of origin, she may think nothing of her own anger when interacting with her NS partner.

The upbringing of the NS partner is also an important factor to consider in the neurodiverse marriage. Many times, the NS partner may have family members with ASD, personality disorders, or alcoholism. It's necessary that both partners and the couples counselor understand how their upbringing affects their behaviors in the marriage.

Trauma Issues

Many women in relationships with men with ASD often report having trauma histories related to family of origin and prior relationships. Many are adult children of alcoholics, have experienced the death of a parent in childhood, or abandonment by a parent. Some have experienced rape, sexual abuse, or infidelity prior to meeting the partner with ASD.

Trauma can often compound ASD traits. It's therefore important to consider the trauma histories of both partners and how that influences their relationship.

♥ JIM AND LAURA'S STORY ♥

Jim, a 35-year-old former U.S. marine grew up in an abusive, alcoholic family. He worked as a security officer at an U.S. embassy overseas. Living in a foreign country, his wife Laura, 28, contacted me via the Internet to discuss her husband's suspected ASD and their marital difficulties. Laura said that in the beginning, Jim was just the type of man she wanted to settle down with. She had been raped by a former boyfriend and struggled with intimacy issues. Jim didn't notice her emotional reticence and the sex was very infrequent.

Two years into the marriage, and with a lot of individual counseling, she felt healed from her sexual trauma. She wanted to feel more emotionally and sexually connected to her husband, but Jim had a hard time overcoming his communication challenges, lack of emotional reciprocity, and his low desire.

Her repeated attempts at trying to get him to talk to her or engage in more sexual activity were unsuccessful. When she confided about her problems to a friend, she told Laura that Jim might have Asperger's Syndrome. Laura then went on the Internet and looked up ASD. She read a book about Asperger's and marriage, and was convinced that Jim might have it.

After working with Laura alone for a few sessions, Jim joined her for couples counseling. Jim was slow to open up. "I don't know what to say," he said. It was evident in the session that Jim really struggled to get his words out. I asked him to write down his thoughts prior to our next session so that he would be better prepared.

"Conversation wasn't big in my family," he read from his notes, "and I don't know how to express myself. That's why I don't talk a lot."

"Being with him can be so tedious sometimes," said Laura, "He won't speak to me for a whole weekend sometimes."

"I don't know what to say. I grew up not saying much. My father was alcoholic and used to verbally abuse and beat my mother until she left him. After that we went to live with my grandparents. They were nice people, but they did not speak much. And they definitely didn't talk about their feelings. Every effort was made to never display anger or negative feelings. Instead of talking things out, my grandfather took me hunting. Nothing unpleasant was ever brought up or processed. I was already a very shy child. Not verbalizing my thoughts and feelings wasn't a big deal."

Laura explained how her past sexual trauma had made her skittish around most men. When she met Jim, his reserve and innocence made her curious and interested in him. Laura felt like she could trust him because of his conservative and old-fashioned manner of courting her. He didn't even try to kiss her until after several dates. Laura felt safe with him. Laura found Jim's social awkwardness and childlike innocence endearing. They were married within eight months.

In Jim and Laura's case, we can see how family of origin patterns and a sexual trauma history intersected with ASD. By learning about ASD, unraveling family of origin information, both Jim and Laura began learning new skills to interact with each other and deepen their relationship.

Cultural Differences

ASD can often be hard to discern for couples that have different cultural backgrounds. Cultural differences might be ethnic, religious, socioeconomic, and geographic. The NS partner, in the beginning of her relationship, might attribute the differences between her partner and her to their different cultural backgrounds. She later learns that their differences are neurological in nature and mainly due to his ASD.

Jenny, an American woman was married to Emanuel from Ghana. She met him while she was on a three-month trip there as a nursing volunteer. It was love at first sight and Emanuel followed her to the U.S. where they were married. Jenny was 23 years old and didn't have much relationship experience. In the beginning, she attributed all of Emanuel's traits to his being African. Emanuel felt more relaxed in America because no one expected him to know what to say and do. He found a job as an IT professional and felt very accepted even though he sometimes experienced racial prejudice.

Due to their highly intellectual nature and the lack of potential life partners due to their weak social skills, individuals with ASD are often more open to dating outside their culture. In my own practice, I see a number of multicultural couples.

Cultural differences can also mask social challenges. For example, in Mexican culture, an individual with ASD will grow up with a lot more social interactions than an individual growing up in the U.S. She may have a built-in network of friends and family that may give a false appearance of being social. On closer examination however, it can become clear that her friends are really family friends; they are not her own friends. And even though her family find her difficult, they love her and spend time with her. This built-in social life insulates her from having to create new social connections. In a neurodiverse relationship, it's important to tease out what are cultural differences versus ASD traits.

Gender Differences

Similar to culture, gender differences seem to matter less to individuals with ASD than they do to their NS peers. They tend to be more fluid in their gender roles. Women with ASD are also flexible in gender roles. They are more likely to accept being the breadwinner in the family, or take up jobs in the military, police, or work in the trades such as being a mechanic or welder. Men with ASD can be happy staying at home and looking after the children, while their partner works. They might also not mind doing household chores such as cooking and cleaning.

That said, a lot of the neurodiverse relationships are based on stereotypical gender roles. In such cases, when the NS partner expresses her challenges to her friends, they might respond by saying, "That's just how men are. They are clueless about our feelings." Her friends might not realize the NS partner's situation and may think that she's overreacting to her husband's behavior. The NS partner can go years thinking that her husband's behaviors are based on him being a man rather than being neurologically different. Once she begins to learn about ASD, she can sift through male versus ASD traits.

Every Neurodiverse Marriage is Unique

Seeing the successes of another neurodiverse couple, the NS partner may be tempted to compare her partner with ASD to that of another woman's husband. Due to the varying factors that can contribute to the neurodiverse marriage, it's important to understand that each neurodiverse marriage is unique.

The life circumstances that contribute to each neurodiverse relationship can be rather specific. Some couples have sexual difficulties, but maybe they do not have financial struggles. Others might have children with special needs, while others might have health issues. For some, the neurodiverse marriage might be their second or third one. The challenges of the neurodiverse relationship will vary depending on the circumstances of each couple.

Customizing Strategies

The strategies recommended and prescribed here are based on my work with the numerous neurodiverse couples I've met in couples counseling and in support groups and workshops. These strategies are based on ASD traits, recurring themes in the neurodiverse relationship, and the practices that seem to be effective for the majority of couples I've worked with. However, not all of these strategies may be equally useful for every couple. Each couple has to brainstorm and troubleshoot their marriage based on what works for their unique situation. While many of the ASD traits are addressed in this book, some are not.

As in any marriage or lasting relationship, understanding, self-awareness, and doing what works is key. With respect and immense amounts of patience and perseverance, anything is possible. The success of each neurodiverse relationship depends on the continued hard work and growth of each partner.

The couples I work with inspire me by their continued resilience and ability to overcome obstacles. The love and persistence I see in them is humbling, and refreshes my hope in the work that I do.

Appendix I

The Appreciation and Gratitude Exercise™

1. Each partner may separately create a list of things that they appreciate and are grateful for in his/her partner. This list can include anything and everything; nothing is too big or small! Don't worry if you only start with a few items.

2. You can either write down the list on a piece of paper or index card, or use your smartphone or computer, to easily access it—at least twice a day. The more places you post it, the more likely you are to use it.

3. As you practice appreciation and gratitude, every day, twice a day, it can easily become second nature to how you think. You may find that you are more easily able to notice the positive qualities and behaviors of your partner. Keep adding new items to the list as you notice your partner doing nice things for you.

4. Repeat the exercise for days, weeks, months, and years—until a "gratitude attitude" sets in, transforming your mindset into one of appreciation, gratitude, and positivity.

Being deeply grateful and appreciative of one's partner can transform a partner at a fundamental level. He or she might become more positive and empathetic, resulting in a reduction in marital conflict. Becoming a more appreciative, grateful, and positive person may result in more harmonious relationships in other areas of your life as well.

Appendix II

Appendix III

Tuning into bodily sensations can help you identify and name your feeling states. You can increase awareness of the physical sensations that occur in particular situations and the emotions connected to these sensations. Learning to express your sensations and feelings to your partner can help you become more emotionally expressive towards her or him.

In a negative situation, you can use your sensation-emotion awareness to practice soothing self-talk, and reduce your stress response. You can then express your feelings of stress or anxiety to your partner if needed.

1. *Situation or event:* Notice and write down (see Table 6.3 and the blank *Sensation-Emotion Awareness Chart* in Appendix V) the particular situation or event. For example, perhaps you just finished watching your favorite television program with your partner.

2. *Physical sensations:* Every person's mind and body is unique, so it's important to notice your own specific physical sensations in response to the situation or event. The situation can be positive or negative. Notice and recognize the physical sensations in your body, no matter how slight or intense they may be. For example, sitting with your partner on the couch after watching your favorite television program gives you a warm and comfortable sensation in your body.

3. *Felt emotions:* Physical sensations in your body can signal different emotions. For example, a warm and comfortable sensation in your body can mean that you're happy and content to be spending time with your partner. Using the *Emotions List* (see Table 6.1 and Appendix IV), you can begin to develop a broader vocabulary for the emotions corresponding to your physical sensations.

4. *Self-talk:* After you label the emotions you're feeling, you can then use self-talk to articulate your sensations and feelings to yourself. Knowing how you're feeling can help you become more aware of your own emotions. For example, you may summarize how you're feeling to yourself, "I feel warm and comfortable in my shoulders and upper arms. She looks sexy in her new pajamas. I want to have sex with her. Wait, maybe I should start by telling her that I love her and that I'm happy that we're spending time together."

5. *Edited communication:* After noticing your physical sensations arising from the situation or event, labeling the corresponding emotions, and self-talk, you can now express how you feel to your partner. However, it's important for you to edit what you say in your mind prior to orally expressing it. For example, you now have exactly the words you want to say to your partner, "Sweetie, I love you. I'm happy that we're spending time together."

Appendix IV

The Emotions List

This is a selected list of emotional words adapted from *Emotional Knowledge* (Shaver *et al.*, 2001). Psychology books, psychotherapy, movies, television, plays, novels, poetry and songs can further provide emotional learning.

CATEGORY	EMOTIONS
Love and longing	adore, affection, love, fond, like, attracted, care, tender, compassion, desire, passion, infatuation
Positive emotions	cheerful, gay, joy, delight, enjoy, glad, happy, elated, satisfied, ecstatic, euphoric, excited, thrilled, content, hope, optimism, bliss
Surprise	amazed, surprised, astonished
Anger	rage, outrage, fury, wrath, hostile, aloof, bitter, hate, loathing, scorn, spite, dislike, resentment disgust, contempt, envy, jealousy torment, irritation, aversion
Sadness	suffering, hurt, anguish, depressed, despair, hopelessness, gloom, unhappiness, grief, sorrow, woe, misery, disappointment, dismay, displeasure, shame, guilt, shame, regret, remorse, isolation, neglect, loneliness, rejection, homesickness, defeat, dejection, insecurity, embarrassment, humiliation, pity, sympathy
Fear	alarm, shock, fear, fright, horror, terror, panic, hysterical, mortified, nervous, anxiety, tenseness, uneasiness, apprehension, worry, distress, dread

Appendix V

The Sensation-Emotion Awareness Chart™

The partner with ASD can also use the *Sensation-Emotion Awareness Chart™* in stressful situations. Once he identifies how the situation or event can trigger him, the sensations he experiences, and the emotions he feels, he can use self-talk to sooth himself and thoughtfully express this distress or thinking-feeling state to his partner. By learning to do so he can revolutionize how he manages his stress, and how he chooses to handle it with his NS partner.

The Sensation-Emotion Awareness Chart™ Example

SITUATION OR EVENT	PHYSICAL SENSATIONS	FELT EMOTIONS	SELF-TALK	EDITED COMMUNICATION
You just finished watching your favorite television program with your wife.	A warm and comfortable sensation in your body, especially shoulders and upper arms.	Happy and content	"I feel warm and comfortable in my shoulders and upper arms. She looks sexy in her new pajamas. I want to have sex with her. I should start by telling her that I love her and that I'm happy that we're spending time together."	Express your *edited* thoughts to your partner: "Sweetie, I love you. I'm happy that we're spending time together."
Being stalled in the car in rush hour traffic.	A queasy feeling in the stomach.	Anxiety	Positive self-talk "There's no need to rush. Just take some deep breaths. One, two, three, four, five. Everyone is sitting in the same traffic. Ok, focus. Let me think what I want to say to my wife"	Express your *edited* thoughts to your partner: "Sweetie, I feel a bit queasy in my stomach. I'm feeling anxious in this traffic. I'm so sorry. This is really hard for me. I'm sorry you've to experience me like this."
After sex.	A warm feeling in the chest	Contentment	"I like having sex with my wife. We fit nicely."	"Being with you feels so good. I love you."
You're coding software. You're interrupted by your wife. She's reminding you to take the garbage and recycling out.	Shooting sensations in the head	Irritation	"I'm irritated, but I need to calm down. It's ok, I can code later. I'll plan to work for two hours longer in the office tomorrow. My wife isn't deliberately disturbing me. Tomorrow is garbage day after all. I'm so glad that she's there to remind me. I'm so grateful for a partner that stays on top of things around here."	"I need ten minutes to transition into taking the garbage out. I'm just wrapping up. I'll do it at exactly 7:25 p.m."

The Sensation-Emotion Awareness Chart™

SITUATION OR EVENT	PHYSICAL SENSATIONS	FELT EMOTIONS	SELF-TALK	EDITED COMMUNICATION

Appendix VI

The Relationship Schedule™

Below are a few of examples of what *The Relationship Schedule*™ could look like. Please note that that each *Relationship Schedule*™ needs to reflect the desires, lifestyle, and personalities of the specific couple. There is no one-size-fits-all; each couple has to negotiate what they need from their respective relationships. *The Relationship Schedule*™ will also have to be adjusted during transitions and life changes.

Examples # 1 and 2 are general examples. Example # 3 is a monthly calendar and it is less detailed. Couples might find it useful to combine the weekly and monthly schedules create a more comprehensive template for their relationship. Example # 4 is an of examples of what *The Relationship Schedule*™ could look like for the parent with ASD.

Example #1 of *The Relationship Schedule*™

TIME	MONDAY	TUESDAY	WEDNESDAY	THURSDAY	FRIDAY	SATURDAY	SUNDAY
6:00 a.m.	Extra long cuddle in bed	Cheerful "good morning" and cuddle	Extra long cuddle in bed			Sleep in	Sleep in
7:30 a.m.	Goodbye hug and kiss	Compliment: "You smell so good." Goodbye hug and kiss	Goodbye hug and kiss	Goodbye hug and kiss	Compliment: "You look good today!" Goodbye hug and kiss	Cuddle and sex	Cuddle and watching Sunday TV
Noon	Text message, "thinking of you"	Email: "Looking forward to seeing you later. It's date night."	Text message, "thinking of you"	Text message, "thinking of you"	Text message, "thinking of you"	Alone time	Go grocery shopping together
3:00 p.m.					Text message, "I'll be home by 6:00 tonight"	Alone time	Alone time
Text message, "I'll be home by 6:00 tonight"							
Text message, "Only a few hours more until our date!"							
Text message, "I'll be home by 7:30 tonight"							
Text message, "I'll be home by 8:00 tonight"							
5:00 p.m.	Phone call to say, "I'm heading home now. Do you need anything from the grocery store?"	Phone call, "See you at the restaurant in 30 minutes. Where do you want to eat?"	Phone call to say, "I'm heading home now. I did have a rough day at work, might need to relax before we hang out."	Phone call to say, "I'm heading home now."	Phone call to say, "I'm heading home now."	Alone time	

cont.

Example # 1 of *The Relationship Schedule*™ (cont.)

TIME	MONDAY	TUESDAY	WEDNESDAY	THURSDAY	FRIDAY	SATURDAY	SUNDAY
6:00 p.m.	Seek out wife, say "hello" with a hug and kiss	Seek out wife, say "hello" with a hug and kiss	Seek out wife, say "hello" with a hug and kiss	Seek out wife, say "hello" with a hug and kiss	Seek out wife, say "hello" with a hug and kiss	Alone time	Dinner and TV together
8:30 p.m.	Half an hour "Conversation Time"	Alone time		Half an hour "Conversation Time"		Alone time	Half an hour "Conversation Time"
10:30 p.m.	Cuddling and sex	Smooch goodnight	Cuddling and appreciation	Cuddling and appreciation	Cuddling and appreciation	Cuddling and compliment	Smooch and goodnight

Example # 2 of *The Relationship Schedule*™

TIME	MONDAY	TUESDAY	WEDNESDAY	THURSDAY	FRIDAY	SATURDAY	SUNDAY
7:00 a.m.	Spooning in bed for 10 minutes	Spooning in bed for 10 minutes	Spooning in bed for 10 minutes	Spooning in bed for 10 minutes	Spooning in bed for 10 minutes	Spooning for longer	Spooning and sex
9:30 a.m.	A 6-second hug and 2-second kiss goodbye	Compliment: "You look great!" A 6-second hug and 2-second kiss goodbye	A 6-second hug and 2-second kiss goodbye	A 6-second hug and 2-second kiss goodbye	Compliment: "You're so beautiful!" A 6-second hug and 2-second kiss goodbye	Go out to breakfast and play a game of Uno at Starbucks after	Cook a leisurely breakfast together
1 p.m.	Text message, "Work busy today, might be late tonight. Miss you"	Text message, "thinking of you... having lunch"	Text message, "thinking of you... having lunch"	Text message, "thinking of you... having lunch"	Email: "Looking forward to seeing you later. It's date night!"	Pick an afternoon activity to do after lunch	Give each other a massage
6:00 p.m.	Phone call to say, "Going swimming after work, see you soon."	Phone call to say, "See you soon, leaving for the train now."	Phone call to say, "Rough day at work, going swimming, see you soon."	Phone call to say, "See you soon, leaving for the train now."	Phone call to say, "See you at the restaurant, leaving for the train now."	Alone time	Alone time
8:00 p.m.	Seek out wife and give her the 6-second hug and 2-second kiss	Seek out wife and give her the 6-second hug and 2-second kiss	Seek out wife and give her the 6-second hug and 2-second kiss	Seek out wife and give her the 6-second hug and 2-second kiss	Seek out wife and give her the 6-second hug and 2-second kiss	Cook dinner together	Alone time
10:00 p.m.	Reading to each other in bed	Alone time	Listening to music together in bed	Alone time	Reading to each other in bed	Alone time	Alone time
11:00 p.m.	Cuddling and express 1 sentence of appreciation	Cuddling and express 1 sentence of appreciation	Cuddling and express 1 sentence of appreciation	Cuddling and express 1 sentence of appreciation and sex	Cuddling and express 1 sentence of appreciation	Cuddling and express 1 sentence of appreciation	Cuddling and express 1 sentence of appreciation

Example # 3 of *The Relationship Schedule*™

FEBRUARY

SUNDAY	MONDAY	TUESDAY	WEDNESDAY	THURSDAY	FRIDAY	SATURDAY
1 Hiking in the Blue Hills	2	3 Conversation, dinner, and movie night	4	5	6 Date night at the Red Tent Restaurant	7 Dinner with new neighbors
8 Reading two chapters of the Asperger book to each other	9	10	11 Date night at the Museum of Fine Arts	12	13	14 *Valentine's Day* Gift: necklace with geometric pendant. Ski weekend
15 Ski weekend	16	17 Conversation, dinner, and movie night	18	19	20 Date night at the Stella's Restaurant	21 Reading two chapters of the Asperger book to each other
22 Concert at the BSO	23	24	25 Conversation, dinner, and movie night	26	27 Conversation, dinner, and movie night	28 Date: Arts and crafts fair

Example # 4 of *The Relationship Schedule*™ for Parents

TIME	MONDAY	TUESDAY	WEDNESDAY	THURSDAY	FRIDAY	SATURDAY	SUNDAY
7:10 a.m.	Good morning to the kids	Good morning to the kids	Good morning to the kids	Good morning to the kids	Good morning to the kids	Good morning to the kids	Good morning to the kids
7:30	Emotional expression: "I love you!" A 6-second hug and 2-second kiss goodbye. School drop off!	Compliment: "Good job on the science project last night!" A 6-second hug and 2-second kiss goodbye. School drop off!	Emotional expression: "I love you!" A 6-second hug and 2-second kiss goodbye. School drop off!	Emotional expression: "I love you!" A 6-second hug and 2-second kiss goodbye. School drop off!	Emotional expression: "I love you!" A 6-second hug and 2-second kiss goodbye. School drop off!	Set the table together with the kids for a family breakfast	Read the children a story in bed
2:30 p.m.			School pick up. 6-second hug and 2-second kiss			Take the kids to the local park	Trip to the dog park
4:00 p.m.			Help the kids with homework			Help the kids with homework	Drive to football practice
6:30 p.m.	Seek out the kids and give them the 6-second hug and 2-second kiss	Seek out the kids and give them the 6-second hug and 2-second kiss	Seek out the kids and give them the 6-second hug and 2-second kiss	Seek out the kids and give them the 6-second hug and 2-second kiss	Seek out the kids and give them the 6-second hug and 2-second kiss	Family board game night	Family movie night
6:45 p.m.	Family dinner	Family dinner	Family dinner	Family dinner	Family dinner	Family dinner	Family dinner
8:30 p.m.	Hug and kiss. Emotional expression: "I love you."	Read the kids a bedtime story. Hug and kiss. Emotional expression: "I love you."	Hug and kiss. Emotional expression: "I love you."	Read the kids a bedtime story. Hug and kiss. Emotional expression: "I love you."	Hug and kiss. Emotional expression: "I love you."	Read the kids a bedtime story. Hug and kiss. Emotional expression: "I love you."	Read the kids a bedtime story. Hug and kiss. Emotional expression: "I love you."

Appendix VII

The Listen, Validate, and Compliment Strategy™

Convey the following three points during your conversational turn. Use no more than three to five sentences for each point.

1. *Listen* to your partner, and paraphrase what you've heard her or him say to show her or him that you've been listening: "I heard you say that you had a frustrating day at work. You said that you've been doing the work of two accountants for almost six months. Is that right?"

2. *Validate* your partner: "That sounds an awful lot of extra work. That must be challenging."

3. *Compliment* your partner: "It sounds like you are doing all you can to do the work of two people. You're such a hard worker."

Appendix VIII

THE MARITAL SATISFACTION SCALE

1	2	3	4	5	6	7	8	9	10

Calling the divorce lawyer   *Completely happy in the marriage*

I ask each partner to use a 1 to 10 scale to rate their satisfaction in the marriage. 1 being that they are about to *call the divorce lawyer* and 10 being that they are *completely happy in the marriage*. Using the marital satisfaction scale both partners can become more aware of the state of their marriage.

References

Amaral, D. G. and Corbett, B. A. (2003) "The Amygdala, Autism and Anxiety," in G. Bock and J. Goode (eds) *Autism: Neural Basis and Treatment Possibilities: Novartis Foundation Symposium 251.* Chichester, UK: John Wiley and Sons, Ltd.

American Psychiatric Association (2000) *Diagnostic and Statistical Manual of Mental Disorders (4th edition) (DSM-5).* Washington, DC: American Psychiatric Association.

American Psychiatric Association (2013) *Diagnostic and Statistical Manual of Mental Disorders (5th edition) (DSM-V).* Arlington, VA: American Psychiatric Publishing.

American Psychological Association [APA] (2013) *Marriage and Divorce.* Washington DC: American Psychological Association. Available at www.apa.org/topics/divorce, accessed January 12th 2015.

Armstrong, T. (2010) *Neurodiversity: Discovering the Extraordinary Gifts of Autism, ADHD, Dyslexia, and other Brain Differences.* Philadelphia, PA: Da Capo Press.

Aron, E. N. and Aron, A. (1996) "Love and expansion of the self: The state of the model." *Personal Relationships, 3,* 45–58.

Aron, A., Aron, E., Norma, C. C., McKenna, C., and Heyman, R. E. (2000) "Couples' shared + participation in novel and arousing activities and experienced relationship quality." *Journal of Personality and Social Psychology, 78,* 2, 273–284.

Aston, M. (n.d.) "Cassandra Affective Deprivation Disorder." Available at www.maxineaston.co.uk/cassandra, accessed July 5, 2014.

Aston, M. (2001) *The Other Half of Asperger Syndrome: A Guide to Living in an Intimate Relationship with a Partner who has Asperger Syndrome.* London: National Autistic Society.

Attwood, T., Evans, C. R. and Lesko, A. (2014) *Been There. Done That. Try This: An Aspie's Guide to Life on Earth.* London: Jessica Kingsley Publishers.

Attwood, T. (2007) *The Complete Gudie to Asperger's Syndrome.* London: Jessica Kingsley Publishers.

Barclay, E. (2012) "Classroom yoga helps improve behavior of kids with autism." Available at www.npr.org/blogs/health/2012/10/12/162782583/classroom-yoga-helps-improve-behavior-of-kids-with-autism, accessed October 7, 2014.

Baron-Cohen, S. (2001) "Theory of mind in normal development and autism." *Prisme, 34,* 174–183.

Bermond, B., Clayton, K., Liberova, A., Luminet, O., Maruszewski, T., Bitti, P. *et al.* (2007) "A cognitive and an affective dimension of alexithymia in six languages and seven populations." *Cognition and Emotion, 21,* 1125–1136.

Centers for Disease Control and Prevention [CDC] (2014) *Autism Spectrum Disorder: Data and Statistics.* Available at www.cdc.gov/ncbddd/autism/data.html, accessed 25 February 2015.

Cell Press (2014) "Low doses of antianxiety drugs rebalance autistic brain, study shows." *Science Daily.* Available at www.sciencedaily.com/releases/2014/03/14031912806.htm, accessed May 11, 2014.

Chapman, G. (2010) *The Five Love Languages.* Chicago, IL: Northfield Publishing.

Cully, J. A., and Teten, A. L. (2008) *A Therapist's Guide to Brief Cognitive Behavioral Therapy.* Houston, TX: Department of Veterans Affairs South Central MIRECC.

Elliott, R. (2003) "Executive functions and their disorders: Imaging in clinical neuroscience." *British Medical Bulletin, 65,* 1, 49–59.

Elliott, R. Jr, Dobbin, A., Rose, G., and Soper, H. (1994) "Vigorous, aerobic exercise versus general motor training activities: Effects on maladaptive and stereotypic behaviors of adults with both autism and mental retardation." *Journal of Autism Developmental Disorders, 24,* 5, 565–576.

Finch, D. (2012) *The Journal of Best Practices: A Memoir of Marriage, Asperger Syndrome, and One Man's Quest to Be a Better Husband.* New York, NY: Scribner.

Finch, D. and Finch, K. (2012) "Yes, You Are Supposed to Hug Me Now: Best Practices for Neurologically-Mixed Marriages and Other Harrowing Relationships." Talk presented by AANE in Waltham, MA. December 1, 2012.

Gaus, V. L. (2007) *Cognitive-Behavioral Therapy for Adult Asperger Syndrome.* New York, NY: Guilford Press.

Goleman, D. (2005) *Emotional Intelligence: Why it can Matter More than IQ.* New York, NY: Bantam Books.

Gottman, J. (1995) *Why Marriages Succeed or Fail and How You Can Make Yours Last.* New York, NY: Simon and Schuster.

Grandin, T. and Panek, R. (2013) *The Autistic Brain: Thinking Across the Spectrum.* Boston, MA: Houghton Mifflin Harcourt.

Higashida, N., and Mitchell, D. (2013) *The Reason I Jump: One Boy's Voice from the Silence of Autism.* (CD, 1st edition, narrator, Picasso, T.) New York: Random House.

Hinshaw, S. P. (2010) "Empathy, Social Connections, and Autism." Origins of the Human Mind. Lecture conducted with The Teaching Company, Chantilly, VA. Available at www.thegreatcourses.com/courses/origins-of-the-human-mind.html, accessed May 28, 2015.

Hua, X., Thompson, P., Leow, A., Madsen, S., Caplan, R., Alger, J., Levitt, J. (2013) "Brain growth rate abnormalities visualized in adolescents with autism." *Human Brain Mapping, 34,* 2, 425–436.

Insel, T. (2009) "Autism and developmental disorders." The Autism and Developmental Disorders Colloquium Series. Lecture conducted at MIT, Cambridge, MA. December 2nd.

Ikeda, D. (2014) "Valiant leaders." *Living Buddhism, 18,* 9, 44–44.

Jayson, S. (2008) "Married couples who play together stay together." *USA Today.* Available at http://abcnews.go.com/Health/Family/story?id=538721, accessed April 15, 2015.

Jekel, D. (2012) Personal communication, December 16.

Khalsa, S. (2013) "Yoga for psychiatry and mental health: An ancient practice with modern relevance." *Indian Journal of Psychiatry, 55*, 3, 334–336.

Knerr, M. (n.d.) "An empirical analysis of the relationship between marital status and job satisfaction." *Undergraduate Research Journal for the Human Sciences.* Available at www.kon.org/urc/v4/knerr.html, accessed September 10, 2014.

Marc, D. and Olson, K. (2009) "Neuroimmunology of Autism Spectrum Disorder." *NeuroScience, Inc.* Available at https://neurorelief.com/index.php?p=cms&cid=409&pid=149, accessed January 27, 2014.

Marshack, K. (n.d.) Asperger and Marriage: Therapy Recommendations for Marriages Impacted by Asperger Syndrome. Available at www.kmarshack.com/Asperger-and-Marriage.html, accessed July 5, 2014.

Mehrabian, A. (1972) *Nonverbal Communication.* New Brunswick, NJ: Aldine Transaction.

Mendes, E. A. (2011) "Bridging parallel play in Asperger marriage: Partnering in exciting and novel activities of play." Master's thesis: The Vermont College of Union Institute and University.

Mendes, E. (2013) "Marriage with Asperger Syndrome: 14 practical strategies." *AANE Journal,* 11, 5–7.

Merriam-Webster (n.d.) Available at www.merriam-webster.com/dictionary/self-exploration, accessed May 26, 2015.

Miller, J. (2012) Autism Spectrum Disorders and Comorbid Conditions. Available from Cigna's Autism Awareness Series site: www.cigna.com/assets/docs/behavioral-health-series/autism/2012>/autismSpectrum DisordersAndComorbidConditions.pdf, accessed April 17, 2015.

Mottron, L., Belleville, S., Rouleau, G., and Collignon, O. (2014) "Linking neocortical, cognitive, and genetic variability in autism with alterations of brain plasticity: The Trigger-Threshold-Target model." *Neuroscience and Biobehavioral Reviews, 47*, 735–752.

Muris, P., Steerneman, P., Merckelbach, H., Holdrinet, I. and Meesters, C. (1998) "Comorbid anxiety symptoms in children with pervasive developmental disorders." *Journal of Anxiety Disorders, 12*, 4, 387–393.

Myhill, G. and Jekel, D. (2008) *Asperger Marriage: Viewing Partnerships Through a Different Lens.* Available at www.aane.org/asperger_resources/articles/adults/asperger_marriage.html, accessed April 15, 2015.

Nigg, J. (2012) "Insights for autism from attention deficit hyperactivity disorder." Available at http://sfari.org/news-and-opinion/viewpoint/2012/insights-for-autism-from-attention-deficit-hyperactivity-disorder, accessed February 7, 2012.

Noles Jr., B. (n.d.) "Secrets of happy couples." Available at www.erehi.com/Article/default.aspx?articleID=596, accessed January 2, 2015.

Page, T. (2009) *Parallel Play: Growing Up with Undiagnosed Aspergers.* New York, NY: Doubleday.

Radesky, J. S., Kistin, C. J., Zuckerman, B., Nitzberg, K., Gross, J., Kaplan-Sanoff, M. *et al.* (2014) "Patterns of mobile device use by caregivers and children during meals in fast food restaurants." *Pediatrics, 10,* 1542, 2013–3703.

Ratey, J. J. and Hagerman, E. (2008) *Spark: The Revolutionary New Science of Exercise and the Brain.* New York, NY: Little, Brown.

Robison, J. E. (2013) "What is Neurodiversity?" Available at www.psychologytoday.com/blog/my-life-aspergers/201310/what-is-neurodiversity, accessed November 14, 2014.

Romero, T. (2002) "The neurobiology of human sexuality." *Serendip*. Available at http://serendip.brynmawr.edu/bb/neuro/neuro02/web2/tromero.html, accessed March 21, 2015.

Rosenn, D. (n.d.) "Is it Asperger's or ADHD?" Available at www.aane.org/aperger_resouces/articles/miscellaneous/apergers_or_adhd.html, accessed September 10, 2014.

Sanderson, C. (2008) "DBT at a Glance". Available at www.behavioraltech.org/downloads/DBT_FAQ.pdf, accessed March 2, 2015.

Seldon, L. (2013) "How Much Does the Average Divorce Really Cost?" Available at www.huffingtonpost.com/galtime/how-much-does-the-average_b_3360433.html, accessed September 10, 2014.

Shaver, P., Schwartz, J., Kirson, D., and O'Connor, C. (2001) "Emotional Knowledge: Further Exploration of a Prototype Approach." In G. Parrott (ed.) *Emotions in Social Psychology: Essential Readings*. Philadelphia, PA: Psychology Press.

Shore, S. (2015) Personal communication, April 11.

Sinclair, J. (1993) "Don't mourn for us." *Our Voice, 1*, 3. Available at www.autreat.com/dont_mourn.html, accessed May 28, 2015.

Simons, H. F. and Thompson, J. R. (2009) "Affective Deprivation Disorder: Does it Constitute a Relational Disorder?" Available at www.affectivedeprivation.blogspot.com, accessed June 8, 2014.

SPD Foundation (n.d.) "Sensory Processing Disorder Explained." Available at www.spdfoundation.net/about-sensory-processing-disorder.html, accessed July 1, 2014.

Tomchek, S. D. and Dunn, W. (2007) "Sensory processing in children with and without autism: A comparative study using the Short Sensory Profile." *American Journal of Occupational Therapy, 61*, 2, 190–200.

Washburn, C. and Christensen, D. (2008) "Financial harmony: A key component of successful marriage relationship." *The Forum for Family and Consumer Issues, 13*, 1. Available at http://ncsu.edu/ffci/publications/2008/v13-n1-2008-spring/Washburn-Christensen.php, accessed April 16, 2015.

Weil, E. (2012) "Does couples therapy work?" *New York Times*. Available at www.nytimes.com/2012/03/04/fashion/couples-therapists-confront-the-stresses-of-their-field.html?_r=0, accessed April 16, 2015.

Index

AANE *see* Asperger / Autism Network (AANE)
acceptance and patience 206
accepting difference 56
active lifestyles 80–1
ADHD *see* attention deficit / hyperactivity disorder (ADHD)
AfDD *see* Affective Deprivation Disorder (AfDD)
Affective Deprivation Disorder (AfDD) 39–40, 82, 103–6
    case study 104–6
alexithymia 103, 140
alone time 143–4
    scheduling 153–6
Amaral, D. G. 66
American Psychiatric Association (APA) 25, 31–2, 138
amygdala 66
anger responses
    by ASD partners 59–61, 63, 72–3
    controlling and managing 63, 72–3, 89, 166–7
    range of emotions 109
    tone of voice 166–7
antidepressants 89
anxiety 66–7
    see also strategies and therapies; stress and ASD
apologizing 98
appearances 119–20
"Appreciation and Gratitude Exercise™ *"* 99, 237–8
apps (smartphones) 188–9
arguments 166–7
    setting ground rules 166
    tone of voice 166–7
Armstrong, T. 18
Aron, A. 141, 145
Aron, E. 145
AS *see* Asperger's Syndrome (AS)

ASD couple's support groups 211, 226
ASD partners *see* NS partners
ASD-specialist clinicians *see* specialist ASD clinicians
ASD-specific couples counseling 216–17
    see also counseling for couples
Asperger / Autism Network (AANE) 15–16
Asperger's Syndrome (AS)
    definitions 17
    diagnosis of 32
Aspie Quiz 36
assessment, neuropsychological testing 36–8
Aston, M. 103–4, 216
attention deficit / hyperactivity disorder (ADHD) 69–72
Attwood, T. 29, 188
Autism Spectrum Disorder / Difference (ASD)
    causes 30–1
    core features 31–2
        behavioral characteristics 27–9
        neurological differences 63–4
        spectrum of traits 32–3
    definitions 17–18
    diagnosis
        deciding to pursue 27–47
        learning to accept 48–56
    learning about condition 57–64, 199–201, 218–19
    prevalence 30–1, 44
awareness of ASD *see* learning about ASD; self-exploration and awareness

Barclay, E. 80
Baron-Cohen, S. 92–3
behavioral therapies
    cognitive behavioral therapy (CBT) 73–5, 226–7
    dialectical behavioral therapy (DBT) 75
Bermond, B. 103

best practice recommendations, in diagnosis 38–42
blame feelings 84, 198–9, 216
bodily sensations, as cues to feeling states 106–8
body language 158–9
brain neurology 63–4
    and ADHD 70
    and anxiety 66
Buddha 179
budgeting 194
    case study 194–6

calendars and chart planners 188–9
    see also "*The Relationship Schedule*™"
case studies 19
    ADHD and ASD 70–2
    barriers to diagnosis 42–4
    co-parenting 176–8
    couples counseling 219–20, 227–9
    difficulties accepting diagnosis 48–9
    financial planning 194–6
    information processing 161–3
    learning about ASD 58–61
    managing expectations 202–4
    meeting sexual needs 125–6
    NS partners with AfDD 103–6
    obsessive compulsive disorder and ASD 68–9
    practising curiosity 200–1
    self-care for NS partners 184–6
    self-exploration needs 85–6, 88–9
    sensory sensitivities 118–21, 123–4
    shared missions 213–14
    social anxiety 112–13
    Theory of Mind practices 94–7, 100–1
    use of behavioral therapies 75–6
    use of planning strategies 77
Cassandra Phenomenon *see* Affective Deprivation Disorder (AfDD)
causes of ASD 30–1
Cell Press 78
Centers for Disease Control and Prevention (CDC) 24
changing behaviors 203–4
Chapman, Gary 133
childcare
    support measures 193
    see also co-parenting
childhood abuse 232–4
children
    emotional needs 174–5
    with special needs 170
Christensen, D. 194

chunking techniques 189–90
Clark, Frank A. 92
clinicians working with ASD *see* non-specialist clinicians; specialist ASD clinicians
co-parenting 169–78
    children with special needs 170
    deciding to have children 178
    discussing duties and tasks 170–1
    getting support 175
    NS children 170
    overcoming difficulties 176–8
    providing quality time 174
    understanding children's emotional needs 174–5
    use of "*The Relationship Schedule*™" 171–3
coaching lessons 192
cognitive behavioral therapy (CBT) 73–5, 226–7
cognitive processes, ASD differences 63–4
communication strategies 157–68
    body language and eye contact 158–9
    editing thoughts 108, 110, 241
    informing vs. connecting 159–60
    initiating and sustaining conversations 163–5
    managing arguments 166–7
    open dialogue 56
    perception and memory differences 160
    and slow processing speeds 160–1
    use of emails and texts 167
complaining behaviors 98
compliments 101
Conrad, Joseph 65
conversations, initiating and sustaining 163–5
Corbett, B. A. 66
corpus callosum 70
counseling for couples 211, 215–29
    ASD-specific 216–17
    benefits for the ASD partner 218
    case stories 227–9
    length of 225–6
    and motivation 222
    and psychoeducation 218–19
    responsibilities 217–18
    safe spaces 220
    strategies for 222
    and "uncoupling" 223
    understanding accountability 221
    value of 224–5
Couple's and Spouse Support Groups 211
criticisms 60
Cully, J. A. 226
cultural differences 234–5
curiosity 199–201

De La Rochefoucauld, Francois 197
decision-making 191–2
decorating and DIY 193
denial of diagnosis 51–5
depression 65–6, 67–8
    in NS partners 105–6
    see also Affective Deprivation Disorder
        (AfDD)
diagnosis of ASD
    assessment and neuropsychological
        testing 37–8
    challenges in getting 34–5
    denial of 51–5
    difficulties recognizing 29–30, 34–5, 40–1
    post-acceptance 55–6
    recommendations for best practice 38–41
    relief after 51
    self-identification 35–6
    strategies for 56
    working in partnership 41
dialectical behavioral therapy (DBT) 75
diary planners 188–9
    see also "The Relationship Schedule™"
Dickens, Charles 116
difference, acceptance of 56
division of labor 196
divorce 223
do it yourself (DIY) 193
domestic cleaners 193
Dunn, W. 116

edited communication 108, 110, 241
    examples of 244
educating about ASD see learning about ASD
Elliot, Jr, R. 80
Elliot, R. 187
email communication 167
emotional expressiveness 165
emotional intelligence 63–4, 102–8
    and alexithymia 103
    strategies to improve 106–15
Emotional Knowledge (Shaver et al.) 109
emotions
    physical sensations of 107–8, 241
    and sex 132–3
"The Emotions List" 109, 242
empathy-building 113–15
endorphins 80–1
Evans, C.R. 188
executive functioning 140–1, 187
exercise 80–1
expectations of marriage 202–6
    case study 202–3
    learning patience 206

management strategies 205–6
expressing emotion 165
eye contact 158–9

family of origin 231–2
fear, range of emotions 109
feedback giving 181–2
felt emotions 107–8, 241
    examples of 244
financial planning 194–6
Finch, D. 179
Finch, K. 179
The Five Love Languages (Chapman) 133
foreplay 134
"Four Horsemen" of divorce (Gottman)
    198–9
Francis of Assisi 146
friendships
    and emotional feedback 181–2
    and social communication 180–1

gaming behaviors 75–6
Gaus, V. L. 73
gender differences 235
gender pronouns 18
gender ratios 44
genetic histories 231–2
Goleman, D. 102
Gottman, J. 198
Grandin, Temple 65, 167
grieving process, and NS partners 49–51

Hagerman, E. 81
Higashida, N. 28, 33
Hinshaw, S. P. 103
hoarding 191
home helps 193
hopelessness feelings 50
household tasks 193
Hua, X. 63
Hugo, Victor 187
hyperfocus 67–8

Ikeda, D. 218
individual counseling 211
information processing 160–3
initiating conversations 163–5
Insel, T. 30
intelligence quotient (IQ), and emotional
    intelligence 102–3
interests and hobbies
    for NS partners 184
    see also special interests

interventions for ASD *see* strategies and
  therapies
interviews with NS partners 37–8
IQ tests 37

Jayson, S. 142
Jekel, D. 49, 62, 216
joint activities 138–9
The Journal of Best Practices (Finch) 179

Khalsa, S. 80
Knerr, M. 225

learning about ASD 57–64, 199–201
  case study 58–61
  importance of 62
  as neurological difference 63–4
  and psychoeducation 218–19
  sources for 62
leaving a marriage 209, 223
Lesko, A. 188
life coaches 192
Life History Questionnaire (Gellar) 39
life mission / goals 184–6
  sharing of 212–14
lifestyles
  active vs. sedentary 80–1
  see also self-care
list making 190
"The Listen, Validate and Compliment
  Strategy™" 164, 252
logic and arguments 166
logical analysis 64
love, range of emotions 109

making judgments 197–9
managing expectations 202–6
  case study 202–3
  patience and acceptance 206
  strategies 205–6
Marc, D. 67
"The Marital Satisfaction Scale" 204, 253
Markman, Howard 141–2
marriage
  terminology 18
  see also neurodiverse marriages /
    relationships
Marshack, K. 181
medications 77–8
  for anger management 73, 89
Mehrabian, A. 158
memory 160

mental health issues
  and ASD partners 65–6
  and NS partners 81–2, 182–3
  see also individual conditions
Merriam-Webster n.d. 83
Miller, J. 35
mimicking others 52–3
mindfulness meditations 75–6, 78–80
misdiagnosis 29–30
  and women 45
"mission-based" marriages 212–14
Mitchell, D. 28, 33
mobile phones 188–9
money issues 194–6
motivation issues, for the partner with ASD
  210
motivational coaches 222–3
Mottron, L. 63–4
Muris, P. 66
mutual interests 138–9, 212–14
Myhill, G. 49, 216

narcissistic tendencies 58–61
negative thoughts 98
neurodiverse marriages / relationships
  definitions and characteristics 25–6
  impact on NS partners 39–40, 82, 103–6
  key challenges 29–30
  managing expectations 202–6
  model of 205
  sharing goals and life missions 212–14
  staying or leaving 209, 223, 229
  as "team work" 212–14
  uniqueness of 230–6
neurodiversity, definitions 18, 30
neurological differences 63–4
  and ADHD 70
  and anxiety 66
neuropsychological testing 37–8
neurotypical (NT) 18–19
new situations, planning for 188
Nigg, J. 70
noise sensitivity 120–1
Noles, Jr. B. 142
non-judgmental approaches 197–206
non-specialist clinicians 40
  case study 42–4
NS (non-spectrum) partners 18–19
  impact of relationship 39–40, 82, 103–6
  mental health issues 81–2
  and PTSD 82
  relief at diagnosis 51
  and self-advocacy 86–7

NS (non-spectrum) partners *cont.*
    self-care needs 179–86
    self-exploration and awareness 84–6
NT (neurotypical) 18–19

obsessive compulsive disorder (OCD) 68–9
    case study 68–9
obsessive interests *see* special interests
olfactory sensitivity 118–19
Olson, K. 67
open dialogue 56
organizational coaches 192
organizers 188–9
    see also "The Relationship Schedule™"
outsourcing tasks and chores 193–4

Page, Tim 136
Panek, R. 65, 167
parallel play 135–45
Parallel Play: Growing Up with Undiagnosed Asperger's (Page) 136
parallel play
    case study 135–6
    reasons for 138–41
    working together and "bridging" play 141–5
parenting *see* co-parenting
Partner and Spouse Support Groups 85, 221, 226
patience and acceptance 206
perception issues 160
perfectionism 67–8
personal organizers 188–9
personality 231
physical appearances 119–20
physical exercise 80–1
physical self-care 183
physical sensations
    as cues to feeling states 106–8, 240–1
    examples of 244
planning 187–96
    as anxiety reduction aid 148
    and decision-making 191–2
    developing skills in 76–7
    division of labor 196
    financial issues 194
    new situations and events 188
    organizational coaching for ASD 192
    outsourcing tasks 193–4
    space management 191
    task management 188–9
    time management 190
    using calendars and smartphones 188–9

Plato 169
positive emotions 109
post-traumatic stress disorder (PTSD) 82
pretending to be normal 52–3
prevalence of ASD 30–1
    gender ratios 44
previous trauma 232–4
psychoeducation 218–19
psychosexual maturity 133
PTSD *see* post-traumatic stress disorder (PTSD)

questionnaires and quizzes
    Aspie Quiz 36
    Life History Questionnaire (Gellar) 39

Radesky, J. S. 174
Ratey, J. J. 81
The Reason I Jump (Higashida and Mitchell) 28
relational consciousness 113–15
"The Relationship Schedule™" 146–56, 246–51
    case studies 150–1
    description 146–7
    how it works 147–50
    ownership of 151–2
    template examples 153–6, 247–51
    use for parenting 171–3
    uses 102, 105–6, 130–1, 141
        in bridging parallel play 142–3
relationships
    terminology for 18
    see also neurodiverse marriages / relationships
relaxation therapies, yoga 80
responsibility for behaviors 198–9
    learning to acknowledge 87–8, 97
Rilke, Rainer Maria 21
Robison, J. E. 30, 35
Romero, T. 129
Rosenn, D. 69–70

SAD *see* Seasonal Affective Disorder (SAD)
sadness, range of emotions 109
Sanderson, C. 75
saying sorry 98
schedules for relationship building *see* "The Relationship Schedule™"
Seasonal Affective Disorder (SAD) 103–4
sedentary lifestyles 80
Seldon, L. 224
self-advocacy
    for the NS partner 86–7

for the partner with ASD 90–1
  see also self-care
self-care 179–85
  case study 184–6
  emotional health 181–2
  mental health 182–3
  physical health 183
  stress management 183–4
  see also self-advocacy
self-diagnosis 35–6
self-exploration and awareness 75–6, 83–4
  for the NS partner 84–6
  for the partner with ASD 87–9
self-medication 78
self-talk 107, 108, 241
  examples of 110, 244
  "The Sensation-Emotion Awareness Chart™*"*
    109–11, 243–5
  "The Sensation-Emotion Awareness Practice™*"*
    106–8, 240–1
sensory sensitivity 116–24
  case studies 118–21, 123–4
  impact on sex lives 127–8
  and meltdowns 123–4
  preventing overload 116–24
  and self-awareness 117–18
  to smells 118–19
  to sounds 120–1
  to touch 121–2
  to visual stimuli 119–20
setbacks 206
sexual needs 125–34
  case study 125–6
  delayed psychosexual maturity 133
  differences in sex drives 128–9
  impact of stress 131–2
  lack of emotional connection 132–3
  lack of energy 130–1
  lack of imaginative play 134
  sensory issues 127–8
Shakespeare, William 230
shared interests 144–5
Shaver, P. 109, 242
Shore, S. 230
Simons, H. F. 39, 82, 104
Sinclair, J. 215
smartphones 188–9
smells 118–19
Smith, Adam 83
social anxiety, case study 112–13
socializing and social communication 180–1
sound sensitivities 120–1
space management 191
SPD Foundation 116

speaking loudly 166–7
special interests
  mutual interests 138–9
  and parallel play 136–7, 138–9
  scheduling of 142–4
  and shared activities 144–5
specialist ASD clinicians, importance of 40–1
"sticky attention" 79
strategies and therapies 19
  behavioral therapies 73–5
  counseling 211, 215–29
  dealing with sensory overload 116–24
  developing shared interests 144–5
  exercise 80–1
  general support measures 193–4, 210–12
  improving communication 157–68
  improving motivation 207–14
  individual nature of 236
  non-judgmental approaches 197–206
  planning skills 76–7
  practising Theory of Mind and EI
    techniques 92–115
  self-awareness and advocacy approaches
    83–91
  use of *"The Appreciation and Gratitude
    Exercise*™*"* 99, 237–8
  use of *"The Listen, Validate and
    Compliment Strategy*™*"* 164, 252
  use of *"The Relationship Scheduler*™*"*
    143–4, 146–56, 246–51
  use of *"The Sensation-Emotion Awareness
    Chart / Practice*™*"* 109–11, 240–5
  use of "The Emotions List" 109, 242
  use of *"The Marital Satisfaction Scale"*
    204, 253
  use of *"The Walking in Your Partner's Shoes
    Practice*™*"* 100–2, 239
  yoga 80
  see also co-parenting; self-care
stress and ASD 53
  effects of exercise 81
  impact of neurodiverse marriage 82
  impact on sex lives 131–2
  management strategies for NS partners
    183–4
  see also anxiety
support measures
  ASD couples support groups 85, 211, 226
  childcare 193
  counseling 211
  domestic help 193
  friends and family 210–11
  see also strategies and therapies
surprises, range of emotions 109

taking responsibility for behaviors 87–8, 97
talking too much 164
task management 188–9
    and outsourcing 193–4
taste sensitivity 122
temperament 231
tests for ASD 36–8
Teten, A. L. 226
texture sensitivity 122
Theory of Mind (TOM) 92–102
    case studies 94–7, 100–1
    description of 92–4
    mindsets of gratitude and appreciation
        98–9
    and parallel play 139–40
    understanding the challenges 97–8
    and *"Walking in Your Partner's Shoes
        Practice*™*"* 101–2
Thompson, J. R. 39, 82, 104
Thoreau, Henry David 27, 48
threats of ending the relationship 209
time alone 143–4
    scheduling 153–6
time management 190
time spent together 141–2
    see also mutual interests
Tolstoy, Leo 207
Tomchek, S. D. 116
touch sensitivity 121–2
    impact on sexual relations 127–8
trauma issues 232–4
Tzu, Lao 135

video gaming 75–6
visual processing 64
    communication strategies 167–8
visual sensitivity 119–20
Vivekananda, Swami 215
voice tone 166

"Walking in Your Partner's Shoes Practice™*"*
        101–2, 239
    case study 100–1
Washburn, C. 194
weekly planners 188–9
    see also "The Relationship Schedule™*"*
Weil, E. 215, 216, 227
women with ASD 44–5
    case study 45–7
    denial abo

Printed in Great Britain
by Amazon